IN SEARCH OF YOUR EUROPEAN ROOTS

Angus Baxter *1912 -*

In Search of Your European Roots

A COMPLETE GUIDE TO TRACING YOUR ANCESTORS IN EVERY COUNTRY IN EUROPE

Second Edition

**GENEALOGICAL
PUBLISHING CO. INC.**

First Edition 1985
Second Edition 1994

Copyright © 1994 by Angus Baxter
All Rights Reserved

Published by Genealogical Publishing Co., Inc.
1001 N. Calvert Street, Baltimore, MD 21202
By arrangement with Macmillan Canada

Library of Congress Catalogue Card Number 94-76791
International Standard Book Number 0-8063-1446-X
Made in the United States of America

For my daughter, Susan, with much love. Aided by
her husband, Thomas Barcsay, she has produced
the ultimate European, our granddaughter
Katherine, who can number among
her ancestors Scots, Hungarians,
English, French, Normans,
Vikings, Italians, and
Germans. She is
proud to be a
Canadian.

Pride in family is pride in ordinary
people—who in our hearts and
minds become extraordinary.
—Anon.

CONTENTS

ACKNOWLEDGMENTS

First and foremost, my love and my thanks to my wife, Nan, who read each chapter as it was produced, and helped me—as she has done with all my books—with sound advice.

I would like to express my gratitude to The Church of Jesus Christ of Latter-day Saints, an organization that shares its genealogical knowledge and vast resources with those of us who are not members of the Church. Their records are too voluminous to list, but you must be sure to check them before you start ancestor-hunting in most European countries, since many of the records of that continent are available on microfilm and microfiche. In the writing of this book and others, and in my own personal genealogical research, I am deeply in their debt.

I must also say thank you to the Everton Publishing Company, of Logan, Utah, for its series of "Handy Guides to Genealogical Records" in various European countries—Austria, Hungary, Italy, and Switzerland. These books are essential for any genealogist researching a family from these countries. You will find more details in the bibliography. This company also publishes *The Genealogical Helper*, another excellent and valuable aid.

I acknowledge with great sincerity my obligation to leading archivists and church officials in Europe—many of whom I met personally during my research, and others who have supplied me with information by mail. I have been in every European country except Albania, Finland, Iceland, and Norway, and I cannot speak too highly of the help and cooperation extended to me by these officials. They have listened patiently to my queries, answered many questions, and pointed me in the right direction for any further help that they could not provide.

I have to say thank you to my son-in-law, Dr. Thomas Barcsay, B.A., D.Phil., of the History Department at Ryerson University, Toronto, Canada, who translated my German and Hungarian correspondence, and shared with me his profound knowledge of European history. Any historical errors of fact which appear in these pages are undoubtedly mine, and not his!

Gratitude is due to various Canadian ambassadors and embassy officials who tried, usually successfully, to help me overcome the many problems I encountered.

In addition to the above, there have been many other people who have helped me—too numerous to list, but not too numerous to be given my gratitude. They include *maires*, *Bürgermeisters*, prefects, administrators, and other municipal officials from provinces, regions, districts, cities, towns, and villages across Europe; local archivists, librarians, historians, and officials of genealogical organizations; and personal friends and acquaintances in many different countries.

Finally, but by no means least, I wish to express my thanks to Flavio Andreatta, President of the Italian Genealogy and Heraldry Society of Canada; Myron Momryk, head of the Multicultural Archives Program of the National Archives of Canada; Miriam Weiner, the noted Jewish genealogist whose charm and determination have unlocked many doors; Gary Mokotoff, the publisher of *Avotaynu*, the Jewish genealogical magazine; and Dr. Lawrence Klippenstein of the Mennonite Church. These five people have graciously shared their wide knowledge of their particular areas of expertise with me, and I am the richer for it.

ANGUS BAXTER

FOREWORD

Why are more and more people tracing their ancestors? All over the world people are in search of their roots, and there must be a reason for this. For members of The Church of Jesus Christ of Latter-day Saints, the answer is simple—they believe that if they can trace their forebears and have them baptized into their own faith, they will be reunited with them after death. But what about the rest of us? Why are we tracing our families back?

There are no easy answers, because our reasons are diverse: some hope to find a title in the family; some hope to discover they are descended from some ancient king; and some want to unlock the key to hidden wealth, to impress their friends with the social standing of a great-great-grandfather, or to find a family coat of arms.

At least two of the hopes are almost certain to be dashed: hidden wealth and a coat of arms. Almost every family has a story that has been handed down about a missing fortune—vast wealth tied up in some court battle because a birth certificate is missing. The tale is always the same, but I have never known anyone to find riches through ancestor-hunting! If you do, as a result of this book, then I shall expect the usual ten percent!

A family coat of arms is just as unlikely. The right to bear arms (heraldic ones, that is) was usually granted by a ruler of a country as a reward for services rendered by some brave soldier or great landowner. Since ninety-five percent of us are descended from farmers and farm workers, the odds against your family having a coat of arms are very great. You may come across one granted centuries ago to someone with the same surname, but there is absolutely no guarantee that there is any family connection; in any case, the right to arms almost always descended in the male line.

However, I suspect that for most of us the motives that move us are quite different and very simple. We have an inborn need to go back and find out where our ancestors came from—not just the name of the country, which we probably know already, but the exact place in that country. We want to know what they did, how they earned a living. Why did they leave? What clothes did they wear? What was happening in that country at that particular time? These are our questions and we are the people who will answer them if we are patient and determined.

Patience and determination. And there is more. You will need money, you will need skill in finding information, you will need charm and good manners in extracting it, you will need time, and you will need luck.

The cost will vary—it will depend on how much you know at the start, on the cost of postage and the cost of paying return postage, on the ease or difficulty of access to records in the "old country," and on how much you will have to pay for an occasional professional researcher. Each family is too individual for me to hazard a guess—but remember that ancestor-hunting is a pay-as-you-go affair! Whenever you think you are spending too much money, stop for a while and let your finances recover. Never, never let searching for your roots be a burden—it should be a pleasure, it should be fun!

Don't spread yourself too wide—take one side of your family at a time; otherwise you will only become confused with the hundreds of names you will acquire as time goes by. You will also find that when you are searching long lists of names (and you will be), it will be much easier to look for *one* surname and not seven or eight. Of course, if two or more sides of your family come from the same village or town, that is quite a different story— you will save time and money by looking for them simultaneously.

How do you start on this magic journey? Well, you start with *you* and with no one else. You go back in time from *you*. You do not find someone with a similar name and trace them down the centuries to you. First, it is impossible, and second, there is little likelihood of a family connection, anyway. Names can be misleading in three ways:

Even within a few generations of a family, the spelling of a name can change, usually because our ancestors could not read or write and so the name would be spelled phonetically (as it sounds). Unfortunately, there was another complication, for a name might sound differently to different people. Just as some people are tone-deaf to music, so other people are tone-deaf to words. That is why in my own family you will find Baxter, Backster, Bacster, Bagster, Bakster, and Bacaster—all the way back to the original Saxon word Bacaestre, meaning baker. So, as you trace back, be prepared for changes of name, and don't assume that because you find a different spelling of your name it is not connected with your family.

Don't assume that everyone with the same name must be related to you somewhere way back in time. Up until the early fourteenth century in almost all European countries there were no surnames. People were known by the first name, and attached to it for identification purposes was a word describing where they lived, or what they did. Then you had John of the hill, or John the baker. As the population grew, this became more than a little complicated, and so the names became John Hill and John Baker. Since almost every village had a hill (except in the Netherlands) and a baker, you can see there is no way that all the Hills and Bakers have any blood relationship.

You may find that your surname was changed a few generations back. This could happen in several ways. It could be a fool or a bigot in the immigration service of this country who might have said, "What's your name—Pryzyborsky? What sort of name is that? I'll call you Price. Next!" It could have been your own ancestor who, finding his new friends and neighbors had difficulty pronouncing his name, changed it himself. When obtaining family stories from relatives and friends, or reading family papers, keep an eye and an ear open for a name change.

Write down everything you are told about your family—where they originated, their religion, their occupations—and write down, too, the names of the persons who gave you the information. You may need to go back to them for a recheck of the details they gave you. Go steadily back from you to your parents and grandparents, and listen carefully to all the family stories—but, having listened to them, don't always believe them! Family stories often become "decorated" with the passing of time. The sergeant in the army becomes a colonel, the tiny cottage becomes a fifty-room mansion, the bricklayer becomes a master builder! If you accept the stories without question you may have created your own dead end, and you will find enough of these along the way without adding to them.

When you start to question your own family, you may meet with resistance. People may say to you, "Leave well enough alone," or "Let sleeping dogs lie," or "Don't go and stir up trouble," or "Don't you bother about our ancestors; they were a bunch of sheep stealers, anyway," and so on. Try and overcome this sort of resistance. They are probably afraid you will find out something to the discredit of the family, some rogue in your ancestry, some skeleton in the closet. Be sure you explain that it is most unlikely you will ever find out anything about the character of your ancestors. You will find out when and where they were born, married, and died—and, probably, how much money they left—but unless they were very prominent in the life of a particular area, you will not find out if they were saints or sinners. So give them the benefit of the doubt, and believe you are descended from a long line of saints!

No one can tell you how far back you can get, as so much depends on the information you find within your own family, and on the records still available in the part of Europe from which your family came. So much, too, depends on you; tracing your ancestors is not easy, and it helps to possess the combined qualities of a Job, a detective, a bloodhound, and an elephant!

Of course, if you have plenty of money and no time you can pay a professional researcher to do all the work for you. The names of researchers can be obtained from genealogical organizations or government archivists, and you will find they are reliable and hard-working. However, they will lack the two things only *you* can provide: love of your family and a deep personal dedication to the task before you. There will, however, be occasions when you will have to use a researcher for a couple of hours because some archives and record offices insist on this.

There is one other important thing you must never forget. Be sure you always send return postage when you send a letter of inquiry abroad. You can do this by buying two International Reply Coupons (IRCs) from your own post office and enclosing them with your letter. Also enclose a self-addressed *airmail* envelope; otherwise your reply may come by surface mail and that has been known to take two months! While we are on the subject of postage, if you are going to be corresponding a great deal with one country, you can save money by writing to the General Post Office in the capital of that country, enclosing whatever sum of money you wish to spend at one time, and asking them to send you a supply of their stamps of the right value for airmail postage to this country. Then you can stick a stamp on the self-addressed airmail envelope and you will have no need to spend money on the two IRCs; there is quite a saving in cost.

When you are writing to archives, or parish priests or ministers, or genealogical organizations, or local officials, remember that they are not compelled to reply to you. There is no international law that says they must. So be sure you write a nice polite letter, give them as much background information as you can about the subject of your query, offer to pay whatever fees are required, and thank them in advance for their kind assistance. You may think this advice is totally unnecessary, and I am sure it is for *you*, but you should read some of the letters—rude and demanding—that are received in Europe from ancestor-hunters overseas!

This book is written to help you trace your ancestors in the old country; it will give you no information about records in *this* country. There are a number of books available for that purpose. We are concerned only with ancestor-hunting "over the water" in the Europe of our forebears.

Remember, you do not need to visit Europe to trace your ancestors. It can all be done by mail and the cost will not be astronomical. It will take up as much or as little of your time as you wish. Of course, one day your natural curiosity will take you back to the land of your forefathers. You will want to walk the streets they walked; to visit the houses in which they lived; to stand in silence in the churchyards where they lie; and to know that where you are, so were they many, many years ago.

In actual fact, it will be to your advantage to visit the old country *after* you have traced the family some way back, because by then you will know so much more about its history and its people. You will have been corresponding with officials of various kinds, librarians, archivists, clergymen, and even newly found distant cousins. Your visit will be so much happier than if you suddenly arrive with no personal contacts, no knowledge of where the records are located, and—quite soon—no time left to do the searching you could have done before you left home.

I mentioned "newly found distant cousins." Many people have found cousins by writing a letter to a local newspaper in the old country. If your ancestor emigrated within the last one hundred years, there may be relatives he left behind whose descendants still speak of the man (or woman) who left home to make good over the ocean. So, if you know the name of the place or the district from which your ancestor came, write to the local paper and ask for information about the family. Give the full name of your ancestor and the date of departure. Keep it brief; in fact, write a letter on the following lines:

> My grandfather, Alexandru Stanescu, emigrated from Pitesti to America in 1890. He was a farmworker. His father was named Nicolae. If there are any relatives still living in Pitesti I would very much like to hear from them.

I should emphasize *local* newspapers because "big-city" ones are not likely to publish your letter, but small ones always will. How do you find out the name of the local paper? Simple; you write to the nearest consulate or embassy of the particular country and ask them. Romania, for example, has a local newspaper in each of its counties, or administrative districts, including ten in Hungarian, and two in German.

You may get letters from people who are not related, complete strangers who are going out of their way to help you. Let me give you a very recent example of kindness I received.

My family originated in a remote valley named Swindale in the Lake District of England. I have traced them back in a proven line to 1340. In fact, there were Baxters there in 1195 but I cannot *prove* descent beyond the later date, and what I cannot prove I do not claim. I visited the valley many years ago but it was a brief visit and all I was able to do was to take a quick look and travel on. I've always meant to go back and spend more time there, but somehow the years have passed and when my wife and I could have been in Swindale we were in Nepal or Tonga or Afghanistan or Egypt or any one of the many places to which our itchy feet have taken us.

So, in 1984 I wrote a letter to the *Westmorland Gazette* (the local paper), explained that my family came from the area, and asked if, by any chance, any reader had any photographs of the houses and farms in which my ancestors had lived (I listed them), and if so, could they lend me a print to be copied, or have a copy made—at my expense, of course.

I had three replies from people who did not have any photographs but who had made a special journey to Swindale to photograph the houses and the scenery of that lovely, lonely valley. In one instance they made up a complete album of pictures with a written commentary; another couple sent me lots of slides and a fifty-foot movie they had made for me; and a third correspondent discovered and photographed the ruins of a very large house reputed to have been built by my family in about 1400. I say "about" because I am in the middle of a whole new project of checking land records and tax rolls to find out more about my earliest ancestral house.

I tell you this story simply to make the point that people are good and kind and friendly, and you should always be prepared to try an unorthodox approach to your ancestor-hunting. A letter to a newspaper may bring you quite extraordinary results.

I could tell you half a dozen stories of people who have done this and have found third and fourth cousins in the old country, have been sent complete family trees and copies of photographs of great-grandparents, and have stayed with their new-found relatives when they eventually visited the country of their ancestors.

So much for these preliminary words of wisdom! With the aid of this book you are starting on an exciting journey, and no one knows where it will take you, or what treasures you will discover along the way. Searching for your roots may not bring you wealth, but the intangible rewards of discovering your own family background may make you a richer person. Good luck!

INTRODUCTION TO EUROPE

People setting out to trace their ancestors in continental Europe face major problems. If you are lacking in patience or are easily discouraged, perhaps you should forget the whole idea. If, on the other hand, you are determined to succeed and are prepared to surmount many obstacles, overcome political and personal resistance, and use charm you did not know you possessed, you have the odds in your favor and the results may exceed your expectations.

Ancestor-hunting in Europe is affected by wars and revolutions, by economic and natural disasters, by religious and political turmoil, and most of all, by four major events that changed the lives of millions of people.

These events were the following:

1. The break-up of the Austro-Hungarian Empire in 1918–19.
2. The dissolution of the Ottoman Empire between 1830 and 1913.
3. The division of Germany and the loss of its eastern territories in 1946 (and the recent re-unification of 1990).
4. The break-up of the Soviet Union, Yugoslavia, and Czechoslovakia in the early 1990s.

Nearly everyone tracing their European ancestors in eastern and central Europe will be faced with problems caused by these events and the boundary changes that followed. Indeed, only Portugal, Spain, and Switzerland of all European countries have had no boundary "rectifications" in this century. The Scandinavian countries have been relatively peaceful, but both Denmark and Finland have had their frontiers varied in recent years.

If you have only traced ancestors in this country, you will have no conception of what awaits you in Europe. Here, records are centralized, generally speaking. There, they are scattered in many different places. Here, records have been preserved in a stable society. There, you must surmount the myriad difficulties caused by wars, revolutions, rebellions, civil disturbances, partitions, plebiscites, conquest, defeat, and boundary changes. Here, we live in an open society where the job of civil servants is to serve the people. There, in many instances, civil servants serve the State and are most reluctant to disclose information of any kind.

Let me give you some examples of what is ahead of you. In France most genealogical records are kept at the local level (the town hall or the parish church), and with no central index your search will be hard unless you have a place-name with which to start. In Germany, which was divided in 1946 and re-united in 1990, some records are in state or Länder archives, others in local archives in each city, town, or village. In Hungary you will find records from Romania, because part of Hungary is now in that country. And the reverse applies; in Romania there are many Hungarian records. In Turkey you will find many records of those Balkan countries that were once a part of the Ottoman Empire.

Let us examine the four major events I have described above in so far as they affect ancestor-hunting:

1. The break-up of the Austro-Hungarian Empire in 1918–19. Eleven distinct national groups lived within the frontiers of the Austro-Hungarian Empire: Austrians, Croats, Czechs, Germans, Hungarians, Italians, Romanians, Ruthenians, Serbs, Slovaks, and Slovenes, plus a number of minor ethnic groups akin to the major races listed above.

The Austrians were found principally in the area of present-day Austria; the Croats in Croatia, Dalmatia, Slavonia and Bosnia-Herzegovina; the Czechs in Bohemia and Moravia; the Germans in the Hungarian province of Transylvania, the Banat, and the Dobrudja; the Hungarians in Hungary proper but also in the Hungarian provinces to the east—Transylvania and the Banat; the Italians in the Bolzano area of the South Tirol and in Istria; the Romanians in Transylvania, the Banat, Bessarabia, Bukovina, Moldavia, and Wallachia; the Ruthenians in the sub-Carpatho-Ukraine; the Serbs in Yugoslavia, Bosnia-Herzegovina, and Croatia; the Slovenes in Slovenia; and the Slovaks in Slovakia.

It was never the intention of the victors in the First World War (France, Great Britain, and the United States) to destroy the Austro-Hungarian Empire. They planned to abolish the Hapsburg Dynasty, to provide some form of local autonomy for the various ethnic minorities, and to establish a Danubian Confederation. All these ideas and others were debated in the corridors of power.

However, various secret treaties had been concluded during the war between the major powers—either acting in concert or alone—and some of the smaller states such as Romania, and these restricted the freedom of the Allies to negotiate, or even to impose their professed principles of self-determination.

Simultaneously, old enmities surfaced among the national groups of the Balkans and the ethnic minorities of central and eastern Europe. The result was the complete dismemberment of the Empire; the emergence of new nations, which proceeded to treat their own minorities as they themselves had been treated by the Hapsburg regime; and the consequent displacement of millions of Europeans from their place of birth. Below you will find details of the transfers of land from the Empire:

THE BANAT: northeast part to Romania; southwest part to Yugoslavia
BOHEMIA-MORAVIA: to Czechoslovakia
BOSNIA: to Yugoslavia
BUKOVINA: to Romania
CROATIA: to Yugoslavia
DALMATIA: to Yugoslavia
GALICIA: to Poland
HERZEGOVINA: to Yugoslavia
SILESIA: to Czechoslovakia and Poland
SLAVONIA: to Yugoslavia
SLOVAKIA: to Czechoslovakia
SLOVENIA: to Yugoslavia
TIROL: southern part to Italy
TRANSYLVANIA: to Romania

This massive transfer of territory solved some problems and created others. You must be prepared for changes in place-names. Grandfather Janos may have told you he came from Nagy Becskerek, in Hungary; however, when you start your ancestor-hunting you will not be able to find it (except on old maps) because it is now named Zrenjanin, and is in Yugoslavia. Pressburg is now Bratislava, Lemberg is Lvov—the list is a lengthy one. The transfer of populations did not solve the minority problems of Europe, for millions of Hungarians were left behind in Transylvania, and millions of Germans in Czechoslovakia; thousands of Austrians found themselves in Italy; thousands of Slovenes were left in Austria; and so on.

Austria itself was reduced to the predominantly German-speaking part of the Empire, and Hungary, which had always enjoyed almost total independence within the Empire, became a small country, having lost all the rich lands to the east and southeast. In Transylvania Hungarians whose ancestors had lived there for a thousand years had to make the choice: flee to Hungary or become second-class citizens in Romania. Most chose the former course, but even today one and a half million still live in Romania.

An example of the problems existing for an ancestor-hunter as the result of boundary changes can be seen with Silesia. Teschen (Tesin in Czech, Cieszyn in Polish) is a former principality and town in the area. It has had a checkered history. It was under Bohemia from 1292 to 1625, then under

Austria until 1918. In 1920 the western part was given to Czechoslovakia and the eastern part to Poland. The town of Teschen was also divided; the eastern part became Cieszyn in Poland, and the western part Cesky Tesin in Czechoslovakia. Poland seized the latter section in 1938, Germany occupied both sections from 1939 to 1945, and then the boundaries reverted to those of 1920.

All this, genealogically, means that a Wilhelm Müller, born in Herrengasse, Teschen, in 1912 and living in the same house all his life, was Austrian at birth and Czechoslovak at his marriage in 1936, and that his children, born in 1937, 1939, and 1940, were respectively Czechoslovak, Polish, and German.

2. The dissolution of the Ottoman Empire between 1830 and 1913. Early in the nineteenth century all the territory known as the Balkans was part of the Ottoman Empire—a vast conglomerate of lands and peoples in the continents of Europe, Asia, and Africa. In Europe alone it ruled nine million people, most of whom were Christians. The area was divided into five provinces: Bosnia, Crete, Djezair (including part of Greece and the Greek islands), Rumelia, and Silistria. In addition, some areas were more loosely attached to the Empire and retained much self-government—the two provinces of Romania, Wallachia and Moldavia, for example.

Strangely enough, in view of the militancy of Islam over the centuries, the Christian subjects of the Empire were not persecuted in any obvious way. Although they could not aspire to any major part in government, they could retain their own religious beliefs (mainly Eastern Orthodox, but there were also Catholic and Jewish areas). However, the obvious power and prestige of the Muslim religion had some effect on the population, and certain areas (Albania, Crete, Bosnia, and Herzegovina) became predominantly Muslim, the converts then enjoying the privilege of first-class citizenship.

The Eastern Orthodox Church was divided along national lines. The Greeks were under the suzerainty of the Patriarch at Constantinople (now Istanbul), while the Serbs looked to their Patriarch at Péc, and the Bulgars to an archbishop at Ohrid. One disadvantage, which all non-Muslim religions suffered, was the law that no new churches could be built, and all male Christians had to pay a special head tax in lieu of military service, which was not permitted anyway for non-Muslims! The Greek Orthodox Church was the most cooperative with the Ottoman authorities, and as a result, in 1766 and 1767 the Serbian Patriarchate and the Bulgarian Archbishopric were abolished. By the early 1800s the Patriarch at Constantinople ruled over eight million Christians.

The beginning of the nineteenth century brought with it the first major rebellions against the Empire, and during the next eighty years Serbia,

Greece, Montenegro, and Romania became independent nations, and Bulgaria was granted autonomy which stopped short of absolute independence. It finally declared its full freedom in 1908.

At the same time the Austro-Hungarian Empire annexed the Ottoman provinces of Bosnia and Herzegovina. In 1912 Albania proclaimed its independence. At this point the old Ottoman Empire ceased to exist and its territories in Europe were now confined to the area around Constantinople. Its remaining territories in the Middle East and Africa were lost after the First World War.

The dates of independence of the various countries mentioned above were: Albania (1912), Bulgaria (1908), Greece (1830), and Montenegro, Romania, and Serbia (1878).

In addition, under the terms of the Treaty of San Stefano (3 March 1878) Ottoman territory was ceded to Romania. In Berlin in July 1881 a conference of the Great Powers returned Macedonia and Thrace to the Ottoman Empire (previously given to Greece in 1878). Greece was consoled by the award of Thessaly and part of Epirus; Russia received Bessarabia; the Austro-Hungarian Empire was given the right to administer Bosnia, Herzegovina, and the Sanjak of Novi Pazar. Few of these awards were to be permanent and all of them provided fertile ground for the seeds of future wars.

If you work back in your research to the days of the Ottoman Empire, you may be able to obtain some information from Turkey. (The countries most affected are Albania, Bosnia-Herzegovina, Bulgaria, Greece, Montenegro, Romania, and Yugoslavia.) The National Archives of Turkey (Topkapi Palace, Istanbul) does not have records of births, marriages, and deaths, taxes, censuses, or wills. They will not provide information about their holdings but suggest you write directly to the Prime Minister's Archives (Baş-Bakanlik Arşivi Müdürlügo, Cağaloğlu, Istanbul).

3. The division of Germany and the loss of its eastern territories in 1946 (and the recent re-unification of 1990). In 1945 the Allies of the First World War—this time with the addition of the USSR—were faced with a similar problem to that of 1919: what should be done with a defeated Empire? Here again the problem was solved by events. It was decided that Germany should remain intact but should be occupied by the four Allies, with a small token occupation in the Rhineland by Belgium. Berlin itself was to be jointly administered, with each power occupying a sector of the city.

The Potsdam Agreement of 2 August 1945 contained a number of clauses that decisively influenced Germany's future. It was agreed that the final German-Polish border should be settled with a peace treaty, but until then the "former" German territories east of the Oder and Neisse rivers should be under Polish administration. It was also agreed that the USSR should get

Königsberg, the north of East Prussia, and Memel. These two decisions affected a quarter of Germany.

In addition, agreement was reached on the return of the Sudetenland to Czechoslovakia. Behind the official wording of the agreement were hidden the roots of a human suffering greater than that of the First World War, and the start of a tortuous chain of events that led to the partition of Germany.

The eastern territories lost to Poland and the USSR consisted of East Prussia, Silesia, and parts of Brandenburg and Pomerania. It was recognized that there should be a "transfer" of Germans from Czechoslovakia, Hungary, and Poland. With this provision one of the great movements of population in history started. Before the Potsdam Agreement four million Germans had fled from the eastern territories as the Russians advanced. Now another five million still living in the Polish-occupied areas were expelled by force, as were three million Sudeten Germans now living in Czechoslovakia. Altogether more than thirteen million Germans were driven from the land on which they had lived for centuries, and probably another million died during the great exodus.

In 1948 that part of Germany occupied by the Western Powers became the Federal Republic of Germany (Bundesrepublik Deutschland, or B.R.D.). This followed the de facto administration set up in the area occupied by the USSR. In 1949 the so-called Russian Zone became the German Democratic Republic (Deutsche Demokratische Republik, or D.D.R.). In 1950 the D.D.R. recognized the Oder-Neisse Line as the frontier with Poland, and in 1970 the Federal Republic followed suit. Germany's boundaries and partition were an accomplished fact, but again suffering followed. Nearly three and a half million people left the D.D.R. for the west between 1948 and 1961.

In 1990 the two parts of Germany were re-united with Berlin as the capital. The government is in Bonn but there is little doubt that this division is only temporary and that the whole country will be administered from Berlin eventually.

4. The break-up of the Soviet Union, Yugoslavia, and Czechoslovakia in the early 1990s. The events in Europe in the 1990s have created additional problems for those searching for records of their ancestors. With the Soviet Union, Yugoslavia, and Czechoslovakia broken up into a number of independent countries, it's not always easy to ascertain the location of genealogical records or to gain access to them.

So, the once mighty empires are no more: the Austro-Hungarian Empire of the Hapsburgs, the Ottoman Empire of the Sublime Porte, and the Third Reich of Germany. The Soviet Union and Czechoslovakia have been broken up, and Yugoslavia has been torn apart in a particularly bloody civil war.

All the problems of European research that I have mentioned, and many more that you will discover for yourself, will not make your search easy, but when you do succeed the results may be beyond your wildest dreams.

You may discover your ancestors took a leading part in freeing a country from brutal oppression; you may find a grim castle on a mountain in Ruthenia as your ancestral home; you may find a fjord in Norway from which your Viking forebears set out to explore the unknown world beyond the sea; you may tread the black soil of Ukraine from which your ancestors fled czarist oppression; you may follow the footsteps of your Huguenot and Mennonite ancestors as they fled religious persecution; you may find ancestral tombstones beside the painted churches of Moldavia; you may sail by caique to Naxos, in the Aegean Sea, and find the whitewashed cottage of your Greek great-grandfather; you will, perhaps, go back to that great estate in Transylvania where your princely ancestors held court; or to that wooden hut in Poland where your family starved and suffered through successive invasions.

You may discover a 250-year-old family portrait (my wife did); you may discover the ruins of the fifteenth-century "great house" of your ancestors (I did); you may find princes and poets and peasants, soldiers and saints and sinners; you may find diaries and letters and documents; you may find unknown cousins. All these things and more may be waiting for you back in the old country.

All this lies ahead of you on the magic and wonderful journey that takes you in search of your roots!

THE LDS CHURCH RECORDS

The initials LDS stand for The Church of Jesus Christ of Latter-day Saints—whose members are sometimes referred to as "the Mormons," a name that is not as widely used as it once was. The LDS Family History Library was founded in 1894 to collect genealogical records and to help Church members trace their ancestors. Located in Salt Lake City (35 North West Temple Street, Salt Lake City, UT 84150; for information call 801-240-2331), it has the greatest collection of genealogical records in the world and is open to the general public without charge. The library consists of 142,000 square feet of space on five floors. When it was designed and built in 1985, allowance was made for an additional three floors to be added at some date in the distant future. With more than three thousand people visiting the library each day, and the steady increase in records, there is no doubt that the extra space will be needed long before the original estimated date.

No one starting off to trace their ancestors should do so without checking the library's records for the country or area in which they are interested. There is no need to go to Salt Lake City to do this because there are more than 1,800 branch family history centers in fifty different countries around the world. You can find the one nearest to you by consulting your local public library or by writing to Salt Lake City at the above address for the information.

There are no strings attached to the use of the library and its wonderful collection of records by those who are not LDS Church members. No one will try to convert you, and to quote the TV commercial "no salesman will call."

The interest of the church members in genealogy is not an idle one, or to be regarded as an interesting hobby as it is by many of us. It is a deep religious need based on their theological belief that family relationships are intended to be eternal, and not limited to a short period of mortality. They believe that husband and wife and their children remain together throughout eternity as a family unit, with all their ancestors and descendants. Members trace their ancestors in order to perform "sealing" ceremonies in temples erected for this purpose. Before the families can be "sealed" together, all the ancestors must be traced so far as is possible.

The library does not have sufficient staff to do detailed research for individuals, but it will answer one or two specific questions. If more detailed information is needed, you will be mailed a list of accredited researchers. When asking for this list, be sure you specify the country in which you are interested, and the state or province if known, since the researchers are specialists in particular regions. You will then make your own financial arrangements with the researcher you have selected. Remember, you are paying for the *research* and not for the result!

Be specific—give all the information you have, distinguish between fact and belief, and give details of the research you have already done. If you are buying a computer printout of the church registers of Graz in Austria, for example, state if you want Catholic or Lutheran registers; if you want army records from Poland specify the rank of the soldier and the name of the regiment, if you know it.

The library is engaged in the most comprehensive genealogical research program ever known. Microfilming and computerization are at the heart of the operation, and every day genealogical records are being copied, filmed, and preserved on compact discs (CDs) and in computers. Documents such as church registers, censuses, civil registration, land records, army and navy lists, deeds, wills, marriage bonds, cemetery records, magazines, and newspapers are all being copied.

The statistics associated with the library are staggering in their immensity. The library contains 1,800,000 reels of microfilm—equivalent to 6 million, 300-page bound volumes. These records contain nearly 200 million names. If these figures amaze you, there is more to come! The collection grows by 5,000 rolls of film and 1,000 books a month. Ancestral File™ records over 8 million *families*, while the International Genealogical Index™(IGI) data base contains over 200 million names and another 7 million are added each year (see below for more information about Ancestral File and the IGI). Visitors to the library in Salt Lake City use over 500 microfilm and microfiche viewers daily, and 60,000 rolls of microfilm are being circulated to local family history centers every month!

The LDS Church has updated and expanded its genealogical record systems to keep up with new developments in the computer field. Many records are now stored on compact discs, as well as the old standbys of microfilm and microfiche.

Now let me summarize for you the most recent developments in LDS Church record-keeping and accessibility.

FAMILYSEARCH®

This is the overall title for the various records and research aids described below. It is a collection of programs developed by the LDS Church to aid its members in their search for their ancestors and is generously made available to those of us of other religions, or of no religion at all.

The various components of FamilySearch can be consulted in the Family History Library in Salt Lake City, in the local family history centers in cities around the world, and in the near future, in public libraries and with genealogical and historical societies. The phenomenal growth in ancestor-hunting has placed a great strain on the family history centers—often beyond available facilities. As a result the LDS has contracted with DYNIX—a supplier of automated systems for libraries—to make its genealogical information widely available in public libraries as well as those of societies and institutions. This is an ongoing project in the process of expansion in coming years. FamilySearch includes the following nine separate segments and all the information is available on compact discs, microfiche, or microfilm:

1. The International Genealogical Index (IGI)
2. The Personal Ancestral File® (PAF)
3. The Ancestral File
4. The Social Security Death Index—USA only
5. The Military Index—USA only
6. The Family History Library Catalog™ and Publications List
7. The Periodical Source Index (PERSI)
8. The Parish and Vital Records List (PVRL)
9. TempleReady

The International Genealogical Index (IGI)
Let us talk first about the IGI because it is vital to your success in tracing your ancestors. Its base is also widely misunderstood by those just starting their search. It consists of information copied from church registers, censuses, wills, and other sources. So far as church registers are concerned it only contains information from those that have been copied. There are a number of church authorities in various countries that do not allow the LDS Church any access to their registers, and so the IGI is not 100 percent complete and probably never will be. For example, the United Church of Canada (which was formed from a merger of Methodists, Congregationalists, and some Presbyterians) is opposed to any copying of its registers in the church archives, and there are other ecclesiastical bodies or individual churches in other countries that share its views. Its attitude is simple to understand. It does not believe its members should be baptized or sealed into another religion after they are dead.

Often, on my lecture tours around the world, people will come up to me and express their worry that they cannot find an event listed in the IGI that they know occurred. "I can't find great-grandfather's baptism in the church in Blanktown though I know it took place." I explain to them that the reason is because the church registers there have not been copied, and that they must get their information from the original church, or in many cases, the local record office, archives, or church headquarters. They are astonished because no one told them the IGI is based on available sources only.

There can be another problem with the IGI. Records are only as good as the accuracy of the copier. Let me tell you a personal story to illustrate what I mean.

A good many years ago I was tracing my CALEY ancestors. I know they came from a particular place in the north of the county of Lancashire, in northern England, called Cockerham. My wife and I visited the parish church (at that time it still held the original registers) and took careful note of all the Caley entries. The earliest entry was the marriage of Henry Caley and Ellen Webster in 1798. Some years later I bought a print-out of the Caley entries for Lancashire in the IGI. I was still searching for the birth-place of Henry Caley. As I read through the list I was astonished to find no mention of his marriage, although the Cockerham registers had been copied and the information included in the IGI. I did find, however, a mention of the marriage of a *Thomas* Caley to Ellen Webster on the same day in the same place! I could not believe I had made a silly mistake. So I wrote to the Archivist of Lancashire who, by then, had custody of the registers of Cockerham, and asked him to check the entry. He replied, telling me that I was correct. Henry had married Ellen and there was no mention of a Thomas. I notified the LDS Church in Salt Lake City, sending them a photocopy of the letter. It took six years for the correction to be made in the IGI.

I do not tell this story in any spirit of carping criticism of the LDS Church, but it illustrates the fact that errors can be made in spite of the double checking of the IGI. I, of course, had copied the registers *before* the LDS did and so the error caused me no problem. However, if I had not, the entry of the fictitious Thomas would have brought me to a dead end. So the moral is to take full advantage of the information included in the IGI but still check the original source if you run into a situation that is creating a problem for you.

Most of the names in the IGI come from the period 1500–1875 and do not include death details. Apart from civil and church sources it also includes information submitted by church members and other individuals. You will find copies of the IGI in the Family History Library in Salt Lake City, in local family history centers, and in many public libraries, and in the libraries of genealogical societies. You can buy print-outs of entries from particular areas, or diskettes with information from these areas or complete countries. Each event recorded in the IGI is coded as follows:

A   Adult christening
B   Birth
C   Christening
D   Death or Burial
F   Birth or Christening of first known child (in lieu of marriage date)
M   Marriage
N   Census
S   Miscellaneous
W   Will or Probate

The individual entries in the IGI include the name and surname, and in the case of births or christenings, the names of the parents. It also gives the region or locality, the date and place of the event, and the source of the information. Remember that deaths and burials are rarely recorded.

As I mentioned above you should also check the original sources wherever possible. If you are fairly certain, from information within the family, that great-grandfather Frank Baker was born in Laindon, Essex, England, on May 12, 1865, and you cannot find the event in the IGI, there may be any one of several reasons for the omission:

1. The register of the church or chapel where the baptism occurred has not been microfilmed by the LDS. Some ecclesiastical authorities do not allow this.

2. The first name you have for him may not be correct. Although he was known in the family as Frank he may have been christened Francis, or he may have been baptized as Zachariah Frank and dropped off the first name because he did not like it.

3. His baptism may not have been recorded in the church register for some reason, or the register may have been destroyed.

4. Although his parents were Protestant he may have been baptized in the church of another religion for some family reason, and the minister of that church may have refused permission to the LDS Church to copy the entries.

5. The LDS Church worker may have missed copying the entry, or entered a wrong name.

There are other obstacles looming ahead of you! If you are searching for an ancestor from the Scandinavian countries, Wales, and certain areas of the Netherlands and Germany you should remember that surnames often changed with each generation (the use of patronymics or creating a surname from the first name of the father—Erik Johansen, for example, or Erik, son of Johan). In Iceland there were also matronymics, and in Norway surnames were taken from the family farm, and changed as the individual moved from one place to another. Fortunately, most Lutheran registers included both kinds of names.

Surnames appear in the IGI as spelled in the original registers, wills, or census returns, but they can be grouped together if they *sound* the same. My own simple name of Baxter, for example, appears over the years as Backster, Bacaster, Bacchuster, and a dozen others.

In its computerized form the IGI has been greatly improved. Originally, it was indexed within a country by county or province (usually the former). If you had no idea of the area of origin within the country you had a lengthy search ahead of you. Now, there is an index for the whole country. There is also a parent index feature. You can search for the parents' names, and so obtain the names of all their children. This often leads to the discovery of hitherto unknown brothers and sisters of your direct ancestors.

Explanatory leaflets available from the LDS Church include:

IGI (on compact discs)
IGI (on microfiche)
IGI (Finding a source)
IGI (Order form for microfiche)

Some microfiche sets are available for purchase, such as Germany (1554 fiche) and Iceland (49 fiche). Contact the LDS Church for prices. An order form is available from the Church Family History Library or your local center.

The Personal Ancestral File (PAF)

This section of FamilySearch contains the world's best home computer genealogical program. PAF allows you to obtain and organize your family history. It provides a wide variety of print-outs such as family group sheets, pedigree charts, descendants charts, and other lists. It also includes in its program the ability to submit your information to the Ancestral File and the IGI. When ordering the components for PAF it is advisable to use the PAF Order Form obtainable from your local family history center or the Salt Lake Distribution Center, 1999 West 1700 South, Salt Lake City, UT 84104.

The items available are:

PAF 5 1/4-inch diskette, release 2.3 for MS-DOS computers
PAF 3 1/2-inch diskette, release 2.3 for MS-DOS computers
PAF release 2.1 for MacIntosh computers

Your own personal requirements are (as specified by the LDS Church):
• An MS-DOS with two double-sided disk drives or 1 double-sided disk drive and a hard drive, DOS 2.0 or above, and 512K memory; or
• A MacIntosh 512, 512e, Plus, SE, II with two disk drives if single-sided, and 512K memory; and
• A printer (for all versions listed). Compressed print (17 characters per inch) for 8 1/2 X 11-inch printouts; or elite print (12 characters per inch) for 14 x 8 1/2-inch printouts.

Ancestral File

This is one of the several files in the FamilySearch system and is available on compact disc. It consists of genealogies of families from around the world and links individuals with their ancestors and their descendants. It differs from the IGI, which records single events, because it can show all the family information in one entry—birth, marriage, and—in most cases—death. It contains information about many millions of individuals, and also contains the names and addresses of people who have submitted the information. The file is updated from time to time.

This is one of the first sources you should check. You can see individual records, family group records, and family trees on the screen. The LDS has three important pieces of advice for those using these records:

1. Some people may have submitted incorrect information.
2. More than one person may have submitted information about an individual you are searching for, and this may cause duplication or discrepancies.
3. Errors may have been made when data was typed into the computer.

You are encouraged to contribute information about your family but try and make sure your information is accurate and not already recorded in the system. By contributing your family information you will help other ancestor-hunters. You can also search the file free of charge, and print copies of records and charts for a small fee, or copy them on a diskette for use in a personal computer.

In addition, you can correct erroneous information you find in the file. For full details of the procedure for doing this you should consult the FamilySearch leaflet *Correcting Information in Ancestral File*, obtainable from the Family History Library in Salt Lake City or from your nearest family history center. Other useful leaflets from the same source are *Using Ancestral File* and *Contributing Information to Ancestral File*.

Social Security Death Index (USA only)

This contains the names of 39.5 million dead persons in the United States. It lists people who applied for Social Security from 1962–1989 and whose deaths were reported to the Social Security Agency. The index gives full date of birth, month and year of death, the Social Security number, the state where the number was issued, and the last residence. There are also *some* records as early as 1937.

The records are from the Social Security Administration and became available through the Freedom of Information Act. As the records are of dead people no rights of privacy are involved.

The index is on compact disc and is updated at intervals. The details of the last place of residence may help you find an obituary in a local newspaper, and the place to which the death benefit payment was sent may enable you to find living relatives.

The Military Index (United States Only)

This is a list of 100,000 men and women who died while serving in the Armed Forces in the Korean and Vietnam wars between 1950 and 1975. It gives birth and death dates, place of residence, place of death, rank and service number, and in the case of the Vietnam War, religion, marital status, and race. The Korean Index covers the period 1950–57 and Vietnam 1957–75. (Deaths in the latter index may have been in Cambodia, China, Laos, North Vietnam, South Vietnam, and Thailand.)

Please note that the index only provides information about the two wars mentioned. It gives no family details or information about place of birth.

Family History Library Catalog and Publications List

This is on compact disc and describes the records, books, microfilms, and microfiche in the Family History Library. It does not contain any records but does describe them in detail. They come from around the world, and include church registers, birth records, marriage records, census returns, wills, family histories, etc. It is also available on microfiche and is updated at regular intervals. It lists over 2 million books, and other materials. You can search by locality or family name, and the call number will bring into your local family history center copies of records from around the world. More information can be obtained from the leaflet *Family History Library Catalog on Compact Disc*, obtainable from Salt Lake City or your nearest family history center.

The Publications List (also obtainable as above) lists all the LDS Church publications designed to help the ancestor-hunter. These are far too numerous to list but are fully described in the leaflet *Family History Publications List*.

Periodical Source Index (PERSI) on Microfiche

This is a subject index to thousands of articles in genealogical periodicals and journals. Using PERSI can help you find articles very quickly and save you a great deal of time in searching through periodicals for a particular subject. It indexes articles from more than 2,000 of them and provides access to about half a million articles. It includes all English language genealogical periodicals, plus those written in French about French-Canadian roots. It indexes articles by locality and family surname as well as generalized subjects. It does not index every name mentioned in the articles or include the actual articles; it also doesn't index queries, family trees, or book reviews.

PERSI contains two separate indexes that are updated annually. The 1847–1985 Index (FHL fiche 6016863) indexes articles in journals in that period, and it is not complete. The Annuals Index (FHL fiche 6016864) covers virtually all genealogical journals from 1986 onwards.

Here again, you can obtain full details of accessibility from the leaflet *Periodical Source Index on Microfiche.*

Parish and Vital Records List (PVRL)

This list, which is on microfiche, shows which records have been extracted and indexed and listed in the IGI for each geographical area and time period. It also shows which records are being indexed at present. This is being done by church volunteers and is updated several times a year.

The list can help you to decide which records to search. If you do not find mention of a particular record it means it has not been extracted yet. The records are listed alphabetically by country, and the United States, Canada, and Germany are subdivided into states or provinces. You can use a micro-fiche printer in the Family History Library in Salt Lake City or in a family history center to copy a page. If your nearest center does not have a printer you can order a copy from the library for a small fee. More information can be found in the Resource Guide leaflet *Parish and Vital Records List.*

TempleReady

This system is primarily of interest to LDS Church members, enabling them to put the names of their ancestors on a computer diskette that can be taken to a temple to provide temple ordinance for ancestors. For more information you should obtain an explanatory leaflet entitled *Introduction to TempleReady.*

All the above information in this chapter will have made it clear to you how far the LDS Church has gone toward simplifying our search for our ancestors. Just pause for a moment and think what our hunt for our family past would be like if the LDS Church did not exist! I am old enough to remember when our searching took place in damp and drafty old churches, crouched in a tiny vestry, or kneeling on a stone floor, or standing up in an unlit corner of a tower. There were also occasions when I sat with the minister in front of a roaring fire drinking his whiskey but they were few and far between!

We have many reasons to thank the LDS Church and its members for opening so many doors for us!

EUROPEAN JEWISH RECORDS

In most European countries over the years, people of the Jewish faith were required to register their vital events with a priest or minister of the State church, whether it was Catholic or Lutheran. Of course, the records were also maintained by the rabbi in the synagogue of the community. Because many Jewish records have been destroyed, it is always wise to check church registers on the appropriate date, at least up to the middle of the last century.

Until recently many people of Jewish descent were convinced of the absolute impossibility of tracing their ancestors. Most certainly there are major problems because of the Diaspora and persecutions, pogroms, and death camps. However, many "lost" records have been rediscovered, a concerted effort is being made to bring all the records together, and the possibility of a successful ancestor-hunt is improving. Remember, too, that you will find your Jewish ancestors recorded in many of the general genealogical records of European countries.

The Jews in Europe were divided into two main groups: the Sephardim (an old Hebrew word meaning Spaniards), who lived in Spain and Portugal; and the Ashkenazim (Germans), who lived in the Rhineland, central and eastern Europe, and Russia. The differences between the two are minor, consisting mainly of a variation in Hebrew pronunciation and some differences in religious practice.

The first Jews to emigrate from Europe went from Portugal to England in the sixteenth and seventeenth centuries, though there had been much individual migration over the English Channel from the time of the Norman Conquest. There was further emigration to the United Kingdom in the eighteenth century from Poland, Germany, France, the Netherlands, and eastern and central Europe. The main migration to North America started in the early 1800s, although the first Jewish immigrants actually arrived as early as 1654.

The American Jewish Archives (Hebrew Union College, 3101 Clifton

Avenue, Cincinnati, OH 45220) has collected every available record of Jews in the United States before 1900. They will not undertake any individual searches but they will tell you if they have the records for a specific community. The American Jewish Historical Society (2 Thornton Road, Waltham, MA 02154) also has a large collection of books, manuscripts, and personal and family papers.

In Israel itself a tremendous amount of information has been collected about European Jews and Jewish communities on that continent. These collections are not in any one place, and if you are planning a visit to Israel be sure you know just where to look for the information you need.

The Central Archives for the History of the Jewish People
Givat Ram Campus, Hebrew University, P.O. Box 1149, Jerusalem

These archives, founded in 1949, have the largest collection of Jewish documents and records in the world. Many of the records are of Jewish communities in Europe, or of microfilmed documents in national and local archives there. The Central Archives also maintain an up-to-date record of all items of Jewish interest in archives in other countries.

For example, the archives in Jerusalem include nearly all registrations of births, marriages, and deaths in Jewish communities in Germany, dating back to about 1800 (with some going back much further) and continuing up to 1876, when state civil registration was started. There is also the Diamant collection. This is the result of the lifelong labors of an Austrian genealogist and contains the genealogies of some three hundred families from Austria, Czechoslovakia, Germany, Hungary, and Poland. However, some of the information is fragmentary, so do not expect to find a complete family tree dating back some three hundred years.

The Central Archives are understaffed and organized in a very amateurish way, and if you visit the building you must not look for anything that resembles our own public archives. If you are writing for information, please don't expect the impossible. They cannot produce a name out of a hat. You must be able to supply them with specific dates and places, and be prepared to wait. The archives are lacking in funds because Israel is a poor country with its own list of priorities on which to spend its money, and these do not include the Central Archives. When you write, be sure to cover the return airmail postage (include at least two International Reply Coupons) and offer to pay whatever fee is required.

Finally, the most complete records are from Austria, France, Germany, and Italy, whereas those from eastern Europe, such as Poland and Russia, are fragmentary. This is because the western countries have maintained good records and their governments are cooperative, while in eastern Europe this has not always been so.

The Jewish National and University Library
Givat Ram Campus, Hebrew University, Jerusalem

This is located quite near the Central Archives but is a separate organization. It has a large collection of birth and death registers (pinchassim) from Austria, France, Germany, Greece, Hungary, Italy, Poland, Romania, Turkey, and the former USSR (including the Baltic countries of Estonia, Latvia, and Lithuania). Here again the records from eastern Europe are very limited but they can certainly tell you if the records of a specific Jewish community are in their collection.

Diaspora Research Institute
The University, Tel Aviv

This is mainly concerned with research into Jewish communities in Bessarabia, Hungary, Italy, and Romania, but the copies of the research papers quite often provide vital information about Jewish families in a particular community.

Archives of the Sephardic Community
Hahavazelet Street 12a, Jerusalem

It is problematical if these archives will be of any great value genealogically, but if you are of Sephardic descent you may find some mention of your family, particularly from areas within the Ottoman Empire.

Ghetto Fighters House
Akko Post Office, Kibbutz Lohamei Haghetaot

This is a museum of the Warsaw Ghetto Rising, but there is also a large document collection containing eyewitness accounts of the rising, and much information about the survivors.

Yad Vashem, Har Hazikaron
P.O. Box 3477, 91034 Jerusalem

If you're on a visit to Israel, this museum will be high on your list because it exists as a perpetual reminder of the Holocaust. It is on the schedule of every organized tour. However, if you have the time, you should go back on your own, and this time avoid the main museum and go to the building on the right, the archives building. This is the main center for books and manuscripts dealing with this particular period from 1933 to 1946. There are a great many accounts of Jewish communities destroyed by the Nazis, particularly in eastern Europe. If you know the exact community from which your ancestors came, your visit may be well worthwhile. You can also, of course, check their information by correspondence. Your main source will be the very large collection of memory (yizkor) books from eastern European communities in some six hundred towns. These books came into existence after the Second World War when survivors of a community had a reunion and produced a yizkor book, which listed details of the area and the names of victims and survivors.

There are copies of most of these books in the YIVO Institute (1048 Fifth Avenue, New York, NY 10028); the Hebraic Section of the Library of Congress; the New York Public Library; the Hebrew Union Colleges in Cincinnati and Los Angeles; and the Robarts Library, Toronto, Canada. Many of them can be obtained through Inter-Library Loan. They can also be bought from Eichler's Books (1429 Coney Island Avenue, Brooklyn, NY).

Two recent developments at Yad Vashem are a computerized list of the 204,000 residents of the Łódź ghetto (the second largest in Europe) and the list of half a million Hungarian victims of the Holocaust.

One problem you will encounter when researching in Israel is that of a change of name. Kanofsky became Kane, Moses became Morris, Martinez became Martin, and so on. Another complication is the literal translation of a name, so that Zevi, in Hebrew, became Hart in English and Hirsch in German. It would be wise to talk to older members of your family, and to examine all family papers, to see if you are going to be affected by a name change.

There are, of course, sources in the different countries in Europe and we should also talk about these. First and foremost, if your immigrant ancestor sailed from Europe, particularly from Germany or central or eastern Europe, then you should check the Hamburg Passenger Lists. You will find full information about them in the chapter on Germany.

Austria

The Jewish records are located in a variety of different places: provincial archives, municipal offices, and magistrates' courts. For more detailed information you should write to Israelitische Kulturgemeinde, Bauernfeldgasse 4, 1190 Vienna, Austria. There are over three hundred Jewish synagogue registers on microfilm in the various Hungarian archives (see chapter on Hungary), and these include the area of the Burgenland that was ceded to Austria by Hungary in 1919. There are also microfilms of the Jewish records for the area located in the Austrian provincial archives at Eisenstadt, the capital of Burgenland (Landsarchiv, Ruster Strasse 12-14, 7001 Eisenstadt, Austria).

Bulgaria

It has not been possible to obtain any definite information about Jewish records in this country. There are reports that some documents are in the National Archives (Centralen Darzaven Arhiv Na Narodna, ul. Slavjanka, Sofia), so you might try writing there for information.

The Czech Republic and Slovakia

There is Jewish genealogical material in the Czech National Archives that dates from the early 1600s. It will be necessary for you to follow the procedure set out in the chapter on the Czech Republic. Remember that this new country consists of the former areas of Bohemia and Moravia. The main archive is located in Prague. The address is: Archívní Správa, Obránců míru 133, 166-21 Prague 6.

There are also some Jewish records in Obvodní Narodní Výbor, Vodičkova 18, Prague. For more information about Jews in this country, please read the chapter on the Czech Republic.

Because Slovakia was joined to the Czech Republic until 1993, some Slovakian records may still be in Prague. The main archive for Slovakia is located in Bratislava. The address is: Archívní Správa, Kriškova 7, 811 04 Bratislava.

For more information about this country, read the chapter on Slovakia.

Estonia

Jewish records from 1918–1946 are located in the State Archives (Maneeźi 4, 200102 Tallinn). More information can be obtained from the Jewish Cultural Society (P.O. Box 2385, 200036 Tallinn).

France

The Jewish people have been in France since the first or second centuries. There is quite a lot of genealogical material about Jews scattered around various archives in France. Most of it has been microfilmed by the Central Archives in Jerusalem. If your ancestors came from a specific area of France, I suggest you should first find out from them whether the nearest archives have Jewish material. If so, then you can deal directly with that particular French archive. In any case, remember that Jews were subject to the normal civil laws. Civil registration, for example, started in 1792 and affected all citizens of France. Read the chapter on France to find out what general records there are of use to you. Be sure, too, that you check the passenger lists for emigrants leaving the port of Le Havre between 1750 and 1898. You will find information about these valuable lists in the same chapter.

Germany

In this area Jews were affected by the same civil laws as were all citizens of the various German states, both up to the unification of the country in 1871 and since then. Civil registration started in 1875 for the country as a whole but had existed long before that year in many of the individual states. You will find full details in the chapter on Germany.

The Weissensee Cemetery in Berlin is the largest Jewish cemetery in Europe. In the offices, there are over 115,000 index cards that give full details of each person buried there for over a century. You can obtain more details from Zentralarchiv der Juden in Deutschland, Fischerstrasse 49, 48477 Dusseldorf. Be sure you send two International Reply Coupons with your letter.

If your Jewish ancestors came from Germany, be sure to read the German chapter, which gives full details of genealogical records in this country, and, of course, remember the Hamburg Passenger Lists. If your ancestor emigrated during the nineteenth century, he or she almost certainly left from either Hamburg or Bremen. The lists for the latter port were destroyed by the authorities or, later, by British bombing, but those of Hamburg survive. They usually list not only the names of the passengers but also their place of origin.

If you are dealing directly with the various German archives you will find the staffs very helpful. You should also check with local libraries (Bibliotheken) because very many of the larger ones have Jewish collections referring to that particular area. These include quite detailed histories of Jewish communities. For example, the Hamburg Staatsarchiv has a register of Jews in the city from 1769.

Hungary

If your ancestors came from this country, don't forget that present-day Hungary is a fraction of its original size. Parts of the old Hungary are now in Croatia, the Czech Republic, Romania, Slovenia, and Slovakia. However, if your forebears did come from a place within the present boundaries you may be very lucky. The Hungarian National Archives (Magyar Országos Levéltár, Bécskapu tér 4, 1014 Budapest) have on microfilm the registers of over three hundred Jewish communities. Most of these date from the mid-1800s but some go back much further—for example, Apostag (1825), Budapest-Nagytétény (1760), Csurgó (1776), Kaposvár (1771), Marcali (1774), Székesfehérvár (1776), and Zsámbék (1769). The final date in all the registers is 1895, when civil registration commenced. The microfilms are also in the various county archives (Megyei Levéltárak) serving each particular area. All this information is listed in the Hungarian chapter.

Italy

Jews have taken an active part in the life of Italy since 100 A.D. and there are extensive collections of Jewish records and documents in many of the major archives and libraries. Unfortunately, there is no one collective list of all this material. Until just over a century ago Italy consisted of a great number of small principalities and states, and nearly all historic documents are still in the various individual archives. The Italians have been meticulous about keeping every possible record, but no one seems to know where they all are. However, the Central Archives in Israel have been active in microfilming many of the Italian Jewish records and if you write, giving the place of origin of your ancestors, they will give you the name and address of the local archive or library if one exists.

Netherlands

All the various records in the Netherlands chapter (except church records) will be of interest to you. In fact, you may even need to check these records as well because in certain places at certain times it was necessary to register the vital events of a Jewish family with the local priest or minister! Jewish people have been in the Netherlands (which then included Belgium) since the Middle Ages. Amsterdam was a main center of Sephardic Jews in Europe, and there are very large Jewish collections in the university library there. The Israel Central Archives also have a very fine collection of Netherlands Jewish records, including marriage contracts and deeds from 1787 (with a number of gaps). Also try contacting the Jewish Family Archive (Nederlands Joods Familienarchief, Amstelkijk 67, Amsterdam).

Poland

This country in its days of grandeur included all the main areas of Jewish settlement in Europe: Ukraine, Galicia, Lithuania, and White Russia (present-day Belarus). So far as modern Poland is concerned, the various regional archives have some Jewish material, and this also has been microfilmed for the Central Archives in Jerusalem. It is mainly from Białystok, Kielce, Kraków, Łódź, Lublin, Poznań, and Warsaw. There is a Jewish Historical Institute in Warsaw (Żydowski Instytut Historyczny, ul. Gen. Świerczewskiego 79, 00090 Warsaw), although it has failed to answer inquiries. There are two museums in Poland with index cards on concentration camp victims. The Państwowe Muzeum (32603 Oswiecim) has about 1,500,000 cards on Auschwitz/Birkenau concentration camp victims; the Krystyna Maddowa (Państwowe ga Muzeum, Droga Meczennikow Majdenska 67, 20325 Lublin) has about 100,000 cards of victims of the Majdanek concentration camp. As you can imagine, there has been a great deal of destruction of Jewish records in Poland, and what could have been a tremendous source of information on eastern European Jewry is, in fact, a genealogical desert.

Romania

I have no information about Jewish records in this country. Under Communism, there appeared to be a policy of total lack of cooperation with genealogical researchers. The Hungarian province of Transylvania was ceded to Romania in 1919 and it is possible that the Hungarian National Archives may have some Jewish records. You can certainly try a letter to the Romanian National Archives in Bucharest (Archivelor Statului, Bulevardul M. Kogălniceanu 29, 70602 Bucharest), but don't hold your breath!

Russia

The government is now cooperating with Jewish organizations on a limited scale. Hebrew manuscripts in the National Library in St. Petersburg are now being catalogued (17,000 file cards) and photocopied. The microfilms are being sent to the Hebrew University in Jerusalem. They are of very limited genealogical interest but—at least—are an example of developing cooperation. Unfortunately, the Russian archives contain masses of uncatalogued material, no adequate financing, and few finding aids.

Before 1772 the Russian government discouraged Jews from living or settling in the country. Then, when Poland was partitioned (see the chapter on Poland), whole areas were included in Russia that had large Jewish populations—eastern Poland, Lithuania, White Russia (Belarus), Galicia, and Ukraine. They were not allowed to move into Russia proper. There were four million Jews in this new area, which stretched from Kovno and Vitebsk in the north to Bessarabia and the Crimea in the south, and from Warsaw in the west to Chernigov in the east. Even within the region, Jews could not live in the cities of Kiev, Nikolaev, Sebastopol, or Yalta without special residence permits.

Over the following years the government forcibly moved Jews who had been living in old Russia into the acquired area. It was this inhumane treatment and the constant harassment, poverty, and population pressures that led to the massive emigration of Jews from Russia to other countries in the 1800s—some two million in all.

Before 1918 there was no civil registration in Russia. Jewish communities kept their own records but few of them survived the pogroms and the various displacements. Perhaps many more exist in the archives of Russia; we do not know. The answer is not *Nyet*. There is just no answer at all.

Yugoslavia, Croatia, and Macedonia

Very little information is available about Jewish records in these countries. You will find details of the general genealogical sources in the Yugoslavia, Croatia, and Macedonia chapters. The main areas so far as the Jewish population was concerned were in Croatia and the Vojvodina (in Yugoslavia), both of which were part of Hungary until 1919. You may well find some Jewish community records in the Hungarian National Archives or in the Hungarian microfilms held by the LDS Church. There is also a Jewish Museum in Belgrade, the capital of Yugoslavia, and the Central Archives in Jerusalem has full details of the genealogical material held there. It covers the period from the mid-1700s to 1952.

There are also some Jewish registers (1750–1832) in the State Archives of Macedonia (Kej Dimitar Vlahov, 91001 Skopje).

The United States and Canada

There are a number of sources of information in the United States and Canada, and I list some of these below:

American Jewish Archives
3101 Clifton Avenue, Cincinnati, OH 45220

Primarily concerned with the history of Jews in the United States and Canada.

American Jewish Historical Society
2 Thornton Road, Waltham, MA 02154

Similar aims and objectives.

YIVO Institute for Jewish Research
1048 Fifth Avenue, New York, NY 10028

The main concern of this organization is European Jewry and it is probably the best source of information outside of Israel. It is particularly good in the main eastern European areas such as Poland, Lithuania, Hungary, and Romania. The institute is not exactly a model of efficiency, but the quantity and quality of their information is outstanding. Place them high on your list.

Leo Baeck Institute
129 East 73rd Street, New York, NY 10021

Its main concern is the preservation of records from German-speaking Jewish areas, including registers and many genealogical collections. If your ancestors are from Germany, Austria, Poland, or the Czech Republic and Slovakia you will find vital records here.

The Canadian Jewish Congress
1590 McGregor Avenue, Montréal, Canada
Primarily concerned with records of Jewish immigrants into Canada.

In both the United States and Canada there are many local Jewish organizations with their own records and collections. The American Jewish Archives and the Canadian Jewish Congress will give you more information about these.

1. The newly opened Holocaust Museum in Washington, D.C., may become a genealogical source in a few years. It has a cooperative agreement with Yad Vashem in an approach to European governments for documents and microfilms of Holocaust-related material. A considerable amount of information is available.

2. Using records left by the Nazis, the Hungarian expert of Yad Vashem hopes to chart family trees for all 800,000 Jews living in the old Austro-

Hungarian Empire before 1919. For further information contact the Jewish Genealogical Society of Greater Washington, P.O. Box 412, Vienna, VA 22183.

As you will now know, all things are possible, and you may go back two centuries or more in your Jewish ancestry. Nothing will be easy, but with patience and determination you will find out a great deal from the various sources I have listed.

Note: If your ancestors came from the area contained within the boundaries of Czarist Russia, you should also read the information about the Russian consular records on page 240.

If you are researching your Jewish ancestry—particularly in eastern Europe—you should subscribe to *Avotaynu: The International Review of Jewish Genealogy.* The address is P.O. Box 1134, Teaneck, NJ 07666. The magazine also publishes some of the books mentioned in the Jewish section of the Bibliography on page 286, and also produces a series of microfiche indexes on such subjects as surnames, name changes, Russian consular records, and family trees.

ALBANIA

The Albanians are supposed to be descended from the ancient Illyrian and Thracian tribes. After the end of the Roman Empire in 395 the area passed to the Byzantines. During the next six centuries the northern part was invaded by the Serbs and the south was taken by Bulgaria. In 1014 the Byzantines reconquered the area, but by 1204 it had passed to the control of Epirus. Then followed invasions over the years by Venetians, Normans, Neapolitans, and Serbs.

In the fifteenth century the Turks of the Ottoman Empire arrived on the scene and stayed for the next five centuries. The First Balkan War (1912) gave the Albanians the chance to proclaim their independence, but during the Second Balkan War (1913) the Serbs occupied the country. A peace conference later in the year ended Albania's dreams of glory when large areas were given to Greece, Montenegro, and Serbia.

With the start of the First World War in 1914 Albania became a battleground for contending armies from Serbia, Montenegro, Greece, Austria, Bulgaria, and Italy. In 1920 the Congress of Lushnje gave Albania complete independence. In 1939 Italy invaded, and a pro-Italian puppet regime declared war on the Allied powers, but guerrilla groups within the country continued the fight against the invaders. In 1946 Albania became a Communist republic.

Albania existed in almost complete isolation from its fellow Communist countries and the rest of the world until 1991. We know little about genealogical sources in the country. Civil registration started in 1929, but before that, records were kept in the mosques and churches. The population was mainly Muslim, but the country is now officially atheist. There was a census in 1921. Until 1929 only religious marriages were allowed. Since 1946 the reverse has applied; only civil marriages are allowed.

It appears that most church records in the country, as well as the churches, have been destroyed. There is a new spirit stirring there, and perhaps some registers will come to light in the future. Meantime, I can offer very little encouragement to anyone of Albanian descent who hopes to trace ancestors.

ANDORRA

This is a very tiny state (population about 53,000) high in the Pyrenees between France and Spain. It is believed to have been first settled by stragglers from the rear guard of Charlemagne's army in 779 when it was returning to France after an unsuccessful campaign in Spain. Deserting soldiers intermarried with local Catalan girls and set up a small community. In the ninth century the Emperor Charles II made the Bishop of Urgel, in Spain, the overlord of Andorra. This led to protests by the counts of Foix, in France, who actually owned the valley of Andorra. The dispute lingered on, but in 1278 the two countries agreed that the Bishop and the Comte de Foix should be joint rulers. The rights of the Comte passed to the King of France by inheritance, and, in due course, from the kings to the presidents of France. So in the present day we still have the Bishop of Urgel and the President of France as co-rulers.

In actual fact, the control is minimal and the country is completely independent. It is governed by a council of twenty-four members, elected from the seven villages that make up the country. The council appoints a secretary-general to administer the affairs of the nation. The seven villages, or parishes, are the following: Andorra la Vella (the capital), Canillo, Encamp, Escaldes-Engordany, La Massana, Ordino, and Sant Julià de Lòria.

There is no form of civil registration, but the parish registers of births and baptisms, marriages, and deaths and burials serve the same purpose. These records are maintained in the church of each parish. Baptismal records started in 1614, and marriages and deaths in about 1694.

Wills are in the custody of the two notaries public (Notaires Publics des Vallées) in the capital and date back to the sixteenth century.

Censuses are conducted intermittently on a parish basis and the returns are located in the town hall (mairie) of each village.

The population is almost entirely Catholic and the language a mixture of French and Catalan.

AUSTRIA

I must start this chapter by emphasizing that it refers to present-day Austria and its existing boundaries. If your ancestors are "Austrian," be sure you know they came from a place within an area covered by the provinces of Burgenland, Carinthia, Lower Austria, Upper Austria, Salzburg, Styria, Tirol, Vorarlberg, and Vienna (in German: Burgenland, Kärnten, Niederösterreich, Oberösterreich, Salzburg, Steiermark, Tirol, Vorarlberg, and Wien).

One major difficulty ahead of you may be that immigration and census records in this country simply describe your ancestor as "Austrian" without giving the exact place of origin. If this is the case, you will have to depend upon either getting more information from within your own family, or basing your research on the apparent ethnic origin of your surname. Of course, the name may not help you at all; your surname, for example, may be Hungarian but your family may have lived in the German-speaking part of the old Austro-Hungarian Empire for centuries!

The following examples show you typical names from the different parts of the "old" Austria, but are only given to illustrate the point I am making:

AUSTRIA:	Müller
CROATIA:	Yankovic
THE CZECH REPUBLIC:	Formanek
HUNGARY:	Szabo
ITALY:	Scarlatti
POLAND:	Pryzyborski
ROMANIA:	Tatarescu
SLOVAKIA:	Lucachko
UKRAINE:	Yaremko

If your "Austrian" ancestors did, in fact, originate in any of the above areas of the Empire, you will have to trace them in the records of that country.

Now let us talk about the main sources of genealogical information to be found within the boundaries of present-day Austria. You must remember that all records are not centralized in one location, so there is no single archive in which you can discover all the information you want. There are state archives located in Vienna (Wien), provincial archives in each of the nine provincial capitals, city archives in the main population centers, family archives in some castles, and other specialized archives in various places.

Present-day Austria is often thought of as a homogenous language unit speaking only German, all the other races of the old Austro-Hungarian Empire having been happily settled in their own independent countries after the First World War. This is not true. Nor is the reverse true: all Austrians are not within Austria's present boundaries—in the South Tirol there are many thousands of Austrians living under Italian rule.

The Province of Carinthia has between 22,000 and 45,000 Slovenes. The Slovenian people originated in what is now Russia and settled in their present area in the sixth century. The majority of Slovenes were incorporated into the new country of Yugoslavia in 1919 and then into the independent country of Slovenia in 1991.

The Province of Burgenland contains about 8,000 Hungarians in the areas of Unterwart, Siget-in-der-Wart, and Oberpullendorf. There are some 25,000 Czechs in the same province in an area stretching from Kittsee in the north to Reindersdorf in the south.

The names and addresses of the state and provincial archives are given below:

State Archives (Österreichisches Staatsarchiv)

The following archives are located in Vienna:

Österreichisches Staatsarchiv
Minoriten platz 1
1014 Vienna

These are the main state archives.

Finanz- und Hofkammerarchiv,
Johannesgasse 6, 1010 Vienna

The most important genealogical records located here are the lists and records of the German colonization of the Banat and Transylvania in the seventeenth and eighteenth centuries. The archives contain reports of the administration of the German colonies and are alphabetically indexed with names of the settlements, but are not indexed with individual surnames. Quite often the place of origin of the family in Germany is given.

Allgemeines Verwaltungsarchiv,
Wallnerstrasse 6a, 1010 Vienna

This is the Archival Administration Office, where you will find administrative and government records, including the Imperial Court and noble families.

Kriegsarchiv
Stiftgasse 2, 1010 Vienna

The military archives are located here. They are of major genealogical importance and will be referred to later in this chapter.

Provincial Archives (Landesarchiv)

Provincial archives are located in the capital city of each province.

BURGENLAND: Rusterstrasse 12-14, Frieheitsplatz 1, 7001 Eisenstadt
CARINTHIA: Herrengasse 14, 9020 Klagenfurt
LOWER AUSTRIA: Herrengasse 11-13, 1014 Vienna
SALZBURG: Michael Pacher Strasse 40, 5020 Salzburg
STYRIA: Bürgergasse 2a, 8010 Graz
TIROL: Herrengasse 1, 6010 Innsbruck
UPPER AUSTRIA: Anzengruber Strasse 19, 4020 Linz
VIENNA: Magistratabteilung 8, 1082 Vienna
VORARLBERG: Kirchstrasse 28, 6901 Bregenz

It is impossible to list in any great detail the records in each of the above provincial archives. There is great variation from province to province, and also great variation in the degree of helpfulness found in each director!

Generally speaking, the provincial archives contain records dating back to the seventeenth century and including internal passports (Passkontrollen); orphans' lists (Waisenbücher); citizens' lists (Bürgerbücher); tax rolls (Steuerbücher); wills (Testamente); city directories (Adressbücher); certificates of domicile (Heimatscheinlisten); labor book registration (Arbeitsbuch-Protokolle); poorhouse records (Armen- und Versorgungshäuser); foundling books (Findelbücher); house records (Abhandlungsakten über Hausbesitz); land and property registers (Bürger Kataster); land records (Grundbücher or Kaufbücher). Please note that not all the provincial archives have all the above records.

Certain of the provincial archives, however, do have very specialized records which can be of great value to you:

Lower Austria

The archives here hold the Feudal Tenure Books (Lehenbücher) from the sixteenth to the eighteenth centuries for the whole of Lower Austria. These list the names of the serfs, their location, and the names of their noble masters.

Salzburg

In 1731–32 the Prince-Bishop of Salzburg expelled some 30,000 Protestants from his province. Some went overseas but the majority settled in North Germany. The provincial archives have records of those expelled, and there are other sources in Germany (see that chapter).

Styria

Very early censuses were held in this province between 1707 and 1853 and the returns are in the archives. Of course, you need to know an approximate address, but generally speaking, if you know the name of the village, that is sufficient. Larger towns such as Graz may present problems, but even there the address should be obtainable.

Tirol

The provincial archives can put you in touch with the local genealogical organization (Tiroler Matrikel-Stiftung) in Innsbruck, and for a small fee its members will search for a particular surname listed in the standard book about Tiroler families (*Tiroler Namenkunde* by Karl Finsterwalder, 1978).

City Archives (Stadtarchiv)

Limited sources of information are also available in the city, town, and village archives (Stadtarchiv). Most of them have some records of genealogical value. The main city archives are listed below, followed by details of those with good genealogical records. The address in each case is Stadtarchiv, Rathaus, followed by the name of the place.

The Stadtarchiv exist in all the main cities and towns and in most villages. The contents vary considerably, from the vast resources of Vienna to a handful of material in such places as Leoben, in Styria. Because of this great variation, no general list of records will be of value, but to give you some guide to the type of records you will find I list below the main items in the Vienna City Archives and then, by contrast, the material in two much smaller places:

Vienna City Archives (Stadtarchiv, Wien)

These archives are combined with the provincial archives for Vienna and are located at the same address: Magistratabteilung 8, 1082 Vienna.

Conscription Lists (Konskriptionsregister), 1740–1820

These give name, date and place of birth, and often, names and addresses of next of kin.

Passport Controls (Passkontrollen), 1795–1901

These are the records of people who left Vienna for overseas, or for another part of the Empire. They give names, dates, and destinations.

Citizen Books (Bürgerbücher), 1600s–1900s

These list names and addresses of people becoming *citizens* of the city and not merely inhabitants. There was a major difference between the two.

Tax Books (Steuerbücher), 1600–1905

These list taxpayers, giving address and occupation. There is an index by name from 1600 to 1748 and by profession or occupation from 1749 to 1812.

Guild Records (Zunftbücher), 1600s–1800s

These are only partially complete but they do give names of masters and their apprentices. The trade guilds were the equivalent of modern trade unions but exercised more power over their members and their occupations. The "closed shop" was invented in Europe in the Middle Ages! These records may be very valuable to you.

Wills and other Probate Records (Testamente)

These run from the early sixteenth century to the present and are indexed.

Certificates of Domicile (Heimatscheinlisten), 1850–91

These are records of identity documents issued; they give place of birth, occupation, and address.

Labor Book Registers (Arbeitsbuch-Protokolle), 1820–91

Everyone who worked had to carry a small book listing his name and address, age, and occupation, and employers for whom he had worked.

City Directories (Adressbücher), 1797 to date

These give name, address, and occupation and are invaluable if you are trying to trace an exact address in order to search census records.

Pedigrees (Abstammungskartei von Personen Jüdischer Abstammung)

These records contain nearly half a million names and are the family trees of Austrians with Jewish blood. The information was collected in 1938–39, and in many cases family information was given dating back to the early nineteenth century.

There are many other sources of information in the Vienna City Archives: poorhouse records, orphans' lists, court records, inquests, mortgages, and a partially indexed list of deaths in the city from 1648 (with some gaps between 1657 and 1677).

Here are some examples of records available in smaller places:

Enns (in Upper Austria): Miscellaneous family documents, 1366–1653

Wels (in Upper Austria): Censuses (Volkszählunglisten) from 1830

Now that you know the main locations of miscellaneous, but important, genealogical records in Austria, let us talk about the major and more obvious sources.

Civil Registration (Standesamt Register)

This is the compulsory registration of births, marriages, and deaths—a vital source of information in this country but of less value in Austria because it did not start until 1938, with the exception of Wiener Neustadt (1872) and Burgenland (1895). The records are in the Standesamt in Wiener Neustadt and Eisenstadt in Burgenland. Before 1938 the only similar records were baptisms, marriages, and burials recorded by the local churches. You will find the civil registration records of each district in the office of the local registrar (Standesamt).

Church Registers (Pfarr Register)

The religions that were officially authorized to keep records of vital events before civil registration were:

1. The Catholic Church
2. The Lutheran Church (Protestant). This was divided into two sects, the Augsburg Confession and the Helvetic Confession.*
3. The Old Catholic Church
4. The Eastern Orthodox Church (Holy Trinity)
5. The Eastern Orthodox Church (St. George)
6. The Romanian-Greek Orthodox Church (Holy Resurrection)
7. The Serbian-Greek Orthodox Church (St. Sava)
8. The Jewish Cultural Community

The great majority of Austrians are Catholic, but until 1849 Catholic priests also had to include in their registers the records of all other denominations. So, even though your ancestors were Lutheran or Jewish, you must search Catholic registers up to 1849. From 1878 until 1917 the Lutherans had to send a duplicate copy of all register entries to the church headquarters: Oberkirchenrat, Severin Schreiber Gasse 3, 1180 Vienna. From 1870 onward other religions, and also people with no religion, registered their names in local magistrates' courts, where the lists are still located.

Catholic Registers

These are, generally speaking, still in the original churches or in city and town archives. A few are in church and provincial archives. There is no point in listing every Catholic parish in Austria since this would, in effect, be a gazetteer listing the name of every city, town, and village in the whole country, including thirty churches for Vienna alone. The starting date of the parish registers varies considerably, but in general, you will find that most of them go back to 1750 and many to the early 1600s. At least one (Thalgau) dates back to 1580.

---

*The headquarters of both sections of the Lutheran Church is located at Severin Schreiber Gasse 3, 1180 Vienna.

The following places have parish archives (Pfarrarchiv) in which church records are located. Not all of them contain church registers, for often these have been lost. You will have to write to the parish priest (Pfarrer) to find out just what he has in his custody. Quite apart from the registers, check to see if he has any of the following records:

Grave Registers (Grabregister)

Church Receipt Books (Einnahme Bücher)

Confirmation Records (Konfirmation Bücher)

Funeral Sermons (Leichenpredigten)

Of course, when you do write be sure you enclose at least two International Reply Coupons and a self-addressed airmail envelope. Also, make it clear you will pay whatever fees are required. Finally, and I know this should be unnecessary advice, be friendly and polite. He does not have to give you any information and a terse, demanding letter won't produce results. Try to write in German, but good English is better than bad German, and if you do write in English you can always end your letter with the magic words "Mit freundlichen Grüssen"—"With friendly greetings."

In this list of parish archives the parishes are given alphabetically under each province:

BURGENLAND: Eisenstadt (Diocesan Archives—Diözesanarchiv).

CARINTHIA: Bad St. Leonhard, Klagenfurt (Diözesan).

LOWER AUSTRIA: Aggsbach, Emmersdorf, Friedersbach, Gmünd, Gresten, Haag, Krems/Donau, Krumau, Laa an der Thaya, Langenfeld, Maria Taferl, Neustadl, Oberleis, Pitten, Ruprechtshofen, St. Egtden, Spitz/Donau, Tribuswinkel, Walterskirchen, Weiten, Weitra, St. Pölten (Diözesan).

SALZBURG: Abtenau, Adnet, Aigen, Alm, Altenmarkt, Badgastein, Bergheim, Berndorf, Bischofshofen, Bramberg, Bruck, Dienten, Dorfbeuern, Elizhausen, Embach, Fusch, Golling, Hallein, Hallwang, Henndorf, Bad Hofgastein, Köstendorf, Krimml, Kuchl, Lend, Leogang, Mariapfarr, Neumarkt, Pfarrwerfen, Piesendorf, Radstat, Ramingstein, Rauris, Saalbach, Saalfelden, St. Georgen, St. Johann/Pongau, St. Veit, Siezenheim, Strasswalchen, Strobl, Stuhfelden, Tamsweg, Taxenbach, Thalgau, Uttendorf, Wagrain, Wald, Werfen, Zederhaus, Zell am See, Salzburg (Diözesan).

STYRIA: Anger, Eggersdorf, Fehring, Feldbach, Gaal, Gleisdorf, Gröbming, Gröming, Grosslobming, Hartberg, Haus, Judenburg, Knittelfeld, Köflach, Krieglach, Kumberg, Leibnitz, Lind, Obdach, Oberzeiring, Paldau, Pols, Purgg, Radkersburg, Ranten, Ratten, Riegersburg, Rottenmann, St. Georgen/Murau, St. Marein/Knittelfeld, St. Marein/Mürztal, St. Oswald, St. Peter/Judenberg, St. Radegund, Spital, Voitsberg, Weizberg, Graz (Diözesan).

TIROL: Innsbruck (Diözesan).

UPPER AUSTRIA: Enns, Freistadt, Grieskirchen, Östermiething, Uttendorf, Wartberg, Windhaag/Perg.

VORARLBERG: Feldkirch (Bishop's Archive—Bistumarchiv).

In addition to the above archives there are many others in various places concerned with religious institutions—nunneries and monasteries, markets, government departments, guilds, etc.

The Lutheran Church

The main archives are at Severin Schreiber Gasse 3, 1180 Vienna.

Lutheran Registers

These, also, are still in the churches, and since the numbers are far fewer than the Catholic ones, it is possible to list those parishes with registers dating back before 1900:

BURGENLAND: Bernstein, Deutsch Jahrndorf, Deutsch Kaltenbrunn, Eltendorf, Gols, Grosspetersdorf, Holzschlag, Kobersdorf, Kukmirn, Lutsmannsburg, Markt Allhau, Moerbisch-am-See, Neuhaus/ Klausenburg, Nickelsdorf, Oberschutzen, Oberwart, Pinkafeld, Pöttelsdorf, Reichnitz, Rust, Sziget, Stadt Schlaining, Stoob, Underschutzen, Weppersdorf, Zurndorf.

CARINTHIA AND EAST TIROL: Arriach, Bleiberg, Dornbach/Gmünd, Eggen/ Kraigerberg, Eisentratten, Feffernitz, Feld-am-See, Fresach, Gnesau, Klagenfurt, St. Ruprecht/Villach, Trebising, Tressdorf/Kirchbach, Tschörau/Bodensdorf, Völkermarkt, Waiern/Feldkirchen, Weissbriach, Wolfsberg, Zlan.

LOWER AUSTRIA: Baden, Mitterbach, Mödling, Nasswald, St. Pölten, Wiener Neustadt.

SALZBURG AND NORTH TIROL: Innsbruck, Salzburg.

STYRIA: Graz, Gröbming, Murzzuschlag, Ramsau am Dachstein, Schladming, Stainach/Irdning, Wald/Schober.

UPPER AUSTRIA: Attersee, Bad Goisern, Braunau-am-Inn, Eferding, Gall- neukirchen, Gmunden, Gosau, Hallstatt, Linz-Innere Stadt, Neukematen, Rutzenmoss, Scharten, Steyr, Thening, Vöcklabruck, Wallern/Trattnach, Wels.

VIENNA: Gumpendorf, Landstrasse, Vienna, Währing.

Many of the above registers date back to the early eighteenth century.

Registers of the Old Catholic Church date back to 1870 when this sect broke away from the main Catholic Church in a dispute over the infallibility of the Pope. The Orthodox Churches started to keep records in 1790.

Wills (Testamente)

These date back to 1600 and can be found in three different locations: provincial archives (Landesarchiv), city archives (Stadtarchiv), and in local magistrate's courts (Magistratsgericht).

Census Returns (Personenstandsgesetz)

These have been held in Austria since the eighteenth century with the actual dates varying from province to province. The first nationwide census was held in 1869 and since then eleven censuses have been held. The first four were for the whole Austro-Hungarian Empire, and the last seven for present-day Austria (1869, 1890, 1900, 1910, 1923, 1934, 1951, 1961, 1971, 1981, and 1991). The records are kept at the Central Statistics Office (Statistisches Zentralamt), Heldenplatz, Neue Burg, 1010 Vienna. Don't forget, of course, the early censuses in the province of Styria mentioned earlier in this chapter.

Movement Registration (Einwohnerlisten)

These records date from the early eighteenth century up to the present day and record all movement within the Empire up to 1918 and in the country from then on. Their location, unfortunately, varies between the National Archives (Österreichisches Archiv, Allgemeines Verwaltungsarchiv, Wallnerstrasse 6a, 1010 Vienna); the various provincial archives (Landesarchiv); and the different city archives (Stadtarchiv).

Marriage Contracts (Eheverträge)

These were necessary whenever the bride owned, or was heiress to, property. They date back to the late 1300s and can be found in city archives (Stadtarchiv).

University Registers (Universitätsmatrikeln)

If your ancestor attended a university, you will find full information about him or her in the archives of each university, or in the archives of the city in which the university is located. Records started in the 1300s.

Genealogical Organizations (Familienverbände)

By far the most important organization in Austria is Heraldisch-Genealogische Gesellschaft "Adler," Haarhof 4a, 1014 Vienna. It is a small private organization with a dedicated membership, but without a government subsidy or any paid staff. The members in general are working on their own family tree as you are, but some of them are prepared to undertake searching for an overseas inquirer for a reasonable fee. The territory of operation is that of the old Empire and not just of modern Austria. All inquiries should be accompanied by two International Reply Coupons and a self-addressed airmail envelope. The organization will give you the name of a member willing to do research and you will agree on the fee with him or her. You must remember there is never any guarantee of success with research, and you must be prepared for this.

You may be sure that the member suggested will be familiar with the records in the place in which you are interested, and the charges will be on a par with what you would pay in this country.

There are three other Familienverbände operating in specific areas of modern Austria:

Arbeitsbund für Österreichische Familienkunde
Bürgergasse 2a, 8010 Graz, Steiermark (Styria)

Oberösterreichische Landesstelle für Familienkunde
Bundesrealschule, 4010 Linz

Tiroler-Matrikel-Stiftung (Peestiftung)
Anichstrasse 18, 6020 Innsbruck, Tirol

MILITARY RECORDS

I have left this part of genealogical research toward the end of this chapter because it is very important and deserves your special attention. You may well ask, "What use are military records to me? My ancestors were farmers, not soldiers!" The answer is simple. In 1868 universal conscription came into effect in the Austro-Hungarian Empire and every male had to serve three years in the army or navy (this was reduced to two years in 1912).

Every conscript was fully documented from his date and place of birth, and all the records exist, they are readily available, and many of them are indexed. They are located in the Military Records branch of the National Archives: Kriegsarchiv, Stiftgasse 2, 1010 Vienna. There is not the space to list all the records, but at least I can tell you about the main ones.

First of all, I should mention that the records do, in fact, cover the period from the sixteenth century up to 1919. In other words, regular soldiers are included (long before the days of conscription a man enlisted for life).

In the armed forces there was no racial discrimination, and if your ancestors were Jewish you may well find a great deal of information about your soldier or sailor forebears, information which, in the civilian records, has been destroyed.

Commissions (Bestallungen)

These contain biographical and personal information about all officers serving in the army from the middle of the fifteenth century.

Muster-Rolls (Musterunglisten)

These contain full information about officers and other ranks serving in particular regiments. You do need to know the regiment in which your ancestor served in order to use these records, but quite often regiments were drawn from a particular area. In that case, if you know the place, you should be able to find out what the regiment was. For example, if your ancestor came from Graz, the odds are that he served in the 62nd Infantry. The regiments usually stayed close to home except in the case of war or rebellion.

The muster-rolls are available for the period 1740–1820 and contain the following: name, age, place of birth, religion, occupation before enlistment, names and places of birth of wife and children, and next of kin. They are indexed for officers.

Enlistment Orders (Stellungslisten)

These separate records give the exact birth date and the names of the enlistee's parents.

Discharge Books (Abgangsprotokolle)

These only cover a period of sixty years from 1859 but list all those discharged from the services.

Conscription Lists (Konskriptionsregister)

These records list the men conscripted for service each year in each particular area, giving the usual personal details and the name and address of the next of kin.

Other records available in the archives include wills (Testamente), 1639–1771, and foundation books (Grundbuchblätter und Stellungslisten). The latter list each soldier on a separate page, with full details of his movements with his regiment, and cover the years 1820–1918. There are also records of the navy organized on similar lines to that of the army.

It should be noted that many of the records for areas no longer in Austria have been transferred to the archives of their present-day countries.

LOCAL ARCHIVES

The various city and town archives in Austria that will be of possible use to you are listed below, alphabetically province by province. However, keep in mind that many small towns and villages, while not possessing archives, do have records in the Rathaus that may contain genealogical information:

BURGENLAND: Eisenstadt, Mattersburg, Neusiedl am See, Pinkafeld, Rust.

CARINTHIA: Friesach, Bad St. Leonhard, Oberdrauberg, Wolfsberg.

LOWER AUSTRIA: Amstetten, Baden bei Wien, Bruck, Drosendorf, Dürnstein, Eggenburg, Gmünd, Gross Enzersdorf, Gross-Siegharts, Haag, Hainburg an der Donau, Herzogenburg, Hollabrun, Hollenstein, Horn, Kloster-neuberg, Korneuburg, Krems/Donau, Laa an der Thaya, Langenlois, Litschau, Mautern, Mistelbach, Mödling, Neunkirchen, Perchtoldsdorf, Pöchlarn, Poysdorf, Retz, St. Pölten, Schwechat, Stockerau, Traiskirchen, Traismauer, Tulln, Bad Voslau, Waidhofen/Thaya, Weitra, Wiener Neustadt, Wolkersdorf, Ybbs an der Donau, Zistersdorf, Zwettl.

SALZBURG: Hallein, Radstadt, Salzburg, Wald, Zell am See.

STYRIA: Bierbaum, Bruck an der Mur, Gaal, Gleisdorf, Hainfeld, Judenberg, Leoben, Murau, Radkersburg, Voitsberg, Weiz.

TIROL: Innsbruck, Kitzbühel, Kufstein, Rattenberg, Solbad Hall.

UPPER AUSTRIA: Braunau am Inn, Eferding, Enns, Freistadt, Gaflenz, Gallneukirchen, Gallspach, Gmünden, Grein/Donau, Greinburg, Haag/Hausbruck, Bad Ischel, Kematen, Neufelden, Neumarkt/Grieskirchen, Ried, Rohrbach, Scharding, Steyr, Vöcklabruck, Wels.

VORARLBERG: Bludenz, Bregenz, Dornbirn, Feldkirch.

ESTATE AND FAMILY ARCHIVES

Many of the old Austrian families (and some new ones!) have maintained estate records over the years. These either are in the original family house (usually a castle or *schloss*) or have been handed over to local archives. If you are descended from one of these families or your ancestors worked on the estate, you may find useful information in these archives. Those known to be available for research are listed below. For further information you should write to, for example, Archiv Kripp, Absam, Tirol:

Place	*Province*	*Family Name*
Absam	Tirol	Kripp
Aistersheim	Upper Austria	Aistersheim
Bleiburg	Carinthia	Thurn
Eberau	Burgenland	Erdödy
Eferding	Upper Austria	Starhemberg
Eisenstadt	Burgenland	Esterházy
Feilhofen	Styria	Liechtenstein
Forchenstein	Burgenland	Esterházy
Grafenstein	Carinthia	Orsini-Rosenberg
Güssing	Burgenland	Battyány
Halbenrain	Styria	Stürgkh
Helfenberg	Upper Austria	Revertera

Place	*Province*	*Family Name*
Himmelberg	Carinthia	Lodron
Hoch Flachau	Salzburg	Plaz
Hohenems	Vorarlberg	Waldburg-Hohenems
Hollenegg	Styria	Liechtenstein
Horn	Lower Austria	Hoyos-Sprinzenstein
Klam bei Grein	Upper Austria	Clam-Martinitz
Murau	Styria	Schwarzenberg
Neulengbach	Lower Austria	Liechtenstein
Patsch	Tirol	Thurn and Taxis
Reideben	Carinthia	Donnersmark
Rosenburg	Lower Austria	Sprinzenstein
Starhemberg	Upper Austria	Starhemberg
Thannhausen	Styria	Gudenus
Waidhofen/Thaya	Lower Austria	Gudenus

GLOSSARY

These are the German words you are most likely to find useful in your search through Austrian records:

Abhandlungsakten über Hausbesitz	House Records
Abstammungskartei von Personen Jüdischer	Jewish Pedigrees
Adressbücher	City Directories
Arbeitsbuch-Protokolle	Labor Book Registration
Armen- und Versorgungshäuser	Poorhouse Records
Auswanderer Listen	Emigration Lists
Bezirk	District
Bezirksgerichte	District Courts
Bistum	Bishopric or Diocese
Bürgerbücher	Citizens' Lists
Bürgerkataster	Land and Property Registers
Eheakten	Marriage Deeds
Eheverträge Verlassenschaften	Marriage Contracts
Einwohnerlisten	List of Inhabitants
Erbverträge	Inheritance Contracts
Findelbücher	Foundling Books
Grundbücher, Kaufbücher	Land Records
Heimatscheinlisten	Certificates of Domicile
Herrschaftsarchiv	Landlord Archives
Kirchenbücher	Church Registers
Konskriptionsregister	Conscription Lists

Land	Province
Lehensbücher	Feudal Tenure Books
Magistratisches Zivilgericht	Magistrate's Court
Musterunglisten	Army Muster Rolls
Passkontrollen	Passport Controls
Personenstandsgesetz	Census Returns
Pfarr	Parish
Rathaus	City or Town Hall
Regierungsgebäude	Government Office
Sonderstandesämter	Special Registers
Staatsarchiv	State Archives
Stadtarchiv	City Archives
Standesamt	Registrar's Office
Steuerbücher	Tax Books
Taufen	Baptisms
Testamente	Wills and Probate Records
Totenbücher	Burial Lists
Trauungen	Marriages
Verfachbücher	Court Records
Volkszählunglisten	Census Returns
Waisenbücher	Orphans' Lists
Zunftbücher	Guild Records

BELGIUM

This country is known as *Belgique* in French and *Belge* in Flemish. Since both languages are official in Belgium, I have tried as far as possible to give names of organizations and addresses in the language used in that particular part of the country. In bilingual areas, such as the capital of the country, I have tried to give organization names and addresses in both languages, with French first and Flemish second, for example Brussels appears as Bruxelles (Brussel). I should, perhaps, explain to my readers of Flemish descent that no slur is intended in placing the Flemish word after the French in this way. It is simply that one has to be first and I have made an arbitrary decision.

The Low Countries (what is now Belgium and the Netherlands) have had a very checkered history and it is quite astonishing that so many genealogical records have survived. Because of the strategic position of the area they were in a constant state of war over many centuries. Originally the Low Countries belonged to the Empire of Charlemagne; later the major part belonged to one of the minor German kings. After 1384 the various provinces were ruled by the Duke of Burgundy, who got them by purchase, marriage, blackmail, threats, and cession—the classic steps on the road to dynastic power in the Middle Ages. In 1548 they passed by marriage into the possession of Spain.

From 1568 to 1648 there was a succession of revolts against the Spanish, and in 1581 the northern provinces of the Low Countries became the country of Holland (the Netherlands). Belgium remained under Spanish rule until 1810 when Napoleon incorporated the whole area into France. In 1815, at the Congress of Vienna, it was decided that both areas should be united in one country. The Belgians did not approve (they had anticipated their freedom for too long) and in 1831 they declared their independence.

Genealogical records in the country are scattered about in many archives, and before we talk about major sources of research we should perhaps think about their locations.

The archives in Belgium are divided into the Royal Archives in Brussels and eight provincial archives, four in the Walloon Provinces (Les Provinces

Wallonnes) and four in the Flemish Provinces (De Vlaamse Provinciën). Generally speaking, the northern provinces are Flemish, the southern ones are French, and Brussels is bilingual.

The Royal Archives are located in the capital, at the address given below in both French and Flemish:

Archives Générales du Royaume	Algemeen Rijksarchief
rue de Ruysbroeck 2	Ruisbroekstraat 2
1000 Bruxelles	1000 Brussel

These central archives include those of the Province of Brabant, of which Brussels is the center. They also contain the government archives; records of contested estates, involving land and/or money; and the parish registers of the Catholic churches in the Province of Brabant. There are also many family archives and genealogical collections donated by families or individual researchers.

The provincial archives contain such items as conscription records dating from 1796; population registers from 1796 (these record births and deaths of family members, addresses, and details of internal migration, and are usually indexed); records of passports issued and destination of emigrants; wills and probate records; civil registration of births, marriages, and deaths from 1795 (many of these are also indexed); parish registers and other church records from the early 1600s, or earlier; census returns where they exist; notarial records (lawyers' notes, papers, property sales or transfers, marriage contracts); genealogical collections and family papers; court records from 1341; guild records (members, date of admission, details of families); burgess rolls (details of people becoming citizens of a city, and not just inhabitants); and tax records.

As you can see, the genealogical material is enormous in quantity and excellent in quality. Not all the provincial archives have all this material, but most of them do, and some have records that are unique to a particular one. Antwerp (Anvers-Antwerpen), for example, has a record of every emigrant from the port in 1855, complete with place of origin, family members, and destination.

The provincial archives are located as follows:

Walloon Provinces (Provinces Wallonnes)

Archives de l'État à Arlon (Aarlen)
Parc des Expositions
6700 Arlon
Province du Luxembourg

Archives de L'État à Liège (Luik)
rue Pouplin 8
4000 Liège
Province de Liège

Archives de L'État à Mons (Bergen)
place du Parc 23
7000 Mons
Province de Hainaut

Archives de l'État à Namur (Namen)
rue d'Arquet 45
5000 Namur
Province de Namur

Flemish Provinces (Vlaamse Provinciën)

Het Rijksarchief Antwerpen (Anvers)
Door Verstraeteplaats 2
2000 Antwerpen
Provincie Antwerpen

Het Rijksarchief Brugge (Bruges)
Academiestraat 14
8000 Brugge
Provincie West Vlanderen

Het Rijksarchief Gent (Gand)
Gerard de Duivelsteen
9000 Gent
Provincie Oost Vlanderen

Het Rijksarchief Hasselt
Bampsplaan 4
3500 Hasselt
Provincie Limburg

Note: In certain of the above provinces the archives do not include a part of
the province that has its own archives. These are shown below:

Walloon Provinces (Provinces Wallonnes)

Archives de l'État à Huy (Hoei)
Ancien couvent des Frères Mineurs
5200 Huy
Province de Liège

Archives de l'État à Saint-Hubert
Abbaye
6900 Saint-Hubert
Province de Luxembourg

Archives de l'État à Tournai (Doornik)
rue du Sondart 12
7500 Tournai
Province de Hainaut

Flemish Provinces (Vlaamse Provinciën)

Het Rijksarchief Beveren-Waas
Kruibekesteenweg 39
2750 Beveren-Waas
Provincie Oost Vlanderen

Het Rijksarchief Kortrijk (Courtrai)
G. Gezellestraat
8500 Kortrijk
Provincie West Vlanderen

Het Rijksarchief Ronse (Renaix)
Biezestraat 2
9600 Ronse
Provincie Oost Vlanderen

Saint-Hubert and Beveren-Waas, although functioning as district archives, are primarily only temporary resting places for archival material destined for other major archives, but for which there is no space available for the time being.

Parish Registers (Registres Paroissiaux— Parochierregisters)

Belgium is one of the few countries in Europe where the early church registers (up to at least 1796) have been handed over to the state archives, and either originals or copies of many of the more recent ones have also been deposited. What is even more exciting is that almost every register has been indexed. They really are a joy to work with and I wish many more countries would follow the example of Belgium. With the limitations of space it is not possible to list all the registers in the archives—although I have been supplied with full details by the Archivist-General of Belgium. However, this presents no problem, because if you have a place and a date, the various provincial archives can very quickly find the particular entry you need.

The archives at Liège have the registers from the former German area of Eupen-Malmedy. Both Catholic and Protestant registers are available for Blegny, Dalhem, Eupen, and Olne. A few years are also available for Bassenge (1770), Eisenborn (1807), Meyrose (1783, 1785), Reuland (1808), Richelle (1813), Saint-André (1813), Saint-Remy (1813), Sourbrodt (1807), Visé (1813, 1814), Waimes (1806, 1807), and Wévercé (1807).

In the archives at Antwerp you will find that many of the parishes have deposited registers as recently as 1885. The same applies to Hasselt but only up to 1870, and to Ronse to the same year.

So far as the Province of Brabant (which includes Brussels) is concerned, its parish registers are in the custody of the Royal Archives (Archives Générales du Royaume, rue de Ruysbroeck 2, 1000 Brussels).

Civil Registration (Registres de L'État Civil— Registers van de Burgerlijke Stand)

Civil registration started in 1796 under the French occupation. One copy of the records is held in the local municipality and the registrar will provide a photocopy for a small fee (inquiries should be sent to M. l'Officier de l'État Civil—M. Officier van de Burgerlijke Stand). The registers are indexed from 1802 onwards. It should be noted that surnames with the prefix "de" are under D and those with the prefix "van" are under V.

There are also population registers, starting in 1850, in the municipal offices. For some reason they are not open to public inspection, but information from them will be given quite freely by the official named above.

Wills (Testaments)

Except for more recent ones these are in the custody of the provincial archives. More recent ones are in the local courts.

Emigration Records

As mentioned above, many of the provincial archives have records of passports issued, and also of police records that show the removal of a family or an individual from one place to another within Belgium. Some police records are in municipal archives and if you do not find anything in the provincial archives you should check locally.

In addition, the provincial archives in Antwerp have the 1855 register for all persons emigrating through the port of Antwerp. Records of other years were destroyed during the First World War. The registers have been indexed by the LDS Church and give the name of the ship, the name of the captain, the destination, the date of departure, the full names of the passengers, and their age and place of birth.

Hotel Registers

These are in the Antwerp Municipal Archives (Stadsarchief—Les Archives de la Ville) and can be very useful indeed. The emigrant vessels did not adhere to a regular schedule and would wait in port until the very last passenger could be packed into an already overcrowded ship. The result was that emigrants would arrive in the port to find that the sailing was delayed. They would have to find a small hotel and, usually, a temporary job until they could board the ship. The available hotel registers date from 1679 to 1811 for foreigners from other parts of Europe, and from 1858 to 1898 for all nationalities.

Genealogical Organizations

L'Office Généalogique et Héraldique de Belgique
Musées Royaux d'Art et d'Histoire
10 avenue des Nerviens
1040 Brussels

This organization is devoted to research in the Walloon areas of Belgium, but failed to answer my inquiries.

Service de Centralisation des Études Généalogiques et Démographiques de Belgique
Maison des Arts
Chaussée de Haecht Schaerbeck 147
1030 Brussels

This is a centralized referral service for genealogical research inquiries in Belgium. It also did not respond to my inquiries.

Vlaamse Vereniging voor Familiekunde
Van Heybeeckstraat 3
2060 Antwerpen-Merksem

This excellent and helpful organization is a credit to any country. If your ancestors from Belgium are of Flemish descent or from the Flemish section of the country, you are lucky to have the V.V.F. to help you. It is staffed entirely by volunteers, and for service and efficiency there is no comparison between the V.V.F. and other organizations with a paid staff.

The organization was set up in 1964 and publishes a monthly magazine called *Vlaamse Stam*, which goes out to each of the 3,000 members. In every Flemish province the V.V.F. has a gouw or district branch, with sub-branches in each important town.

At the national headquarters in Antwerp the staff answer all written, telephone, and personal-call questions, totaling over 4,500 a year. They will try to answer your simple queries without charge (if you cover the return postage with two International Reply Coupons), but if your inquiry is more complicated you will be referred to one of their members, who will do research for you for an agreed fee. You will find the association particularly willing to help overseas inquirers. Donations will be welcome, of course. Your query can be sent in English.

The V.V.F. library is growing by 800 books a year from all over the world, and by 100 genealogical magazines a month. The V.V.F. also holds seventy-five percent of all indexes and inventories of genealogical sources from all over the world; the electoral registers of nearly all the Belgian municipalities; over 100,000 obituaries; half a million "In Memoriam" cards; a growing collection of press clippings; family and local histories in both published and manuscript form; and a large collection of genealogical manuscripts from 1500 to the present day.

Obviously the V.V.F. is fast becoming a document collection center for all genealogical material. It also has access to an on-line computer. In Belgium, as in many other countries, this is a very visible part of genealogical research.

If you join the organization, you can also make use of the Question and Answer Section (Vraag en Antwoord) of *Vlaamse Stam*. Use of this section could well put you in touch with distant relatives, or with other members who are expert and knowledgeable about a particular district in Belgium.

Belgian Minorities

There are over 100,000 people of German descent living in the Province de Liège. This is the result of the transfer of the Eupen and Malmedy districts to Belgium after the First World War. Church and civil records for this area are located in the provincial archives at Liège (for address, see earlier in this chapter).

Census Returns

Censuses are held every tenth year (starting in 1846) with occasional gaps. The returns are not normally available for public search, but consideration will be given to a special application on legal grounds, accompanied by proof of descent. Application can be made to the Institut National de Statistiques (Nationaal Instituut voor Statistiek), Brussels. The odds, however, will be against you.

There are some early census returns that are open for search. There were censuses in the city of Namur in 1745, 1766, 1775, 1784, 1794, 1804, and 1812 that are in the state archives there. Censuses also took place in the Province of Brabant in 1693, 1709, and 1755, and these are in the National Archives in Brussels.

The Low Countries

If you get back far enough you will enter the period when Belgium and Holland were controlled by either Austria or Spain. Some records exist in the National Archives of both countries, but in Spain you may have trouble in running them to earth. In this area the V.V.F. (see above) can be very helpful.

In Antwerp V.V.F. has an inventory of sources of information about men from the Southern Netherlands (Belgium) who served in the Austrian army. It also has inventories of genealogical material from the occupation period, most of which is now located in the archives at Dijon, Lille, and Paris, in France, and also in the Simancas Archives in Spain.

Details of the holdings in the archives at Lille are very important as it was once part of the Earldom of Flanders, which included the Flemish areas of

Belgium. The archives at Lille have a great deal of genealogical material for Flanders during that period. So far as French Flanders is concerned, the V.V.F. holds a great deal of material from Bergues St. Winoque, which was a Flemish-speaking district in a Walloon area.

BOSNIA-HERZEGOVINA

This country is divided into two regions—Bosnia in the north and Herzegovina in the south. The capital is Sarajevo, in Bosnia. The chief city in the south is Mostar. The language of the population is Serbo-Croat and the main religions are Muslim, Catholic, and Orthodox. There is an ethnic brew scattered in pockets throughout the area.

Bosnia was originally a Roman province, and became fully independent in the twelfth century after being settled by Serbs after the Roman departure. Later it acknowledged the Hungarian kings as overlords. By the fourteenth century Bosnia was a powerful state controlling much territory on its borders. It annexed the Duchy of Hum and doubled its size. The latter area declared its complete independence of Bosnia in 1448 under the name of Herzegovina. There was considerable religious warfare in both countries at this time, and the Turks invaded Bosnia in 1463 and Herzegovina two years later in order to protect the Muslim population and expand still further into Europe.

The two countries remained under Turkish control for several centuries but a peasant rebellion in 1875 led to Russian intervention against the Turks. At the Congress of Berlin—held at the end of the war in 1878—Bosnia and Herzegovina were placed under the control of the Austro-Hungarian Empire. They were completely annexed in 1906.

In 1918 Serbia took control and joined with them and other areas to form the new kingdom of Yugoslavia. In World War II they were joined to Croatia by the Germans, but in 1946 the united country of Bosnia-Herzegovina became one of the founding republics of the Yugoslav republic. It was an uneasy alliance in view of Serbia's attempts to dominate the republic. In 1992 Bosnia-Herzegovina declared its independence. This was recognized by the United Nations and the European Community (EC).

There are a number of archives in the country and their addresses are given below:

Archives of Bosnia
Save Kovačevića 6
71001 Sarajevo

Historical Archives
Koturova 3
71001 Sarajevo

Archives of Herzegovina
Trg 1 maja 17
79000 Mostar

Bosanska Krajina Archives
Aleja JNA 1/1
78000 Banja Luka

Archives of Central Bosnia
Omladinska 8
72270 Travnik

Regional Historical Archives
Moše Pijade 13
75001 Tuzla

Regional Archives
Ismeta Kapetanovića 43
74000 Doboj

Be aware that because of the civil war in the early 1990s, many records have been destroyed. In addition, there's been widespread forced relocation of people from their ancestral homes.

Other records that might be useful are described in the chapter on Yugoslavia later in this book.

BULGARIA

Bulgaria occupies the area of ancient Thrace and Moesia, which was settled by Slavic peoples in about 600 and later by the nomadic Bulgars. It is believed they originated in the Volga area of what is now Ukraine. Sofia was taken from the Byzantines in 811. By this time the Bulgars and the original Slavs had merged into one race, speaking a Slavic language.

In 1018 the Byzantines reconquered the country and it remained under their control until a rebellion in 1186. During the next century Bulgaria reached its period of greatest expansion, controlling nearly all the Balkan area with the exception of Greece. At the end of two centuries of grandeur it was conquered by the Ottoman Empire. There were frequent unsuccessful revolts during the next five centuries until the country was liberated by Russia in 1878. The Bulgarians you meet in your visit to the homeland of your ancestors will be quick to tell you that they have twice been liberated by their "Russian brothers" from the "Imperialists" (the other time being in 1944).

After the Congress of Berlin in 1878, North Bulgaria became a vassal state of Turkey, while South Bulgaria (then known as Eastern Rumelia) and Macedonia were ruled directly from Constantinople. In 1885 Eastern Rumelia was reconquered by the Bulgars, and in 1908 Bulgaria declared the complete independence of the reunited country.

Bulgarian claims to Macedonia led to the Balkan Wars of 1912–13 in which Bulgaria made wide conquests of Balkan territory. In 1915 the country, led by its German-born king, "Foxy Ferdinand," joined the First World War on the side of Germany and the Austro-Hungarian Empire. It was a disastrous move, because in the Peace Treaty of Neuilly that followed the Allied victory, Bulgaria lost its outlet to the Aegean Sea to Greece, the South Dobrudja to Romania, and some territory to Yugoslavia.

In 1940 Bulgaria reclaimed the South Dobrudja and joined the Axis powers in 1941. The USSR declared war on Bulgaria in 1944—belatedly because in 1941 the Bulgarians had declared war on the United States and Great Britain, and had occupied parts of Greece and Yugoslavia. Since the population of Bulgaria was very pro-Russian, no action was taken against the USSR at that time. However, the USSR did declare war in due course, and this was followed by an immediate armistice. Bulgaria then declared war on Germany. In 1945 a republic was declared and in 1947 a peace treaty allowed Bulgaria to retain the South Dobrudja.

The capital of the country is Sofia and the administrative districts are Blagoevgrad, Burgas, Gabrovo, Haskovo Choumen, Iamdol, Kakdjali, Kustendil, Lovetche, Michailovgrad, Pazardjik, Pernik, Pleven, Plovdiv, Razgrad, Russe, Silistra, Sliven, Smolian, Sofia (city), Sofia (district), Stara Zagora, Targovichte, Tolbouhin, Varna, Veliko-Tarnovo, Vidin, Vratza.

Each of the above-mentioned districts has its own archives. For information about a particular area you should write to the Director, Dăržaven Istoričeski, followed by the name of the city. For more general information contact the National Archives (Centralen Dăržaven Arhiv, ul. Slavjanka, Sofia).

Civil Registration

This started in 1893 for births, marriages, and deaths. The records are kept in the various districts in the People's Council Office, which acts as the local registration office. Birth, marriage, and death certificates may be obtained for a small fee.

Church Registers

These appear to have started as recently as 1800 in most places and are kept in the local churches. It was at this time that the Bulgarian Orthodox Church broke away from the Eastern Orthodox Church. Eighty-five percent of the Bulgarians belong to this church, the remainder being Muslims. The churches can supply certificates of marriage and baptism. Be sure you ask for the full details, including names of witnesses or godparents.

Wills

These are limited in number, because very few Bulgarians owned enough property or real estate to make a will necessary. They are in the custody of the Ministry of Justice, in Sofia.

Censuses

These took place in 1881, 1893, 1905, 1920, 1926, and 1934. It is not known what information is contained in the census returns; whether any have been held since 1934; where the returns are located; or whether anyone tracing their Bulgarian ancestors may have access to them.

There must surely be other records of genealogical value in the various archives, but under Communism the Bulgarian government was totally non-informative about its records. I failed to obtain any details during my visit to the country, nor was I any more successful by correspondence with Sofia. However, the Cultural Attaché of Bulgaria in Ottawa, Canada, was most helpful in answering a few questions. I suggest you try writing directly to the National or District Archives first, and if that fails, try your nearest Bulgarian Embassy.

One result of the disappearance of Communist regimes in Eastern Europe has been greater cooperation with the LDS Church. This is particularly true of Bulgaria. The LDS has recently concluded agreements to microfilm civil registration and church records of all denominations for the period from 1800 to 1945.

CROATIA

Croatia includes within its borders such areas of historical renown as Dalmatia, Slavonia, and parts of Istria. The majority of Croats are Catholic, but there are minority groups that include Serbs, Slovenes, Hungarians, and Germans.

Croatia became an independent kingdom in the tenth century but became linked with Hungary in 1091. However, it continued to elect its own rulers and retained its own *Diet*, or Parliament. In 1526 it came under Turkish rule, and this forced the Croats to accept the Hapsburgs as their kings in return for military assistance in expelling the Turks.

When the Austro-Hungarian Empire was first established in 1867, Croatia and Slavonia were included in Hungary, and Dalmatia and Istria in Austria. The following year Croatia was granted local autonomy but was restless under Hungarian control and efforts to Magyarize it. In 1918 the country joined with Serbia and Slovenia in creating Yugoslavia—the kingdom of the Serbs, Croats, and Slovenes as it was called. It was not long before sporadic uprisings occurred because of Serbian efforts to centralize government in Belgrade.

In World War II Croatia was granted limited independence under joint German-Italian control. Civil war followed with the majority of Croats under Tito (himself a Croat) fighting the Germans. In 1945 it became one of the founding states in a reconstituted Yugoslavia. Croatia declared its independence in 1991, and this was recognized by the United Nations and the European Community (EC).

National Archives

The National Archives are located in Zagreb at the below address:

Archives of Croatia
Marulićev trg 21
41001 Zagreb

Historical Archives

Historical archives are located in various provincial centers. The locations are given below:

Opatička 29	Vladimira Nazora 26
41001 Zagreb	51400 Pazin
Pavlinks Majur Trstenjakova 7	Ive Lole Ribara 4/III
42000 Varaždin	58000 Split
Trg Jedinstva 3	Palača Sponza
43000 Bjelovar	55000 Dubrovnik
Nikole Demonje 1	Park Vladimira Nazora 2
Osijek	51000 Rijeka
Augusta Cesarca 1	Džemala Bijedića
55000 Slanonski Brod	47000 Karlovac
Rade Končara 21	Letnjikovac Hanibala Lucića
44000 Sisak	58450 Hvar

Note: Much damage was sustained in these areas in World War II and in the recent civil war.

Civil Registration

Civil registration started in 1946. Before that year vital events were recorded in the churches.

Church Registers

Croatia is regarded as a Catholic country, but there are also Orthodox and Lutheran churches.

Censuses

Most of the early censuses are missing, but fragments exist for 1673 and 1815. These are in the National Archives in Zagreb (see above). Other records are described in the chapter on Yugoslavia later in this book.

At the time of publication, negotiations were still taking place on the question of the exact boundaries of Croatia. It is possible that some of the places listed above may be transferred to Serbia.

CYPRUS

Cyprus has been inhabited since 4000 B.C. The Phoenicians settled the island in 800 B.C and subsequent invaders included Assyrians, Egyptians, Persians, Romans, Byzantines, Venetians, and Turks. It was part of the Ottoman Empire from 1571 to 1878, when it was placed under British administration. In 1914 Great Britain annexed the island, which became an independent republic in 1960.

In 1974 after many years of tension between the Greek and the Turkish communities, the country was invaded by Turkish forces, which occupied the predominantly Turkish-speaking north of the island. As a result, many Greeks in the north fled to the south, and many Turks in the south fled to the north. Although peace talks have continued sporadically since then, the situation is basically unchanged. Access to the Turkish-controlled one-third of the island is generally obtained by entry from Turkey. However, recently there has been some traffic allowed between the south and the north. If you are proposing to visit Cyprus, be sure you check the present situation and obtain all the necessary travel documents before you leave home. You should obtain information from both the Turkish and Cypriot embassies if you plan to travel between the two parts of the country. Entry to the south only, including the capital of Nicosia, can be obtained from any of the nearby countries such as Greece, Italy, Egypt, and Israel.

It is not easy to obtain genealogical information from Cyprus, but your best sources of information are the Ministry of the Interior or the Archbishop of Cyprus, both located in Nicosia. Other local offices are listed below.

Religions

Islam is the predominant religion in the north, Christianity in the south. The latter is mainly Greek Orthodox, but there are also small numbers of Catholics, Armenian Gregorians, and Maronites. The church registers are still in the original churches and have not been centralized.

Civil Registration

This commenced in 1895 for births and deaths, and in 1923 for marriages. The records are kept in local registration offices in each district. For information before these dates you will be dependent on church registers, which date back to about 1870 in the Christian churches and to 1850 in the mosques.

Censuses

These were held at ten-year intervals from 1881 to 1931. Since then there have been censuses in 1946 and 1960, the last full censuses to be taken on the island. However, there was a partial census in 1973 for certain areas, and in 1976 for the non-Turkish part of the country. Information from the census returns can be obtained by writing to the Ministry of the Interior, Nicosia.

Wills

These are in the custody of the probate registrar in each district. If you do not know the exact address of your ancestor, you should write to the Ministry of the Interior in Nicosia.

THE CZECH REPUBLIC

Until 1993 the Czech Republic was joined with Slovakia to form Czecho-slovakia. Although Czechoslovakia was only created as a separate country in 1919, its historical roots go deep into central Europe. After the Treaty of Versailles the new country consisted of four provinces: Bohemia (Cechy), Moravia (Morava), Silesia (Slezsko), and Slovakia (Slovensko). The area of Ruthenia (Podkarpatská Rus) was also included.

The name Bohemia originated after the area was first populated by the Boii, a Celtic tribe, under the leadership of Boiohemus. However, the name is not used in the present-day Czech Republic. The official name is Cechy and the people are called Cechové or Czechs.

By the seventh century the four provinces mentioned had joined with Austria and Poland to form the Moravian Empire. The Magyars invaded in the tenth century and Slovakia became a part of Hungary. When the Moravian Empire disappeared, the Czechs and Moravians joined together in the Duchy of Bohemia and Moravia, and—together with Silesia—became part of the Holy Roman Empire. In 1198 the area became the Kingdom of Bohemia, and this survived until 1620, when the area came under the control of the Hapsburg Dynasty.

After the First World War, Czechoslovakia was created out of the ruins of the old Austro-Hungarian Empire. Although its creation was hailed as a great victory for democracy in central Europe, all was not sweetness and light. Many Slovakians would have preferred to remain within Hungary rather than join with a people with whom they shared neither religion nor language, and the boundaries of the new country included large numbers of Germans and Hungarians now separated from their homelands.

In 1938 the German-speaking areas, the Sudetenland, were incorporated into Germany, and in 1939 a German protectorate of Bohemia and Moravia was proclaimed. Slovakia became nominally independent under German control.

After the Second World War, there was a total and drastic expulsion of all Germans from the country, followed by a mass exodus of Hungarians.

Ruthenia was seized by the USSR and is now known as the Oblast of Zakarpatskaya, an administrative district of Ukraine.

In 1949 the original system of provincial administration was abolished and administrative districts (oblasti) were set up. The lower division is a county (okresy) and several okresy together form an oblast. An alternative name for an oblast is a kraj.

The seven oblasti are listed below, together with the name of the chief administrative city in each oblast:

Západočeský (Plzeň)
Severočeský (Ústi nad Labem)
Středočeský (Prague)
Jihočeský (České Budějovice)
Východočeský (Hradec Králové)
Jihomoravský (Brno)
Severomoravský (Ostrava)

When dealing with place-names it may be helpful to know that North is Severo, East is Východo, South is Jiho, West is Západo, and Central is Středo.

The seven oblasti listed above each contain the following counties (okresy):

ZÁPADOČESKÝ: Cheb, Domažlice, Havlíčkův Brod, Karlovy Vary, Klatovy, Plzeň (Jih), Plzeň (Sever), Rokycany, Sokolov, Tachov.

SEVEROČESKÝ: Česká Lípa, Chomutov, Děčín, Jablonec nad Nisou, Liberec, Litoměřice, Louny, Most, Teplice, Ústí nad Labem.

STŘEDOČESKÝ: Benešov, Beroun, Kladno, Kolín, Kutná Hora, Mělník, Mladá Boleslav, Nymburk, Praha (Východ), Praha (Západ), Příbram, Rakovnik.

JIHOČESKÝ: České Budějovice, Český Krumlov, Jindřichův Hradec, Pelhřimov, Pisek, Prachatice, Strakonice, Tábor.

VÝCHODOČESKÝ: Chrudim, Hradec Králové, Jičín, Náchod, Pardubice, Rychnov nad Kněžnou, Semily, Svitavy, Trutnov, Ústí nad Orlici.

JIHOMORAVSKÝ: Blansko, Břeclav, Brno Město, Brno Venkov, Gottwaldov, Hodonin, Jihlava, Kroměříž, Prostějov, Třebíč, Uherské Hradiště, Vyškov, Zďár nad Sázavou, Znojmo.

SEVERMORAVSKÝ: Bruntál, Frýdek-Mistek, Karviná, Nový Jičín, Olomouc, Opava, Přerov, Sumperk, Vsetin.

A very useful book, if you can find a copy, is *Die Deutschen in der Tschechoslowakei, 1933–1947* by Vacloc Kral. It lists place-name changes from German to Czech and Slovak. Luckily the people of the various parts of the former Czechoslovakia have always been great record-keepers, either with oral histories passed down through many generations, or in family papers lovingly preserved within families over centuries.

The Czech government is reasonably helpful to ancestor-hunters and does now permit individuals to make personal searches in the various archives—providing that application is made through the nearest consulate, and details of reasons for search and of relationship are given. However, the government does encourage you to let it organize the searching for you. The reason given is that problems of language will make it hard for you to do your own research. This is very probably true, but you will be charged for this kindly gesture!

At any rate, let me explain the system. You give the name of the person whose ancestry is being searched, place of birth, marriage, and death, and dates of the same; in the case of a birth certificate the names of the parents (including the mother's maiden name); and the religion.

The minimum fee per certificate, at this moment of writing, is $10, but it may be higher if the search is difficult or the information you gave was not exact. The cost of what they call a "running account"—tracing back from the records over several generations—is based on time spent on the project. The government states that it is not possible to quote a figure in advance and you should be aware that the fee you pay is for research and not for results.

Some lines can be traced back to the seventeenth century; in other cases no records can be located. It may be several months before a report can be sent to you. You must apply to the nearest consulate for a request form, and when completed it should be mailed to the following address: Department of Archives, Obránců míru 133, 166-21 Prague 6. (It is essential that you give the religion of your family and the name of the district in Prague.)

However, it seems likely you may be spared all this official form-filling. The LDS Church has now concluded an agreement with the government that will enable it to microfilm all church registers of all religions from 1599 to 1896. Check with your nearest LDS family history center for up-to-date information.

Language

Try to buy a good Czech dictionary and study it. You should also buy a very good book about ancestor-hunting in the area. *Genealogical Research for Czech and Slovak Americans* by Olga Miller (Gale Research Co.: Detroit, 1978) has first-rate information about the language and a very good bibliography of books in Czech about records.

Church Records (Matriky)

These are your most valuable sources of information in both the Catholic and Protestant churches. Even if you are using the records of the LDS Church it is always wise to check original sources, and so you should read the following paragraphs with care—particularly if you are planning a personal visit to your ancestral homeland.

Catholic

Some of these registers date back to the early 1500s in Bohemia, and to 1600 in Moravia. Officially, the registers started in 1563 after the Council of Trent, but only for baptisms and marriages. Deaths or burials were listed after 1614. When the Hapsburgs took over in 1620, only the Catholic Church was permitted to record vital events.

The original matriky were loose sheets of paper which were bound together later. The entries could be from several widely scattered villages, but all within the same parish, and often included other events not normally found in church registers such as accounts of murders, floods, civil disturbances, and feasts and galas.

In the mid-1700s a new law ordained that in future the matriky should include in the baptismal entries the full names of the parents and all four grandparents, together with their addresses and occupations. Latin or German were to be the languages used instead of Czech. In the early 1800s priests started to include dates of birth and death.

In 1790 the indexing of the matriky was ordered and in 1802 the new law was made retrospective to include all earlier entries back to the beginning. This was not a very popular idea with the hard-worked priests, and the retrospective indexing was done in a very half-hearted way and is not at all reliable. I suggest you can trust the indexing after 1802 but before that you should check the entries themselves one by one around the dates in which you are interested. Even though you may find some family members in the index, there is no guarantee there are not more unindexed.

In 1799 the practice of duplicate entries was started so that an extra copy could be sent to the bishop. This was good because in many cases the originals have been lost and the duplicates are available. On the other hand, the duplicates are not always as reliable as the original—there was no carbon paper in those days!

Protestant

In 1771 the Protestants (mainly Evangelicals and Lutherans) were allowed to keep their own matriky for the first time, but they had to give copies to the Catholic priests, who included them in their own registers. At this time the Protestants did not have their children baptized, so you will find few of these entries.

Other Religions

Jews had to report their vital events to the Catholic priest in most parts of Bohemia. However, the matriky information was also used as a basis for conscription, and since the Jews did not welcome military service they often registered the birth of a son as that of a daughter. As they lived within their own enclosed community, there was little chance the false entry would be discovered. I suppose the local Gentiles might have done the same thing if it were not for the certainty of speedy discovery!

Jews were subjected to many restrictions on registration and religious observances, and there are a number of surviving records of these from various parts of Bohemia. They can be found in the Obvodní Narodní Výbor, Vodičkova 18, Prague.

The other religions in the Czech Republic were Bohemian and Moravian Brethren, Hutterite, Greek Orthodox, and Anabaptist. Most of their records have been lost over the years, but those that survive are in the District Archives. However, you may also find their vital events recorded in the Catholic Registers, as at various times these sects were not allowed to perform their own ceremonies.

One problem with the matriky is the naming system. Surnames could be based on the father's first name, on the name of the family farm, or on normal surname descent. The surname could change if the father changed farms, and if he inherited a farm through his wife he could even change his name to hers. It was all very complicated, but such changes are usually recorded in the matriky by hyphenating the names together (the family and any other) or by use of the word Kdysi or Vulgo, which roughly translated means "also known as."

Archives

The central state archives are in Prague (Státní Ústřední Archiv, Malá Strana, Karmelitská 2, 118 01 Prague 1). They contain the main government records but not much of value to the ancestor-hunter.

The administrative headquarters for the Archives of Bohemia and Moravia is: Archívní Správa, Obránců míru 133, 166-21 Prague 6.

The district archives for each of the seven districts (oblasti) listed earlier in this chapter are known as Státní Oblastní Archívy. They contain all documents connected with the history and administration of a district and are the most valuable from an ancestor-hunter's point of view.

In addition there are county archives (Okresní Archívy) and municipal archives (Městské Archívy). The latter exist in all cities, towns, and large villages.

Civil Registration

This began in 1918 but was only compulsory for those people not belonging to a church. Church members, both Catholic and Protestant, registered all vital events with their priest or minister as they had always done. In 1950 all registers were taken over by the state. A copy of a certificate will be issued for a small fee by the National Committee (Místní Národní Výbar) in the place where the event occurred.

Before 1869 only the church registers recorded baptisms, marriages, and burials. In some registers you may find that dates of birth and death are recorded, but don't count on it!

In 1869 some priests refused to marry people who were not Catholic. For this and other reasons, the recording of vital events was taken over by local municipal officials. The churches still had the right to keep records, but only official registration was accepted as legal proof that the event had occurred. These records are also held by the National Committee mentioned above.

In 1920 a law was passed authorizing central civil registration records. Births and deaths had to be reported to the Central Statistics Office and consisted of doctors' reports on baptisms and burials, and details of marriages and divorces received from the civil authorities.

Birth records will give the name, date and place of birth, full names of parents, occupations, ages, names of their parents, witnesses and/or godparents, and their relationship to the child.

Marriage records include date and place, full names of bride and groom, their ages and place of birth, occupations, and full names of all parents and their addresses.

Death records give date and place, full name, age at death, and name of surviving spouse and parents (whether living or dead).

These civil registers are kept in the offices of the local municipality, and there is no central index, or even a local one.

Census Returns (Sčítání Lidu)

Censuses in the Czech provinces have been held intermittently since the seventeenth century, but many returns were destroyed after the heads had been counted. Many were used as a basis for conscription and only males were recorded. In any case, the government does not at present make them available for genealogical research. I hope this policy will change, since the census records are almost as valuable for an ancestor-hunter as the church registers. The argument is used that since the matriky records are so complete there is no need to make census records available. I question this, but we have to accept the policy as it now stands.

The 1651 Census of Population for Bohemia (Soupis Obyvatelstva v Čechách, 1651) has survived for many villages and towns. The object was to check the number of Catholics, and so the religion is noted, as are numerous personal details of all family members. No indexes are available, but you should check with the nearest embassy or the district archives in the county to find out if the census is available for your ancestral village.

In case circumstances change in the future, I will describe in very general terms what may one day be available. In Bohemia censuses have been held at intervals ever since the 1651 census mentioned above, and the surviving documents can be found in the state archives in Prague (Archívní Správa, Obránců míru 133, 166-21 Prague 6). The last one taken under Austrian rule was in 1910, and the first since independence was in 1921. Since then they have been held every ten years.

If you know where an ancestor was living in a particular year, and can send evidence of your descent from that person, it is worth taking a chance and writing to one of the above addresses. Maybe you will be lucky! The 1869 census has been microfilmed by the LDS Church and is available through your nearest family history center.

The information in the more recent censuses includes name, sex, relationships, age, place and date of birth, religion, occupation, name of employer, and length of residence in that place. However, you cannot search the census returns in person but must apply to the state archives for the information you need.

Wills (Poslední Vůle)

These date back to the fourteenth century but are limited in value, since only people with substantial wealth or property needed to make a will. They are lodged with the State Notary (Státní Notářství) in the nearest main city or town, and are then transferred to the district archives. Application for any information from them must be made through the Archívní Správa in Prague. Be sure to include proof of your descent. Wills were originally kept in the office of the notary concerned, but were all passed to the archives in 1949.

Tax Lists (Berní Ruly)

These date to about 1654, and many have been published for various villages by the archives, and many more are in preparation. Here again you must consult with the state archives in Prague.

Land Records (Pozemkové Knihy)

These date back to the 1500s and are one of the best sources of information if you are descended from someone who owned land. They are in the district archives but only available to you through governmental search at a fee.

Military Records (Vojenské Zaznamy)

Many have been lost but a few date back to 1630. The records of Czechs conscripted into the armed forces in the days of the Empire were transferred from the Military Archives in Vienna when the new country was born. They are in several different places, and you should check with the Archívní Správa in Prague. So far as recent military records are concerned, these are not available for you to search, although the archives may do so for you.

The Calendar

Before searching records, do not forget the changes in the calendar. The original Julian Calendar was introduced by Julius Caesar in 325 and divided the year into 365 days, plus an extra day every fourth year. However, astronomers later calculated that this system meant that the calendar year exceeded the solar year by eleven minutes. By 1582 there was a difference of eleven days. Since this had an effect on the calculations for Easter, Pope

Gregory XIII ordained that ten days be dropped from the calendar. He also changed the beginning of the year from March 25 to January 1. The new calendar became known, of course, as the Gregorian Calendar. Catholic churches observed the change almost immediately; Protestant ones were slower to follow. In Bohemia the year started on 6 January 1584, in Moravia on 4 October 1584, and in Silesia on 12 January 1584.

Other Records

In the district archives you will find records of the ancient craft guilds, particularly from Prague and other major cities; early newspapers and directories; passport records (mainly internal); and many records of the noble estates, which contain lists of tenants and employees.

Newspapers can be particularly important. Obituaries were a great feature (very often paid advertisements, which went to great lengths to eulogize the late departed). You should check for the existence of newspapers with the district archives for your area.

Emigration

No lists have survived, except in a few unrelated places, but don't forget that most Czechs emigrated overseas through the German ports of Hamburg and Bremen. Although the latter records were destroyed during the Second World War, the Hamburg records exist for the period 1850 to 1934 (except for the early part of 1853 and the years 1915 to 1919). You will find many more details about these records in the chapter on Germany.

Finally, remember it is essential you know the place in the Czech Republic from which your family came. Dig deep into your family memories and papers. Then you have three ways to go: use the facilities and records of the LDS Church so far as they go; do your research through the state archives in Prague; or go to the country and do it yourself. Personally, I would try the first one, then the second, and, finally, the third. By then you may have enough preliminary information to make your journey really pay off.

The German genealogical society concerned with researching ethnic Germans in the former Czechoslovakia is: Vereinigung sudetendeutscher Familienforscher (VSFF), Juttastrasse 20, 90480 Nürnberg, Germany. All letters should be in German or clear non-idiomatic English, and two International Reply Coupons must be enclosed.

If your ancestors were Germans you should bear in mind that although they were mainly in the northern and western areas of the country, there were also many German enclaves in other purely Slavic areas. They were mainly Catholic, but many registers were destroyed in World War II. There are some duplicates for 1780 to 1820 for western Bohemia in the custody of the Bishop of Regensburg, Germany (see page 106).

DENMARK

Denmark is now a peaceful country but once upon a time the Danes were feared from Ireland to Russia and south to the Mediterranean. With their neighbors the Norwegians and the Swedes they formed the brave, warlike race known as the Vikings. From 1018 to 1035 Denmark, England, and Norway were united under King Canute (Knut). The south part of Sweden was part of Denmark (with some interruptions) until 1658, as was Iceland until 1944. Today Greenland and the Faeroe Islands are part of Denmark, but have local autonomy. In 1397 Denmark, Norway, and Sweden were united under the Danish Crown. The union was dissolved in 1523, but Denmark's union with Norway lasted until 1814. In that year Denmark lost Norway to Sweden.

In 1848 Denmark, with some disregard for reality, started a war with her larger and much more powerful neighbor, Prussia, over the status of the two duchies of Schleswig and Holstein. These two areas were ruled by the Danish kings on a personal basis, and were not an integral part of the kingdom itself. Since the majority of the inhabitants were German-speaking, Prussia kept an eye on their interests. Denmark won this war and included the duchies in her territory. A long period of confusion followed. In 1852 Denmark agreed that the status of the duchies should, after all, remain as in 1847; in 1855 Denmark reincorporated them; in 1858, under pressure, she canceled this; in 1863 they were incorporated once again; in 1864 Prussia and Austria declared war on Denmark, and won. Schleswig went to Prussia and Holstein to Austria. In 1867 these two countries fought over the spoils and Austria lost. Both the duchies were then included in Prussia.

If all this is confusing to you, you are not alone. The British Foreign Secretary at that time said, "Only three people understand the Schleswig-Holstein question: Prince Albert, who is dead; a professor who is now insane; and myself, and I have forgotten."

After the First World War Denmark regained north Schleswig after a plebiscite in 1920. Some 23,000 German-speaking people still remain in that area (which is now South Jutland, or Sønderjylland). Roughly speaking, the present frontier between Denmark and Germany is a horizontal line across the Jutland Peninsula just north of the city of Flensburg, in Germany. Records for the part of Schleswig that remained German after the 1920 plebiscite are in the custody of the Landesarchiv Schleswig-Holstein (Schloss Gottorf, 24837 Schleswig, Germany). An exception is the census records of the area, which are still in the Danish National Archives (Rigsarkivet). See below for address.

You should also know that in 1970 the number of counties in Denmark was reduced and many changed their names. The original counties were Aabenraa-Sønderborg, Aalborg, Aarhus, Assens, Bornholm, Frederiksborg, Haderslev, Hjørring, Holbaek, Københavns, Maribo, Odense, Praestø, Randers, Ribe, Ringkøbing, Roskilde, Skanderborg, Sorø, Svendborg, Thisted, Tønder, Vejle, and Viborg.

The new counties are Aarhus, Bornholm, Frederiksborg, Fyn, Københavns, Nordjylland, Ribe, Ringkøbing, Roskilde, Sønderjylland, Storstrøm, Vejle, Viborg, and Vestsjaelland.

It may be useful to you to know the areas covered by the counties before that date. The mainland of Jylland included the counties of Hjørring, Thisted, Aalborg, Ringkøbing, Randers, Viborg, Skanderborg, Aarhus, Ribe, Vejle, Haderslev, Tønder, and Aabenraa-Sønderborg.

The island of Fyn had two counties—Odense and Svendborg. The islands of Sjaelland and Møen included the counties of Frederiksborg, Holbaek, Københavns, Sorø, and Praestø. The two islands of Lolland and Falster formed the county of Maribo. The island of Bornholm formed a county of the same name.

Archives

The National Archives (Rigsarkivet) are at Rigsdagsgården 9, 1218 Copenhagen K. In addition to the censuses mentioned above, they hold records of administration and government, but generally, you will find your major sources of genealogical information in the four state archives. These are known as Landsarki*ver*. The individual archives are known as Landsarki*vet* and are in the following locations:

Landsarkivet for Sjaelland
Jagtvej 10, 2200 Copenhagen N

Landsarkivet for Fyn
Jernbanegade 36, 5000 Odense

Landsarkivet for Nørrejylland
Hansgade 5, 8800 Viborg

Landsarkivet for de sønderjyske Landsdele
Haderslevvej 45, 6200 Aabenraa
(This archive has North Schleswig records and also copies of census returns for Holstein.)

Of course, you will want to know which particular state archive covers the area from which your ancestors emigrated. If you do not already have a map of Denmark, or cannot find one in a local library, I suggest you (a) write to your nearest Danish embassy or consulate or (b) write to the National Archives mentioned above. By all means write in English. It is a generality to say all Danes speak English, but certainly English is a required language in the schools. You will find Danes are extremely helpful and patient in dealing with your queries.

Civil Registration

This does not exist in the form that applies to most other European countries. The Lutheran Church (which is the official state church) is responsible for the registration of vital events, as births, marriages, and deaths are called, and so it is in the church registers and other ecclesiastical records that you will be searching for your ancestors.

However, there are certain civil records that exist outside of the churches:

1. The civil registration of births, marriages, and deaths for the counties of Aabenraa-Sønderborg, Haderslev, and Tønder exist from 1874 and are located in the state archives (Landsarkivet) at Aabenraa.

2. Death certificates for the districts of Zealand, Fyn, Bornholm, and Lolland-Falster from 1857 are in the Landsarkivet in Copenhagen.

3. Some civil marriages were recorded from 1851 and these can be found in state or city archives.

4. Records of marriage licenses for the city of Copenhagen only (1735–1868) are in the city archives (Byarkiverne) in Copenhagen. They are called Kopulations-protokoller.

Church Records

Before we examine church records in any detail, there are several things to be said. A major problem in ancestor-hunting in Denmark is the duplication of personal names and place-names. It is essential that you find out all you can about the location from which your emigrant ancestor departed for his or her new country. There are some emigration records available and we will talk about them later, but the multiplication of place-names is the major problem. In fact, there are problems within problems, because you must also consider farm names as well. In addition, you must be concerned with patronymics, which is a surname taken from the given name of the father; the system was widespread in Denmark up to the closing years of the last century.

So, if all you know is that your ancestor Jens Nielsen came from a place named Skovlund in Denmark, you have a problem. Nielsen is an extremely common name and there are 114 places in Denmark named Skovlund.

However, even if you do have this problem, there is an excellent organization in Denmark that will help you solve it. I will tell you more about this later, but in the meantime let us assume you know the exact location of your ancestors in Denmark and want to know what you can find out in the church records.

Registers (Kirkebøger)

Although the state church is Lutheran, there are other church registers available. The *recognized* non-Lutheran churches were the Roman Catholic Church (Romersk Katolske Kirke); the Reformed Churches (Reformerte Menigheder); the Episcopal Methodist Church (Biskoppelige-Metodistiske Trossamfund); and the Jewish Communities (Mosaiske Trossamfund). These recognized churches were permitted to record vital events in their own registers. Any other religion or sect was not recognized and the members of those churches were compelled to register their family events in the registers of the Lutheran Church. No other religious organizations were recognized until early in this century.

In 1645 a law was passed requiring the Lutheran ministers on the island of Sjaelland to record all births, marriages, and deaths in their parishes. In the following year the law was extended to the whole country. Some ministers had begun keeping such records even earlier. As a matter of fact, some seventy-five parishes have entries pre-dating 1645. In many cases the ministers did not conform exactly with the civil law, preferring to record baptisms rather than births, and burials rather than deaths.

Many of the earlier registers have been lost to fire, damp, and rats; many are beautifully written, others almost impossible to decipher. Before 1814 many ministers recorded the events as they occurred in chronological order; others kept separate sections in the registers for the different events. In addition, the sexes were not separated, After 1814 there were separate lists of male and female christenings, confirmations, and burials.

All the church registers of all denominations up to 1891 are located in the state archives (Landsarkivet) covering the particular district. Since 1891 a copy of the parish register has been sent to the state archives thirty years after it has been completed. Generally speaking, registers or copies of registers up to 1925 are now in the archives.

So far as birth or baptism is concerned, the entry lists the name of the child, the date of birth and/or baptism, the names of the parents (the mother's name is often left out or she is identified by her maiden name), and the names of witnesses and their relation to the child. The baptism took place within a few days of the birth, usually on a Sunday.

Before 1814 the marriage register often recorded only the names of the bride and groom and the date. After 1814 the registers give the date and place of birth of each, details of any previous marriages, and names of witnesses.

Most death or burial records give name, address, date, and age. After 1814 the cause of death is usually included.

Betrothal (Trolovelse)

These are the equivalent of the banns of other churches. Not all the ministers recorded them, but it is worth checking for them because quite often they give more information than the marriage register.

Confirmation (Konfirmation)

In 1736 a law was passed requiring that every child be confirmed at the age of fourteen. Most parishes recorded all confirmations from that year on but often listed only the name and age of the child. After 1814 it was customary to list the names of the parents.

Introduction (Introduktion)

After each child was born, the mother was regarded as "unclean." After a period of several weeks she was regarded as cleansed and the minister then introduced her to the congregation and she was able to take her place in church again. After 1814 the date of the woman's "introduction" was usually included in the birth or baptism records.

Communion (Kommunion)

These records date back to 1645 in many places and usually include name and address.

Absolution

These records started in the mid-1600s and were discontinued in 1767. They give the name of the person absolved for transgression and, often, details of the transgression.

Vaccination

Strangely enough, these records were also regarded as a matter of church business. They started in 1800, and though the records are still kept, they are now found included in the confirmation or marriage records. They give the child's name and address, and the name of the doctor.

Lutheran Parish Register Extracts (Kirkebogsuddrag)

These cover some two hundred years between the seventeenth and nineteenth centuries. The entry is identical with that in the parish register but is usually confined to prominent or noble families. If you find that a particular parish register has been lost or destroyed, and if you think the above description fits your own family, it will be worthwhile to check the extracts.

Arrival Lists (Tilgangslister)

From 1814 to 1875 the minister was required to record arrivals and departures from the parish. He noted the name of the person concerned, his or her age and address within the parish, and the name of the parish from which he or she came. I should mention that the law was never enforced in cities but only in rural areas.

Removal Lists (Afgangslister)

The details in the previous paragraph apply here, except that the parish to which a person was moving was listed, instead of the one from which he or she had arrived.

General Schematic Register (Almindeligt Jevnførelse Schema)

These registers were started in each parish in 1814. Although intended to be a register of every person recorded in the church records, with reference to the page of the book in which the original entry was listed, many of these registers were never kept, and many are incomplete. However, they are in the state archives and you may just find some vital fact not recorded elsewhere.

So much for all the church records in Denmark. My own reaction to this formidable list is that a conscientious minister would have to make a choice between his records and his parishioners. I really can't see how he could possibly look after both!

There are, of course, a number of other available records, many of which will be essential to you:

Police Census (Politiets Mandtalslister)

This covers the period from 1869 to 1923 and lists the names of residents of Copenhagen and their children over ten, with place of birth, occupation, and address. The records from 1869 to 1900 are in the city archives, and those from 1901 to 1923 in the Statistical Office, Copenhagen.

Censuses (Folketaellinger)

These have been held from as early as 1787 and the returns from all of them are in the custody of the National Archives (Rigsarkivet, Rigsdagsgården 9, 1218 Copenhagen K. The questions asked by the census-takers varied greatly over the years. The returns available for search are 1787, 1801, 1834, 1840, 1845, 1850, 1860, 1870, 1880, 1890, and 1901. Those for 1906 and 1911 are available by special permission, and with proof of descent. There is no access to the later returns: 1916, 1920, and every fifth year from then on (the 1935, 1945, and 1955 returns were destroyed). There are also many local censuses that were taken in various years and for these you should check with the municipal archives for the particular place in which you are interested. Check with the LDS Church for microfilm copies.

Emigration (Udvandrings-journaler)

These records were kept from 1868 to 1959 and are in the Landsarkivet for Sjaelland.

Passport Records (Pasprotokoller)

These are to be found in the various Landsarkiver for the period 1780–1920.

Marriage Licenses (Kopulations-protokoller)

These are for the city of Copenhagen only for 1720–1868 and are in the city archives (Rådhuset, Rådhuspladsen, 1550 Copenhagen V).

Army Service (Stambøger)

The military records are in the Haerens Arkiv, Copenhagen. There are lists of officers and men serving in the army from the mid-1700s to the present date (some muster-rolls dating back to 1693), and also lists of men liable for service in the local units of the militia. These Military Levy Rolls (Laegsdsruller) are on a parish basis and date from 1789. There are similar records for the navy from 1802 and these are in the National Archives.

Deeds and Mortgages (Skøde og Panteprotokoller)

These date from 1580 and contain names and addresses of the contracting parties and descriptions of the property involved. They are in the state archives and also in the nearest municipal archives.

Trade Guilds (Lavsprotokoller)

In Denmark, as in most European countries, the trade guilds were powerful organizations very similar to present-day trade unions except that they were concerned with skilled crafts rather than with general industry. The records date from 1527 and give personal details of all applying for membership including place of birth, age, and names of parents. The guilds were usually established only in principal cities unless a small town was the center of a major craft. The records are in several locations, but the National Archives will help you locate the records for a specific guild in a particular place. You will find them in state and city archives, in museums, and in some cases, still in the possession of a guild.

Servants (Tyendeprotokoller)

These records were kept from 1828 to 1923 and are in the state archives. They give the names of domestic employees, dates and places of birth or baptism, and changes of address.

Trade Licenses (Rådstue og borgerskabs protokoller)

These are to be found in city archives and date from 1596. They should not be confused with guild records. They are, in effect, a license to operate a business in a particular municipality. They give the usual personal details of name, address, occupation, and place and date of birth.

Schools (Skoleprotokoller)

These records are either in the state archives or in the original schools. They go back to 1584 and list pupils, matriculations, endowments and scholarships, and the probate records of the teaching staff.

Probate Records (Skifteprotokoller)

These records go back to the fourteenth century in a few cases, but in general they start in the second half of the sixteenth century. They are located in the state archives, with more recent records in the custody of the local courts. Details are given of the deceased, family members, and the inventory and disposition of his or her property.

Court Records (Tingbøger eller retsprotokoller)

These records are in the National Archives and state archives and can often be of great value, since they are concerned not only with crime, but with real estate transfers, marriage settlements, mortgages, and guardianship applications.

You will find that the various archives will usually undertake a quick search (i.e., when you can supply exact date, name, and place) without charge. However, a fee will be charged for anything more general. The archive may undertake the work itself, or may refer you to a list of approved researchers.

Genealogical Organizations

There are two genealogical organizations in Denmark; the first is Samfundet for Dansk Genealogi og Personalhistorie (The Society of Danish Genealogy and Personal History), Grysgaardsvej 2, 2400 Copenhagen. They will not undertake research but can suggest the names of members willing to do work for overseas inquirers for a fee.

The second organization has the potential to become a major source of assistance to people of Danish descent tracing their ancestors. It is Det Danske Udvandrerarkiv (The Danish National Collection of Books and Documents on Emigration History), v/Vor Frue Kirke, P.O. Box 731, 9100 Aalborg.

Its goal is to collect and preserve all kinds of material concerning Danish emigration to countries all over the world. The small staff will answer all letters from overseas concerning genealogical questions. In the organization archives is a name register of emigrants, but it contains only five percent of the total number who emigrated. However, it is being added to all the time and may be worth checking.

Their main source of emigrant information is the list compiled by the Copenhagen police between 1868 and the 1930s. The list is in the Landsarkivet for Sjaelland in Copenhagen, but the organization has microfilms for 1869–1910. They give the name of the emigrant, age, address, place of birth, occupation, destination, and in some cases, the name of the ship on which the emigrant was to travel overseas. The lists are in chronological order and it is essential, of course, for you to be able to supply the actual year of emigration. If you can do this, there is a fair chance they can find the parish of origin. Once you have that, you can get in touch with the Landsarkivet for the area, and away you go!

If the exact information needed is given by you, they will not charge for the brief search (provided you have sent two International Reply Coupons with your letter), but if a more detailed search is needed, they will make a small charge. If you need an extended search over a long period, they suggest you write to the Landsarkivet for the area in which you are interested, and obtain their list of researchers.

As you will see, there are many good sources of information in Denmark, and you will find archives and individuals prepared to be most helpful to you. However, as I told you at the start of this chapter, you need to know a place of origin for your emigrant ancestor. There is no central index and no shortcut. The LDS Church has microfilmed a major portion of the available Danish records and has indexed some of them. Be sure you make use of these records through your nearest family history center before you visit the country of your ancestors, or spend money on search fees and postage.

Patronymics

This naming system was common to all the Scandinavian countries until about 1860. For example, the son of a man named *Anders* would be called *Andersen*, and his daughter would be *Andersdotter*. However, permanent surnames were established in Denmark between 1771 (in the south) and 1828 (in the north). Many people continued to use patronymics but usually a church entry contained both names.

Having told you all this I must also point out that the nobility, clergy, and prominent citizens had often been using normal surnames since the sixteenth century.

ESTONIA

The Estonians, who are ethnically close to the Finns, were conquered in 1219 by the Danes and a German military order named the Livonian Brothers of the Sword, or the Livonian Knights. The Danes took the northern part of Estonia and the Knights the southern part. In 1346 the Danes sold their share to the Knights, under whose control Estonia remained until 1561, when the northern part was taken by Sweden and the southern by Poland. In 1629, after a war between the two countries, Sweden took control of the whole country. In 1710 Russia seized control of Estonia and Livonia.

Estonia declared its independence in 1918 but under the German-Soviet Pact of 1939 all three Baltic states, including Estonia, were absorbed by the Soviet Union. In 1991 Estonia declared its independence once again.

The Estonian archival system is complicated by the fact that there are two central archives—the State Historical Archives (J. Liivi 4, 202400 Tartu) and the State Archives (Maneeźi 4, 200102 Tallinn). The former hold records up to 1918, and the latter from that date up to the present day.

Civil Registration
The records of births, marriages, and deaths up to 1926 are in the State Registry Office (Lossi plats la, 200103 Tallinn). Records since that year are in local municipal offices.

Church Registers
Registers up to 1926 are in the State Registry Office mentioned above, but there are also copies in the State Historical Archives in Tartu (see above) and the City Archives (Tolli 4, 200001 Tallinn). There are also copies in many of the churches.

The addresses of the headquarters of the various churches are:

CATHOLIC: Rev. Rein Òunapuu
              Vene 18, 200001 Tallinn
ORTHODOX: Rev. Kornilius
              Pikk 64-4, 200001 Tallinn
LUTHERAN: Archbishop K Oajula
              Kiribu 8, 200001 Tallinn
BAPTIST: Presbyter U. Meriloo
              Pargi 9, 200016 Tallinn
ADVENTIST: Rev. R Kalmusm
              Nere pst 3, 200001 Tallinn
METHODIST: Rev. O Pärnamets
              Apteegi 3, 200001 Tallinn

Ancestor-hunters of Estonian descent are welcome to visit the archives and do their own research. At present, there is no charge for this. Written applications for information will be answered—provided that return postage is covered by two International Reply Coupons. A fee will be charged for a search—the amount will depend on the type of inquiry.

People of Jewish descent will find records for the period 1918–1946 in the State Archives in Tallinn. More information can be obtained from the Jewish Cultural Society (P.O. Box 2385, 200036 Tallinn).

FINLAND

The capital city of Finland is Helsinki (or Helsingfors, in Swedish). Both Finnish and Swedish are official languages of the country, even though only eight percent of the people are Swedish-speaking. The main Swedish areas are in the west (Osterbotten) and in the south (Nyland). Until 1809 Finland was part of Sweden. In that year it was annexed by Russia and ruled by the Czar in his capacity as Grand Duke of Finland. It declared its independence in 1917 at the time of the Russian Revolution. In 1939 Finland was attacked by the USSR and quickly subdued. By the treaty of Moscow (1940) Finland ceded the Rybachi Peninsula, part of the Karelian Isthmus (including Vyborg), and an area on Lake Ladoga. In addition, the USSR was granted a thirty-year lease of the port of Hango.

When Germany attacked the Soviet Union in 1941, Finland allied itself with Germany in the hope of regaining the lost territories. It was forced to sign an armistice with the USSR in 1944, and the terms confirmed the cession of territory in 1940, except that in place of the lease of Hango the USSR was given a fifty-year lease of the Porkkala Peninsula, near Helsinki. In the 1947 Peace Treaty, which followed, Finland also ceded Pechenga (Petsamo) in the far north of the country, and also some additional border districts in the east. About half a million Finns left the ceded areas and were resettled in Finland. In 1956, after some years of tactful relations with the USSR, Porkkala was returned to Finland. Over 90 percent of the population is either Lutheran or Greek Orthodox.

The country is divided into twelve provinces. These are listed below with the name of each provincial capital in parentheses: Uudenmaan Lääni (Helsinki), Turun JA Porin Lääni (Turku), Hämeen Lääni (Hämeenlinna), Ahvenanmaan Lääni (Mariehamn), Kymen Lääni* (Kouvola), Mikkelin Lääni (Mikkeli), Kuopion Lääni* (Kuopio), Pohjois-Karjalan Lääni (Joensuu), Keski-Suomen Lääni (Jyväskylä), Oulun Lääni (Oulu), Lapin Lääni* (Rovaniemi), Vaasan Lääni (Vaasa). These provinces each have their own archives, except for those marked with an asterisk. The National Archives (Valtionarkisto) are located in Helsinki (PL 258, 00171 Helsinki).

Church Registers

Although it should not be necessary to write for information in any language but English (the Finns are excellent linguists), I think I should give the Finnish and Swedish descriptions that you may need to make certain your request is clearly understood:

English	Finnish	Swedish
Catholic Records	Katolisen Kirkon Luettelot	Katolska Kyrkans Böcker
Lutheran Registers	Luterilaisen Kirkon Historialliset Aikakirjat	Historieböcker
Greek Orthodox	Kreikkalaiskatolisen Kirkon Luettelot	Grekisk-Katolska Kyrkans Böcker
Lutheran Main Books	Luterilaisen Kirkon Pääkirjat	Kommunion-Eller Huvudböcker

The Lutheran church registers date back to 1648 in some cases, the Greek Orthodox to about 1779, and the Catholic to 1800. There are over 500 parishes in Finland, and over 300 have now transferred their records to the National Archives and provincial archives. The more recent registers from 1860 onward are still in the original churches (an exception to this is that the registers from the areas ceded to the USSR are all in special archives; more about these later). I have not listed all the parish registers now in the archives because the list would be out of date very quickly. The transfers are being speeded up and should be completed within a year or so. This transfer of registers applies to all religions.

The inclusion of civil registration in the church records (Pääkirjat, or Main Books) began between 1650 and 1700 depending on the decision of the church authorities in different parts of the country. The records are fairly complete from 1700 and are on microfilm in the National Archives up to 1850. Entries since then are normally closed to public search, but special exceptions can be made if there is a valid reason (including genealogical research or evidence for inheritance), and application should be made to the National Archives (address above).

Lutheran Church Registers

These contain the following information:

BIRTHS: Names, dates of birth and baptism, parentage, occupations of parents, names of witnesses at baptism, places of residence.

MARRIAGES: Names, ages, dates of banns and marriage, addresses, and sometimes, names of parents.

DEATHS: Names, ages, cause of death, occupations, dates of death and burial, and place of death.

MISCELLANEOUS: Church accounts, minutes of meetings, and details of absolutions and misdemeanors.

There are also transcripts of the entries that contain the above information, with some variations, and these are also in the National Archives on microfilm, with copies in the possession of the Genealogical Society of Finland (Suomen Sukututkimusseura, Snellmaninkatu 9-11, 00170 Helsinki 17).

Greek Orthodox Church Registers

The registers for birth, marriage, and death give names, parentage, address, occupations, ages, dates, and godparents and witnesses. Copies are also in the provincial archives at Mikkeli.

Catholic Registers

These give the same information as above.

Lutheran Membership Movements (Luterilaisen kirkon muuttaneiden luettelot)

These give names of persons arriving in the parish or leaving it, with previous or future locations, marital status, and sometimes, date and place of birth. They date from about 1800 to the present and are in the local church. There are a few of these records that go back to the early eighteenth century. There are also Certificates of Movement (Muuttokirjat), which give similar information but often in greater detail and dating from 1800. They are also in church custody and also on microfilm in various provincial archives.

Lutheran Pre-Confirmations (Luterilaisen kirkon luettelot lapsista)

Some of these lists start as early as 1696 and give details of children eligible for confirmation with full personal details of age, address, and parentage.

Tombstone Inscriptions (Hautakivien muistokirjoitukset)

These have been recorded from the early eighteenth century and the records are in local churches and cemeteries, and also in the custody of the Genealogical Society of Finland.

Lutheran Main Books (Luterilaisen kirkon pääkirjat)

These are probably the most important and comprehensive records you will find in your ancestor-hunting in Finland. They are also known as Population Registers and contain a tremendous amount of information about each parish. They started in about 1667, but were not widespread until 1700. Details are given of the whole population of a parish, grouped by families, including not only family members, but servants, lodgers, and estate workers, with every personal record you can possibly imagine.

You will find dates of all vital events, changes of address, origins and later destinations, standards of religious knowledge, relationships with other families, legitimacy of children—the list is endless. It certainly suggests that Big Brother was watching—or at least the Lutheran minister was, or is, because the records continue right up to the present! From a genealogical point of view the system is terrific. The records are in local church custody with microfilm copies in the various archives. Here, again, access to recent information is restricted, but special permission may be granted for you to obtain some information, provided that you prove descent.

The Greek Orthodox Church was also permitted to maintain Main Books from 1779, but some are available from earlier dates. The oldest ones are in the archives in Kuopio and Mikkeli, but most are still in church custody.

Civil Registration

Records under this heading, as we know them in this country, only started in 1922 and registration is only required from non-members of the Evangelical-Lutheran Church. Each community keeps its own register, which is located in the municipal offices.

Head-Tax Registers

This tax was first imposed in 1634, and was abolished in 1924. Until 1652 the records of taxes paid were kept by the ministers of the church, and from then until 1779 by state list writers. Up until that date only males between eighteen and sixty were listed, but after 1780 everyone was listed. One copy is in the National Archives, one in the provincial archives, and one in local municipal offices. The lists are alphabetical within each village or town.

Property Taxes

The provincial archives have copies of these lists from 1539 onward.

Guilds (Ammattikuntaluettelot)

These records are in some of the provincial archives, since the guilds, in the main, were only established in major towns. They were craft guilds similar to modern trade unions and the records give details of apprenticeship, qualifications, personal information, place of birth, and parentage. The period covered is from the early eighteenth century to the late nineteenth.

Wills and Probate Records (Perukirjat)

These start in about 1650 and are in various locations. Up until 1809 they are in the National Archives, from 1809 to 1860 in the various provincial archives, and since then in either the National Archives, the provincial archives, the district courts, or even local libraries. Bear in mind that wills are not too common in Finland because of the widespread use of estate inventories (Bouppteckningar).

Census Returns (Henkikirjat)

The first census (for tax purposes) was held in 1634 and a census has been held each year since then. However, before 1925 only the taxpayer (normally the head of the family) was named. Since 1925 all members of the household have been listed by name. The returns are in the National Archives and are open for public access up to 1860 only. In actual fact, they are not so vital in Finland as in other countries because of the wealth of documented information available about almost everyone from several other sources.

Land Records (Maakirjat)

If your ancestors owned or leased land, these records may provide you with some extra information. They cover a period from 1630 to 1758 and are in the National Archives.

Court Records (Oikeuden päätokset)

Don't assume that these records will be of no interest to you because your very respectable ancestors would never have appeared in court! Don't be so sure; not only did the courts deal with the usual criminal cases, but they approved the transfer of real estate, mortgages, leases, tenancies, marriage settlements, guardianship records, etc., and all these records can contain a great deal of genealogical information. The records are in the National Archives, the provincial archives, and in local courthouses.

Register of the Inhabitants of Finland (Suomen asukasluettelot)

This is yet one more record designed to keep tabs on the Finns and provide work for bureaucrats. This ambitious project was started in 1539 and discontinued in 1809, although it is still being added to as new information about individuals is discovered. Basically, it is genealogical data collected from churches. It lists addresses and names and refers you to the locations of records on file for a particular person. The register is in the National Archives.

Military Records (Sotilasasiakirjat)

These are muster-rolls of various regiments from 1537 to the present. All these military records, and others, up to 1809 are in the War Archives in both Helsinki and Stockholm (Sweden); records after that date are in the National Archives.

Don't overlook the fact that records of military interest can also be found in odd places. For example, in the provincial archives at Mikkeli you can find church registers and Main Books for various military installations in the area, or for regiments stationed there:

EVANGELICAL LUTHERAN: Military Academy in Hamina (1821–1902)

5th Sharpshooter Battalion (1855–69)

GREEK ORTHODOX: 8th Russian Sharpshooter Battalion (1908)

Infantry Regiment of Lesnoi (1914)

Military Parish on the Journey (1872–1904)

Infantry Regiment of Novotorzski (1873–1912)

Finnish Sharpshooter Regiment (1892–1914)

Military Parish in Tuusula (1856–1918)

Russian Military Hospital, Tuusala (1856–60)

Garrison in Viipuri (1802–1924)

Genealogical Organizations

The name and address of the national organization is listed earlier in this chapter, but there are also local organizations throughout Finland. I list them below and you can obtain the current address of the secretary by writing to the national headquarters:

Forssa, Hamina, Helsinki, Hyvinkää, Ilmajoki, Jakobstad, Jyväskylä, Kerava, Kokkola, Kuopio, Lahti, Lapua, Mariehamn, Oulu, Pargas, Pori, Riihimäki, Salo, Tampere, Turku, and Vaasa.

Archives

The provincial archives are in eight of the twelve provinces, and the four deprived provinces have their records in other archives. These archives are located as follows: Ahvenanmaa, Hämeenlinna (and Uusimaa), Joensuu, Jyväskylä (and Lapland), Mikkeli (and Kymi and Kuopio), Oulu, Turku, and Vaasa. Note that owing to lack of space many of the records of Oulu are at Jyväskylä.

THE LOST TERRITORIES

These are the parts of Finland taken by the USSR. The church registers and Main Books of the Evangelical Lutheran churches (and two Orthodox ones) are in the custody of a special archives *within* the provincial archives at Mikkeli (Lakkautetettujen Seurakuntien Keskusarkisto, PL 78, 50101 Mikkeli 10). Those of you whose family members fled from Soviet-held Finnish territory during and after the Second World War will find these books and registers of major importance.

The parishes are as follows:

EVANGELICAL LUTHERAN: Antrea, Äyräpää, Harlu, Heinjoki, Hiitola, Ihantala, Ilmee, Impilahti, Inkerin (Viipuri), Jaakima, Jääski, Johannes, Käkisalmi, Kanneljärvi, Kaukola, Kirvu, Kivennapa, Koivisto, Korpiselkä, Kuolemajärvi, Kurkijoki, Lavansaari, Lumivaara, Metsäpirtti, Muolaa, Pälkjärvi, Persamo, Pyhäjärvi, Räisälä, Rautu, Ruskeala, Säkkijärvi, Sakkola, Salmi, Seiskari, Soanlahti, Sortavalan, Suojärvi, Suursaari, Terijoki, Tytärsaari, Uusikirkko, Vahviala, Valkjärvi, Viipuri (rural parish), Viipuri (cathedral parish), Vuoksela, and Vuoksenranta.

Note: The starting dates vary considerably for both the church registers and the Main Books. The rural parish of Viipuri dates back to 1686, but the majority start about 1750, and all of them end in the period 1949–53 (except Ilmee, which ends in 1900).

GREEK ORTHODOX: Korpiselka, Petsamo, Salmi, Viipuri.

FINNISH ORTHODOX CHURCH: Viipuri (1930–50)

As you will have gathered by now, Finland is a genealogist's dream, at least for the last 250 years. Before that, the going gets tough, but at least the odds are heavily in your favor that you will get off to a very good start.

FRANCE

Little is known of the area we call France before the Roman Conquest in the first century B.C. During several centuries after the Roman occupation, France, then known as Gaul, was torn apart by dynastic wars. In 800 the Emperor Charlemagne brought order to France and other areas under his rule. However, his son Louis could not maintain the order established by his father, and when he died the three sons he left behind divided the lands among them (Treaty of Verdun, 843). Charles, King of the West Franks, was recognized as ruler of the area that is now France.

From then until the end of the sixteenth century, France had to contend with Viking and English invasions, the rise to power of great feudal nobles, wars against the Hapsburgs, questions of succession, religious rebellions, assassinations, strong and weak kings, honest and venal administrators, and long-suffering peasants.

In 1789 the inevitable revolution occurred, and since then France has been a republic with strong central control located in Paris.

Archives

The address of the National Archives (Archives Nationale) is 60 rue Francs Bourgeois, 75003 Paris. With the decentralization of so many French records in the various départements and cities this is not of such major importance to ancestor-hunters as in other countries but it does hold Protestant records, records of wills, some notarial records, and nationalization lists.

There are ninety-five départements in France, each administered by a préfet responsible to the government in Paris. A département is roughly equivalent to a county, and is divided into districts (arrondissements), municipalities (communes), and cantons. Each département has its own archives (Archives Départementales), and since you will most certainly be corresponding with them, I list all the addresses below. If you are already familiar with the départements, and perhaps have a map showing their locations, you should be warned that in 1964 there were some major changes in boundaries in the Paris area. The Départements of the Seine and Seine-et-Oise were abolished. The twenty arrondissements of Paris were formed into the Département de Paris, and the remaining eighty communes of the Département de Seine were redistributed among the Départements of Hauts-de-Seine, Seine-Saint Denis, and Val-de-Marne.

The Département of Seine-et-Oise was broken up and formed to the west of Paris the Département de Yvelines and the Département de l'Essonne, and to the north that of Val-d'Oise. Its remaining communes joined with the eighty from the Seine mentioned above to form the three new départements.

Note: Correspondence for each of the following Archives Départementales should be addressed to Le Préfecture, followed by the city and the postal code given below:

Ain, 01000 Bourg
Aisne, 02000 Laon
Allier, 03400 Yzeure
Alpes de Haute-Provence, 04000 Digne
Alpes (Hautes-), 05000 Gap
Alpes-Maritimes, 06000 Nice
Ardèche, 07000 Privas
Ardennes, 08000 Charleville-Mézières
Ariège, 09000 Foix
Aube, 10000 Troyes
Aude, 11000 Carcassonne
Aveyron, 12000 Rodez

Bouches-du-Rhône, 13006 Marseilles

Calvados, 14000 Caen
Cantal, 15000 Aurillac
Charente, 16000 Angoulême
Charente-Maritime, 17000 La Rochelle
Cher, 18000 Bourges
Corrèze, 19000 Tulle
Corse, 20000 Ajaccio
Côte-d'Or, 21000 Dijon
Côtes-du-Nord, 22000 St. Brieuc
Creuse, 23000 Guéret

Dordogne, 24000 Périgueux
Doubs, 25000 Besançon
Drôme, 26000 Valence

Essonne, 91100 Corbeil
Eure, 27000 Évreux
Eure-et-Loir, 28000 Chartres

Finistère, 29000 Quimper

Gard, 30040 Nîmes
Garonne (Haute-), 31000 Toulouse
Gers, 32000 Auch
Gironde, 33000 Bordeaux

Hérault, 34000 Montpellier

Ille-et-Vilaine, 35000 Rennes
Indre, 36000 Châteauroux
Indre-et-Loire, 37000 Tours
Isère, 38000 Grenoble

Jura, 39000 Lons-le-Saunier

Landes, 40000 Mont-de-Marsan
Loir-et-Cher, 41000 Blois
Loire, 42000 St. Etienne
Loire (Haute-), 43000 Le Puy
Loire-Atlantique, 44000 Nantes
Loiret, 45000 Orléans
Lot, 46000 Cahors
Lot-et-Garonne, 47000 Agen
Lozère, 48000 Mende

Maine-et-Loire, 49000 Angers
Manche, 50000 St. Lô
Marne, 51000 Châlons-sur-Marne
Marne (Haute-), 52000 Chaumont
Mayenne, 53000 Laval
Meurthe-et-Moselle, 54000 Nancy*
Meuse, 55000 Bar-le-Duc
Morbihan, 56000 Vannes
Moselle, 57000 Metz*

Nièvre, 58000 Nevers
Nord, 59000 Lille

Oise, 60000 Beauvais
Orne, 61000 Alençon

Paris, 75004 Paris
Pas-de-Calais, 62000 Arras
Puy-de-Dôme, 63000 Clermont-Ferrand
Pyrénées-Atlantiques, 64000 Pau
Pyrénées (Hautes-), 65000 Tarbes

Pyrénées-Orientales, 66000 Perpignan

Rhin (Bas-), 67000 Strasbourg*
Rhin (Haut-), 68000 Colmar*
Rhône, 69000 Lyon

Saône (Haute-), 70000 Vesoul
Saône-et-Loire, 71000 Maçon
Sarthe, 72000 Le Mans
Savoie, 73000 Chambéry
Savoie (Haute-), 74000 Annecy
Seine (Hauts-de-), 92500 Rueil-Malmaison
Seine-Maritime, 76100 Rouen
Seine-et-Marne, 77000 Melun
Seine-Saint-Denis, 93000 Bobigny
Sèvres, 79000 Niort
Somme, 80000 Amiens

Tarn, 81000 Albi
Tarn-et-Garonne, 82000 Montauban
Territoire de Belfort, 90000 Belfort

Val-de-Marne, 94100 Saint-Maur
Val-d'Oise, 95300 Pontoise
Var, 83000 Draguignan
Vaucluse, 84000 Avignon
Vendée, 85000 La Roche-sur-Yon
Vienne, 86000 Poitiers
Vienne (Haute-), 87000 Limoges
Vosges, 88000 Épinal*

Yonne, 89000 Auxerre
Yvelines, 73000 Versailles

Since many of you will be affected by the changes in the départements in the Paris area, and the consequent transfer of records of arrondissements and communes from one département to another, it may be helpful to list these transfers:

From the former Département of Seine-et-Oise to:

HAUTS-DE-SEINE: Bagneux, Bourg-la-Reine
SEINE-SAINT DENIS: La Courneuve, Île-Saint-Denis, Noisy-le-Sec, Romainville, Rosny-sous-Bois
VAL-DE-MARNE: Arcueil, Bonneuil-sur-Marne, Champigny-sur-Marne, Choisy-le-Roi, Thiais, Villejuif

---

*The archives marked with an asterisk are of interest to people of Alsace-Lorraine descent.

From the former Département of the Seine to:

HAUTS-DE-SEINE: Antony, Asnières, Bois-Colombes, Boulogne-Billancourt, Châtenay-Malabry, Châtillon, Clamart, Clichy, Colombes, Courbevoie, Fontenay-aux-Roses, La Garenne-Colombes, Gennevilliers, Issy-les Moulineaux, Levallois-Perret, Malakoff, Montrouge, Nanterre, Neuilly-sur-Seine, Le Plessis-Robinson, Puteaux, Sceaux, Suresnes, Vanves, Villeneuve-la-Garenne

SEINE-SAINT-DENIS: Aubervilliers, Bagnolet, Bobigny, Bondy, Le Bourget, Drancy, Dugny, Épinay-sur-Seine, Les Lilas, Montreuil, Pantin, Les Pavillons-sous-Bois, Pierrefitte-sur-Seine, Le Pré-Saint-Gervais, Saint-Denis, Saint-Ouen, Stains, Villemomble, Villetaneuse

VAL-DE-MARNE: Alfortville, Brie-sur-Marne, Cachan, Charenton-le-Pont, Chevilly-Larue, Créteil, Fontenay-sous-Bois, Fresnes, Gentilly, L'Hay-les-Roses, Ivry-sur-Seine, Joinville-le-Pont, Le Kremlin-Bicêtre, Maisons-Alfort, Nogent-sur-Marne, Orly, Le Perreux-sur-Marne, Rungis, Saint-Mandé, Saint-Maur-des-Fossés, Saint-Maurice, Vincennes, Vitry-sur-Seine

So much for the locations of the archives. Their holdings are immense, incredibly ancient, uncountable, and in many cases not catalogued and indexed. The volume of documents continuously arriving is not merely a flood but a total inundation at times. If you have wandered, as I have done, in some of the remote storage areas of some of the archives, you would not credit that any particular document could ever be found in the mass of records. Yet, thanks to the memories and the energies of the wonderful and hard-working men and women of the archives, the document you need will be produced with speed and efficiency.

The system of genealogical record-keeping in France differs from those of most other European countries. Once you understand it, you will find it very easy and reasonably inexpensive. The key to ancestor-hunting in France is the system used to maintain a permanent record of an individual during his or her life. For example, in the registers of birth, marriage, and death kept in the local town halls (or mairies) are wide margins. These margins are used for notes to be added later in order to update the information about the individual.

Since 1897 the birth certificate has shown in the margin the date and place of the subsequent marriage of the infant, and his or her divorce or remarriage. Since 1922 it has also shown the date and place of the marriage of the infant's parents. Since 1945 the marginal notes have given details of the eventual death of the infant. The marriage certificate includes full details of witnesses. The death certificate includes details of the date and place of birth of the deceased.

It is important, too, that you remember there is a "100 years law" governing the information that may be given to an inquirer. Information within the last 100 years will not be divulged in full so far as birth certificates are concerned unless (a) you are the person named on the certificate, or (b) you can prove your descent from him or her. These restrictions are simply to protect the privacy of people who may still be alive. However, even when you write for a certificate copy more than 100 years old, you should always specify that you want a *full* copy—in English, "an exact copy of the birth certificate"; in French, "Extrait des Registres des Actes de Naissance (Copie littérale)." If you do not specify this, you will receive an abridged copy without any details except the date and place of birth. Be sure you send two International Reply Coupons.

The government of France has issued a very clear and concise explanation of the method of keeping vital records in the country. The keeping of these records originated with two customs started by the Catholic Church:

Baptismal Records

These enabled a priest to discover a person's family background, and he could therefore avoid performing a marriage ceremony between a man and woman related to a degree prohibited by canon law.

Marriage and Death Records

These were types of account books in which the priest entered the gifts and offerings to the church received at the time of these sacraments.

It is generally accepted that baptismal records date back to the beginning of the thirteenth century and marriage and death records to the fourteenth century.

The parish records maintained by the clergy became increasingly useful to the state for the purposes of taxes, land disputes, military service, etc., and the government began to regulate them. In 1539 baptismal records were made compulsory by state law, and in 1563 a similar ordinance was issued for marriage records. Finally, in 1579 death records were also included under the Ordinance of Blois.

The records, of course, were only maintained by Catholic clergy, but in 1791, at the time of the Revolution, it was ordered that public officials would be responsible for the keeping of all such records. The Catholic records continued to exist alongside the civil records, but only those records kept before 1792 by the clergy could be used as legal documents.

The civil records are maintained in each commune in two separate registers. At the end of each year the second copy is sent to the registrar of the civil court of the first instance, while the first copy remains in the town hall. The law requires that any changes in the civil status of the individual (marriage, separation, divorce, adoption, death, and the birth of children) be entered in the margin of the original birth entry. Each document contains the date information was received and the names, ages, occupations, and addresses of everyone named.

The mayor is the registrar of each commune, but he may delegate his authority to a named local official.

French nationals living abroad, whether temporarily or permanently, may either use the forms used in their country of residence and register them with a French consul, or have the French official documents completed by the consul.

There is one final thing to remember before we leave the subject of French vital records and their systems. The death certificate will not record the place of burial. To find this, you will need to write to the parish priest of the district giving him the date and place of death. This may cause you some difficulties because many churches have been closed and a local priest may not exist in that particular parish. The registers may have been transferred to an adjoining parish, but there may be several of these. If you run into this difficulty, you should write to the Archives Départementales (addresses listed above), give them the story, and ask for their assistance.

So much for French records and record-keeping. Now let us talk— finally—about the various sources of information you may need in your search for those missing French ancestors.

Civil Registration

As you already know, this was established under French law in 1791, and the records start in 1792. This is the most important source of genealogical information in France since that date. The records are located in the town or village of origin, with a copy in the Archives Départementales up to the year 1870 approximately, and since then in the local court of the first instance (Greffe du Tribunal de Prèmiere Instance) located in the chief city of the préfecture or département (see above for address). Both the town hall and the provincial archives have yearly and ten-year indexes to births, marriages, and deaths, so there is no problem in tracing an entry as long as you have a name, date, and place to start with. If you require information about French citizens living overseas,you should write to Civil Registers of French people overseas (Direction des Affaires Administratives, Ministère des Affaires Étrangères, Boîte Postale 1056, 44035 Nantes).

If you are checking the indexes in person and not by correspondence, you should be aware that names such as De Lussac are indexed under D and not L, and you will find Leclerc under L and not C, even if the name is divided as le Clerc. Finally, bear in mind that the ten-year index I mentioned is not made up at the end of each ten-year period but is rewritten at odd intervals, so that though a name is listed by its initial letter, each letter is in chronological order:

L. 1876 5 Mars   Lavoie, Jean
L. 1876 4 Avril   Lacoste, Charles
L. 1876 7 Avril   Luétte, François
L. 1876 6 Mai   Lenoir, Marcel

Church Registers

These are in the Archives Départementales up to 1792 and since then in the individual churches, or in adjoining churches to which they have been transferred. Many of them have been indexed. The information in the registers includes not only baptisms, marriages, and burials but also confirmations and banns. Confirmation usually took place when a child was about twelve years old. Witnesses to baptisms are also listed, usually with addresses, and relationship, if any, to the child being baptized. These remarks apply, of course, to Catholic church registers only.

Protestant Registers

These are usually Lutheran from 1525 and Calvinist from 1559. The records are similar to the Catholic, except that confirmation usually did not take place until a child was sixteen years of age. The location of the registers is, unfortunately, scattered. Some are still in the local church, some in town halls, some in the Archives Départementales, some in the Library of the Protestant Historical Society (Société d'Histoire du Protestantisme Français, 54 rue des Saints-Pères, Paris), and for part of southern France, the Archives Départementales du Gard, 30040 Nîmes.

Huguenot Records

The majority of French Protestants were Huguenots, many of whom fled the country because of religious persecution. They are fairly well documented in various places.

1. The Huguenot Society (Miss Irene Scouloudi, 67 Victoria Road, London W8 5 RH, England) has parish registers, marriage contracts, wills of Huguenots who went to England, and many documents giving details of place of origin in France.

2. The Centraal Bureau voor Genealogie (Postbus 11755, 2502 AT, The Hague, Netherlands) indexed records of Huguenots who lived in some cities of France, Germany, Belgium, and the Netherlands.

3. Both the Archives Nationales and the Archives Départementales also have some Protestant records.

4. The City Archives (Stadtarchiv) of Frankfurt-am-Main, Germany, has records of financial and other assistance given to Protestant refugees. These include names of family members, relationships, places of origin, and intended destination.

The Calendar

For a short period from September 1792 to December 1805 the Gregorian calendar was replaced by the French Revolutionary calendar. You may find dates that include such months (or periods) as Pluviôse, Ventôse, Germinal, Floréal, Prairial, Messidor, Thermidor, Fructidor, Vendémiaire, Brumaire, Frimaire, and Nivôse. Although the names as I have given them correspond roughly with the months January to December, they do not match up exactly. There are methods of conversion from one to the other, but I doubt if I could explain them clearly, quite apart from the complications of three leap years in the period. I suggest you write down the dates you come across in the above period, and then gently persuade a friendly French archivist to convert them for you to the existing calendar.

Censuses (Recensements)

The first of these was held as far back as 1590 in at least one area; the Archives Départementales of Bas-Rhin have these on file for their area. There were other censuses in various places over the centuries, but often only the head of the family was named, and sometimes only the number of people in the house. Check with the Archives Départementales and also with the town hall. Censuses have been held regularly since 1836 at intervals of five years. Some have been lost in various wars, but those that survive are in the Archives Départementales, often with copies in town halls. The returns usually named complete families in the house, with age, occupation, and religion. The actual place of birth was not included before 1872.

In addition to the national censuses there were many local or municipal censuses, and here again you must check with the town hall. Since 1795 the municipal censuses have included the place of birth of all those present in the house.

Notarial Archives (Les Archives des Notaires)

These are probably the next most important source of genealogical information in France. Notarial documents are in existence as far back as the twelfth century, but to all intents and purposes you cannot rely on finding notarial records before the middle years of the sixteenth century. What is a notarial record? It is a document drawn up by a lawyer. These documents come under literally hundreds of headings, but as ancestor-hunters we are mainly concerned with marriage settlements, land sales, wills, inventories after death, and the division, or partition, of inheritances of land and property.

In 1928 a state law authorized notaries to deposit their documents older than 125 years in the Archives Nationales or the Archives Départementales. Papers less than 125 years old remain in the possession of the notaries. The problem has been that all the notarial records are regarded as the personal property of the notary concerned. The state recognized this claim in 1928 by allowing the notaries to retain ownership, even though the documents themselves were deposited in the archives. An example of the immense burden suddenly placed on archival resources is that of the Département de Seine (now defunct), which received documents from 144 existing notarial offices, for a total of nearly ninety million documents. That is just one département out of ninety-five!

The **marriage settlements or contracts** give us the full names of the contracting parties, their parents, the witnesses (with the relationship to the parties), and the date and place of the projected marriage.

The **inventories after death** are just that, a description of the personal papers of the deceased, the principal events of his or her life—birth, marriage, military service, children living and dead (and their marriages), property bought and sold, houses occupied, and, finally, death. Almost the whole of a man's or woman's life is set out on paper.

The **inheritances of land and property** give full details of the heirs and descendants of the deceased.

Wills and probate records are in the Archives Nationales and the Archives Départementales. Donations to heirs are records in this same general area (Donations entre vifs) and are usually gifts of property from old parents to their family. They date from the fifteenth century and are in the Archives Nationales, Départementales, and Municipales, or if filed within 125 years, in notaries' offices.

Administration of Estates (Partages de Succession)

These give names and addresses of deceased persons, their legal heirs, and the date and place of death. They can be found in the three levels of archives (national, departmental, municipal) and in notaries' offices. They date from about 1450, generally speaking.

Land and Property Records (Achats et Ventes de Terres)

These date from the mid-1400s in most localities and include details of renters, buyers, and sellers of land and buildings, with names, dates, addresses, and relationship (if any). They are in the three levels of archives or in notaries' offices.

Court Records (Archives Judiciares)

These exist from the early 1400s in many areas and are in the three levels of archives. They record not only crimes but also all civil actions involving land and property disputes, administration of estates, marriage contracts, and the buying and selling of real estate and buildings.

Schools and Universities (Écoles et Universités)

There are many records of pupils at educational institutions dating back to the fourteenth century and they give names, ages, and addresses, and names of parents. They are to be found in the three levels of archives, and also in the National Library (Bibliothèque Nationale, 58 rue de Richelieu, Paris).

Cemetery Inscriptions (Inscriptions Mortuaires)

These date from the twelfth century and are located in cemetery offices (Bureaux des Cimetières) in larger cities, or in churches, or in various archives. In the latter case they are likely to be indexed.

Burgess and Guild Records (Registres des Citoyens et des Corporations de Métiers)

These records apply only to major cities and are in one of the three levels of archives. They date from the twelfth to the eighteenth century and list those being accepted as burgesses or citizens of a city (much more important than being a mere inhabitant!), or those granted membership in a trade guild.

Electoral Lists (Listes Électorales)

These date from the early nineteenth century and list names, addresses, ages, and occupations of males only (until 1945) in each electoral district. (Women were granted the vote after the Second World War.) The records are in town halls and Archives Départementales.

Internal Passports (Passeports pour l'Intérieur)

These were in use from about 1800 to 1870 and were needed for movement between one location and another within France. They include the usual personal details, plus a physical description, and are in a certain number of Archives Départementales.

Conscription Lists (Registres de Conscription)

Since 1800 every French male has been liable for military service. These records show those who served, those who were exempted from service for one reason or another, and those who deserted either to avoid service, or while serving. Males over twenty-one years of age are included, and are listed by cities, towns, and communes or cantons. They are often indexed in alphabetical order of personal names, and are in the Archives Départementales.

Emigration Records (Registres d'Émigrés)

These date from 1788 to the present and list all those granted permission to emigrate. The records give place and date of birth, address, occupation, physical description, and names of family members traveling with the person listed. The intended destination is also included.

Passenger Lists (Rôles des Passagers)

These date mainly from the early eighteenth century and are listed under the names of the ships. They list the usual personal information, including country of origin since many passengers through French ports were from other European countries. The records for Le Havre (1750–1898) are in the Archives Départementales de la Seine-Maritime, 76100 Rouen. The archives are prepared to make a search if you can give precise information— name of vessel, name of passenger(s), and date of sailing. Similar records for Bordeaux (1713–87) are in the Archives Départementales de Gironde, 33000 Bordeaux.

Naturalization Records (Lettres de Naturalisation)

These date from 1635 to the present and, of course, give the country of birth of those becoming French citizens by naturalization. They are in the custody of the Archives Nationales and the Archives Départementales.

Military Records (Registres Militaires)

These are extensive and it is only possible to list some of the items available.

The records start in the seventeenth century and continue to the present day. Details are available at the Army Historical Service (Service Historique de l'Armée de Terre, Château de Vincennes, 94300 Vincennes) of all officers and most men serving in the army during that time. So far as the navy is concerned, the address is Service Historique de la Marine, Pavillon de la Reine, Château de Vincennes, 94300 Vincennes. The records list all personal details including next of kin and their address, dates of marriage and birth of children, children's names and ages, name and address of wife, injuries and death, and personal description.

Army records in most countries, including France, are your only source of information about the physical appearance of your ancestors. They are very detailed, listing height, weight, color of hair and eyes, "wart on chin," and so on. The description had only one purpose: to make it easier to catch a deserter from the armed forces. Conditions, up to modern times, were so bad for serving soldiers, particularly those in the ranks, that desertions were common.

There are also records from 1817 of disability pensions paid to ex-servicemen and pensions paid to widows. These are indexed.

I should, perhaps, mention at this point that if you intend searching archives personally on a visit to France, you should be sure to bring with you (a) proof of descent from the original emigrant from France, (b) a letter of introduction from a priest, minister, lawyer, or doctor translated into French, (c) half a dozen passport-size photographs. If you visit the National Archives first, you will be issued with an identity card, and this is usually sufficient to also give you admission to archives at a lower level—département, ville, commune. However, some local archives insist on checking your bona fides and issuing you with their own archival identity card.

Genealogical Societies

There are one or more genealogical societies or associations in each of the ninety-five départements. It is pointless to list the names and addresses of the secretaries of each of these because they change so often. If you are interested in a particular area, I suggest you write to the Federation (Fédération des Sociétés Françaises de Généalogie, d'Héraldique et de Sigillographie, 11 boulevard Pershing, 78000 Versailles)—which includes among its members most of the regional organizations in France—and ask for the address for your location.

In case you are wondering, *Sigillographie* means the study of seals—not the cuddly kind, but the big blobs of red wax that appear on ancient documents!

Be a little careful in your dealings with professional researchers and be sure they are on the approved list of an archive or a genealogical organization. There are many people in France who check the probate records, discover someone who died without a known heir but with a large estate, and try to trace a descendant, or near relative. Once found, the inheritance is split fifty-fifty. These inheritance searchers call themselves genealogists and advertise as such in newspapers and magazines.

The usual final word: **Don't forget the return postage!**

GERMANY

It is probably harder to trace your ancestors in Germany than in any other European country. It can also be said that if you are of German descent your roots may not be in Germany at all, at least may not have been for centuries. I don't want to discourage you in any way, but you must arm yourself for the fray with patience, determination, a sense of order, and an infinite capacity for hard work—in fact, with all those admirable characteristics associated with your German ancestors.

Let me set out for you the causes of the problems you will face:

1. Germany as an undivided nation existed only from 1871 to 1945, a brief period of seventy-four years. By comparison, such countries as France and England have been unified since the thirteenth and fourteenth centuries. In the seventeenth and eighteenth centuries the area we know as Germany consisted of 1789 kingdoms, principalities, grand duchies, dukedoms, electorates, free cities, right down to tiny personal estates of only a few acres. Each political unit had its own laws, archives, and systems of record-keeping. You cannot say, for example, that "censuses were first taken in Germany in 1871." That is true for the unified country of Germany, but censuses were taken in Württemberg in 1821, in Prussia in 1831, and so on. The only unifying and centralizing force in the Germanic area was the church, first the Catholic Church and later the Lutheran Church as well.

2. In the first half of the nineteenth century, because of the Congress of Vienna and growing German nationalism, the number of states was reduced to thirty-four. Some of these formed the German Confederation and in 1867 the North German Federation (Norddeutscher Bund) came into existence under the leadership of Prussia. In 1871 Prussia defeated France, and the south German states then joined with the Federation to form the German Empire (Deutsches Reich). Suddenly, in the very center of Europe, a powerful new country existed.

3. The new Empire included the following territory:

(a) Kingdoms of Bavaria, Prussia, Saxony, and Württemberg

(b) Grand Duchy of Baden

(c) Free Cities of Hamburg, Bremen, and Lübeck, and Anhalt, Brunswick, Darmstadt, Hesse, Lippe, Mecklenburg, Oldenburg, Reuss, and the various states comprising Thuringia

(Justice, education, health, and police were left under the control of the individual states.)

4. The unification of Germany ended in 1945 when parts of it were given to Czechoslovakia, Poland, and the USSR. What was left was then divided between East Germany (Deutsche Demokratische Republik, or D.D.R.) and West Germany (Bundesrepublik Deutschland, or B.R.D.). This division of Germany into two countries lasted until 1990. You may be dealing with six countries as well as Germany—if you include Belgium, Denmark, and France, which obtained German territory in 1919. All this may be ahead of you, plus the fact you may be dealing with the records of some of the original German states!

5. During the period when Germany was unified, little or no attempt was made to centralize records in one place such as Berlin; instead, they remained in the capital cities of the original states. In retrospect, this was a blessing to ancestor-hunters because the destruction of records in Germany during the Second World War was surprisingly small. Imagine what would have happened if everything had been in Berlin!

6. Even though you are of German descent, your roots may not be in Germany. Over the centuries, Germans from the Germanic area settled in other parts of Europe. Many tens of thousands settled in Ukraine and the area of the Volga Basin, others established themselves in Transylvania (Hungarian until 1919, Romanian since then), and still more are to be found in parts of Hungary and Yugoslavia. There were also nearly four million Germans in Czechoslovakia, but they were expelled by force after the Second World War.

7. The postwar dismemberment of Germany mentioned in (4) above is set out below:

TO CZECHOSLOVAKIA: Part of Silesia (Schlesien)

TO POLAND: The eastern parts of Brandenburg and Pomerania (Pommern), the southern part of East Prussia (Ostpreussen), Posen, Silesia (Schlesien), and West Prussia (Westpreussen)

TO THE USSR: The northern part of East Prussia (Ostpreussen)

The remaining part of Germany was then divided into the eastern part occupied by the USSR and the western part occupied by Britain, Belgium, France, and the United States. These two parts later became the German Democratic Republic or East Germany (Deutsche Demokratische Republik, or D.D.R.) and the Federal Republic of Germany or West Germany (Bundesrepublik Deutschland, or B.R.D.). Details of this division were:

EAST GERMANY (D.D.R.): Anhalt, Brandenburg (western part), part of Brunswick (Braunschweig), Mecklenburg-Schwerin, Mecklenburg-Strelitz, Reuss, Sachsen-Altenburg, Sachsen-Meiningen, Sachsen-Weimar, Schwarzburg-Rudolstadt, and Schwarzburg-Sondershausen. Also four provinces of the State of Prussia (the parts remaining after territory taken by Czechoslovakia, Poland, and the USSR).

WEST GERMANY (B.R.D.): Baden, Bavaria (Bayern), part of Brunswick (Braunschweig), Coburg, Lippe, Oldenburg, Schaumberg-Lippe, part of Thuringia (Thüringen), Waldeck, Westphalia (Westfalen), Württemberg; five provinces of the State of Prussia—Hanover (Hannover), Hessen-Nassau, Rhineland (Rheinland), Schleswig-Holstein, and Sigmaringen.

After the division in 1945, various changes were made within each of the two Germanys and they were then divided as follows:

EAST GERMANY (D.D.R.): Originally this consisted of five Länder or provinces. These were then abolished and replaced by fifteen districts (Kreise). However, the D.D.R., unlike the B.R.D., was not a federal state, and all power was centered in the capital (East, or Ost, Berlin).

WEST GERMANY (B.R.D.): The country consisted of ten federal states (Bundesländer or just Länder): Baden-Württemberg, Bavaria (Bayern), Bremen (city-state), Hamburg (city-state), Hesse (Hessen), Lower Saxony (Niedersachsen), North Rhine-Westphalia (Nordrhein-Westfalen), Rhineland-Palatinate (Rheinland-Pfalz), Saarland, and Schleswig-Holstein. The city-state of Berlin (West) was also integrated into the legal and economic system of the Federal Republic.

Following unification in 1990 the fifteen districts of East Germany (D.D.R.) mentioned above were replaced by the five original provinces or Länder. All the states of Germany are listed below with the name of the capital city:

Baden-Württemberg (Stuttgart)
Bayern (Munich)
Berlin
Brandenburg (Potsdam)*
Bremen
Hamburg
Hessen (Wiesbaden)
Mecklenburg-Vorpommern
　(Schwerin)*
Niedersachsen (Hannover)
Nordrhein-Westfalen
　(Düsseldorf)
Rheinland-Pfalz (Mainz)
Saarland (Saarbrüken)
Sachsen-Anhalt (Magdeburg)*
Sachsen (Dresden)*
Schleswig-Holstein (Kiel)
Thüringen (Erfurt)*

The Länder marked * are the new political divisions of the old East Germany, which replace the fifteen districts. The names of these districts or Bezirkes now within each of the five Länder are:

BRANDENBURG: Berlin, Cottbus, Frankfurt, Potsdam

MECKLENBURG-VORPOMMERN: Neubrandenburg, Rostock, Schwerin

SACHSEN: Dresden, Karl-Marx-Stadt, Leipzig

SACHSEN-ANHALT: Halle, Magdeburg

THÜRGINGEN: Erfurt, Gera, Suhl

Note: Karl-Marx-Stadt has now reverted to its original name of Chemnitz.

We can now start to talk about the main German sources of genealogical information, beginning with the various church registers. However, there will be a slight delay at this point because it is essential you know all about the organization and archival policies of the various churches before you hear about the registers and other church records.

In your search of records remember that it was common in Germanic areas in the middle 1700s to use only the *second* baptismal name in official records later in life. The first name was that of a parent or grandparent and was given as a compliment, but never used officially. So Oskar Georg Weber would only appear as Georg Weber.

THE EVANGELICAL CHURCH

The Evangelical Church in Germany (Evangelische Kirche in Deutschland) is a union of largely independent territorial Lutheran, Reformed, and United churches. These are listed below, and I have also included three smaller communities that are affiliated with the Evangelical Church but are not members of it.

As you can see, in the past the Protestant churches in Germany were divided into several sects. If your ancestors were members of the Evangelical Church, it will help you in your search if you can discover from within your family what particular sect they belonged to.

Evangelische Landeskirche Anhalts
Kavalierstrasse 35, 06844 Dessau

Evangelische Landeskirche in Baden
Blumenstrasse 1, 76133 Karlsruhe

Evangelisch-Lutherische Kirche in Bayern (Bavaria)
Meiserstrasse 11/13, 80333 Munich (München)

Evangelische Kirche in Berlin-Brandenburg
Neue Grünstrasse 19/22, 10179 Berlin

Evangelisch-lutherische Landeskirche in Braunschweig (Brunswick)
Neuer Weg 88/90, 38305 Wolfenbüttel

Bremische Evangelische Kirche
Franziuseck 2/4, 28199 Bremen

Evangelisch-lutherische Landeskirche Hannovers (Hanover)
Rote Reihe 6, 30169 Hannover

Evangelische Kirche in Hessen und Nassau (Hesse and Nassau)
Paulusplatz 1, 64285 Darmstadt

Evangelische Kirche von Kurhessen-Waldeck
Wilhelmshöher Allee 330, 34131 Kassel

Lippische Landeskirche
Leopoldstrasse 27, 32756 Detmold

Evangelisch-Lutherische Landeskirche Mecklenburgs
Münzstrasse 8, 19055 Schwerin

Nordelbische Evangelisch-Lutherische Kirche
Dänischestrasse 21/35, 24103 Kiel

Evangelisch-Lutherische Kirche in Oldenburg
Philosophenweg 1, 26121 Oldenburg

Protestantische Landeskirche der Pfalz (Palatinate)
Domplatz 5, 67346 Speyer

Pommersche Evangelische Kirche (Pomerania)
Bahnhofstrasse 35, 17489 Greifswald

Evangelisch-reformierte Kirche in Nordwestdeutschland (NW Germany)
Saarstrasse 6, 26789 Leer

Evangelische Kirche im Rheinland (Rhineland)
Hans-Böckler Strasse 7, 40476 Düsseldorf

Evangelische Kirche der Kirchenprovinz Sachsen (Saxony)
Am Dom 2, 39104 Magdeburg

Evangelisch-Lutherische Landeskirche Sachsen (Saxony)
Lukasstrasse 6, 01069 Dresden

Evangelische-Lutherische Landeskirche Schaumburg-Lippe
Herderstrasse 27, 31675 Bückeburg

Evangelische Kirche der schlesischen Oberlausitz
Schlaurother Strasse 11, 02827 Görlitz

Evangelisch-Lutherische Kirche in Thüringen (Thuringia)
Dr. Moritz-Mitzenheim-Strasse 2a, 99817 Eisenach

Evangelische Kirche von Westfalen (Westphalia)
Altstädter Kirchplatz 5, 33602 Bielefeld

Evangelische Landeskirche in Württemberg
Gänsheidestrasse 4, 70184 Stuttgart

Evangelische Kirche der Union (E.K.U.)
Herrenhauser Strasse 12, 30419 Hannover

Evangelische Brüder-Unität (Moravian Church)
Zittauerstrasse 24, 02747 Herrnhut (Oberlausitz)

Europäisch-Festlandische Brüder-Unität (Moravian Church)
Unitätshaus, 73087 Bad Boll

Bund Evangelisch-reformierter Kirchen (Federation of Reformed Churches)
Untere Karspüle 11a, 37073 Göttingen

Archiv und Bibliothek des Evangelisch Ministeriums (Archives)
Schmidtstedter 42, 99084 Erfurt

You will find the various church headquarters staff anxious to be of help to you but you must not ask for the impossible. For example, people have been known to write to the North Elbian Evangelical Lutheran Church to the effect "My great-grandfather was a member of the Evangelical Church and came from somewhere near you. He was born in 1870 or thereabouts. Can you look up the baptism entry in the register?" The North Elbian area covers Schleswig-Holstein, Hamburg, Eutin, and Lübeck. You can imagine how impossible it would be to even start a search.

When you write to a church organization, or a small individual church, please remember to enclose an addressed airmail envelope and at least two International Reply Coupons. I am sorry to have to keep repeating myself on this subject, but if you do not pay the return postage you may not get a reply. In addition, it will not hurt your chances of successful cooperation if you offer, in advance, to pay whatever search fees are required. If the search is an easy one you may not be charged anything.

Finally, if you can, write in German. If you cannot, then at least end your letter with the words "Mit freundlichen Grüssen" (With friendly greetings).

The address of the Evangelical Church headquarters (E.K.D.) is:

Rat der Evangelischen Kirche in Deutschland
Jebensstrasse 3
10623 Berlin

German Lutheran Churches in Memel

When Memel was transferred to the Soviet Union in 1945 the Lutheran registers for the area churches disappeared and many of the churches themselves are now closed. It seems probable that the registers are now in the

State Parish Register Archives of Lithuania (Lietuvos valstybinis metriku archyvas, 21 Kalinausko, Vilnius). It may be worthwhile writing to them—be sure you enclose two International Reply Coupons.

The parishes concerned are Coadjuthen, Dawillan, Crottingen, Heydekrug, Kairinn, Karkelbeck, Kinten, Laugszargen, Nattkischken, Nidden, Paleiten, Paszieszen, Piktopen, Plaschken, Plicken, Prokuls, Ramutten, Rucken, Russ, Saugen, Schwarzort, Szugken, Wannagen, Wieszen, and Wischwill.

Evangelical Churches in East Prussia (Ostpreussen)

Before the invasion of East Prussia by the Red Army, the parish registers and church books (Kirchenbücher) from about 500 parishes were removed to West Berlin. They are in the Central Archives of the Evangelical Church (Evangelisches Zentralarchiv in Berlin, Jebensstrasse 3, 10623 Berlin).

There are some missing and many gaps in the ones that survive, but if your ancestors came from East Prussia and were members of the Evangelical Church, these records may be vital to you. There is no listing of the parishes available, but the archives are planning a book about them.

Although 500 parishes are represented, there are in fact over 6,800 books involved, so you can see that the transfer and saving of these records were a major undertaking which reflects great credit on all the people concerned in this enterprise.

You should also enquire about the existence of Kirchenbüchduplikate. This is a duplicate of register entries sent each year to the nearest headquarters of the particular church.

THE CATHOLIC CHURCH

The Catholic Church in Germany is organized in ecclesiastical provinces (each under an archbishop), bishoprics (Bistum), and the local parish (Pfarr). There are twenty-seven church archives. These hold the earlier parish registers, as well as confirmation and communion records, and in many cases, the Family Books (Liber de Statu Animarum). There is no countrywide accepted date for the surrender of early records to the various archives.

The Family Books were first introduced in 1614 and include full details of each family in the parish, together with the names of any servants, and the occupation of the head of the family. The books were kept in Latin and German and are more complete in some areas than in others. It was compulsory for the priest to maintain the books up to 1918, but since then it has been quite voluntary.

The division of Germany after World War II did not affect the boundaries of the various dioceses, and so the re-unification in 1990 had no effect on ecclesiastical divisions.

The addresses of the various Catholic Archives are set out below. It should not be difficult for you to decide to which address you should write. If, for example, your ancestors came from Wanzleben, a gazetteer or a good map in your local library will show you it is near Magdeburg, and the list below will give you the address for that diocese. Generally speaking, you will find that the headquarters of each Bistum is located in the largest city of the area:

AACHEN: Postfach 210, Klosterplatz 7, 52062 Aachen

AUGSBURG: Fronhof 4, 86152 Augsburg

BAMBERG*: Domplatz 3, 96049 Bamberg

BERLIN: Wundstrasse 48/50, 14057 Berlin

DRESDEN: Käthe-Kollwitz-Ufer 84, 01309 Dresden

EICHSTÄTT: Leonrodplatz 4, 85072 Eichstätt

ERFURT: Herrmannsplatz 9, 99084 Erfurt

ESSEN: Postfach 100464, Zwölfling 16, 45127 Essen

FREIBURG*: Herrenstrasse 35, 79098 Freiburg

FULDA: Postfach 147, Paulustor 5, 36037 Fulda

GÖRLITZ: Carl-von-Ossietzky-Strasse 41, 02826 Görlitz

HILDESHEIM: Postfach 100263, Domhof 18-21, 31134 Hildesheim

KÖLN*: Postfach 108014, Marzellenstrasse 32, 50668 Köln

LIMBURG: Postfach 1355, Rossmarkt 8, 65549 Limburg

MAGDEBURG: Max-Josef-Metzger-Strasse 1, 39104 Magdeburg

MAINZ: Postfach 1560, Bischofsplatz 2, 55116 Mainz

MÜNCHEN*: Postfach 360, Rochusstrasse 5, 80333 Munich

MÜNSTER: Postfach 1366, Domplatz 27, 48143 Münster

OSNABRÜCK: Postfach 1380, Hasestrasse 40a, 49074 Osnabrück

PADERBORN*: Postfach 1480, Domplatz 3, 33098 Paderborn

PASSAU: Residenzplatz 8, 94032 Passau

REGENSBURG: Postfach 110163, Niedermünstergasse 1, 93047 Regensburg

ROTTENBURG: Postfach 9, Eugen-Boltz-Platz 1, 72108 Rottenburg

SCHWERIN: Lankower Strasse 14, 19057 Schwerin

SPEYER: Postfach 1160, Kleine Pfaffengasse 16, 67346 Speyer

TRIER: Postfach 1340, Hinter dem Dom 6, 54290 Trier

WÜRZBURG: Domerschulstrasse 2, 97070 Würzburg

Note: The headquarters of the Catholic Church is Sekretariat der Deutschen Bischofskonferenz, Kaiserstrasse 163, 53773 Bonn. The places above marked with an asterisk (*) are archbishoprics, the rest are bishoprics.

If you know the exact location of the place from which your ancestor came, you can probably identify the particular archive that may have the registers. If you cannot, then I would write to the Sekretariat and ask where the registers for that particular church are now.

OTHER CHURCH GROUPS

The two largest of the Protestant free churches, the Methodists and the Evangelical Community (Evangelische-Gemeinschaft), joined in 1968 to form the Evangelical Methodist Church (Evangelisch-Methodistische Kirche). There is also the Alliance of Free Evangelical Congregations (Baptists) (Bund Evangelisch-Friekirchlicher [Baptisten]), as well as Mennonites, Quakers, and Jews. By and large, all these organizations leave the registers and other records in the individual churches.

In 1933 there were over half a million Jews living in Germany. Today there are thirty-five thousand and about seventy Jewish congregations. Nearly a third of the members are in Berlin and Frankfurt-am-Main. The address for the Jewish headquarters is:

Zentralrat der Juden in Deutschland
Fischerstrasse 49
40477 Düsseldorf

THE CALENDAR

Before searching German records, you should be aware of changes in the calendar which, over a period of some years, produced either opposing and contradictory systems, or two different systems existing side by side.

Until 1582 the Julian calendar, established by Julius Caesar, was used in Germany and, indeed, in all civilized countries. This calendar divided the year into 365 days, plus an extra day every fourth year. The system was in operation until 1582, but astronomers had discovered that it exceeded the solar year by eleven minutes—or three days every four hundred years. Between the date when the Julian calendar was established in 325 and the year 1582, the difference amounted to eleven days. Since this affected the calculations for Easter, Pope Gregory XIII decreed that ten days be dropped from the calendar in order to bring Easter to the correct date. To prevent a recurrence of the problem, he also ordered that in every four hundred years leap year's extra day be omitted in a centennial year when the first two digits could not be divided by four without a remainder.

Are you still with me? Well, it means that it was omitted in 1700, 1800, 1900 but will not be omitted in 2000. The Pope also changed the beginning of the New Year from March 25 to January 1, and this new system became known as the Gregorian calendar.

Generally speaking, the new calendar came into force in Germany between 1582 and 1585, depending on the locality. There were some places that started it later and the most important of these are listed below:

Prussia (Preussen)	1612
Pfalz-Neuburg	1615
Osnabrück	1624
Minden	1630
Hildesheim	1631
Friesland	1700

Basically, the Protestant areas were reluctant to make the change, while the Catholic areas started as soon as possible after the papal decree was issued. So you will find places where the Catholic Church accepted the New Year as starting on January 1 and so called September the ninth month, while the Lutheran Church in the same place regarded March 25 as the New Year and regarded September as the seventh month.

When the change did take place, it led to confusing entries of dates in church registers for a brief period. Once the reason is clear to you, you will not be puzzled to find that an ancestress of yours had one child born in one year and a second born a few months later. It was the calendar that changed and not the nine-month gestation period, so all is well!

CHURCH RECORDS

Some church records date back to the fifteenth century, but in fact you should not expect to find many of them before about 1563 for the Catholic Church and a few years later for the Lutherans. Some of the exceptions are to be found in Baden and Württemberg, where there are Lutheran registers dating back to 1531 and 1545 respectively.

Although civil registration did not come into force until recent times, very early church registers often contained detailed information about individuals in the parish. Remember, of course, that most church records showed only dates of baptism, marriage, and burial and you may never find out the dates of birth and death.

Many of the registers have been destroyed as the result of civil wars, rebellions, and invasions over the centuries, but in some cases duplicates were kept in a separate location, so all is not necessarily lost. In Mecklenburg, for example, copies were kept from 1740 onward.

If you are searching church registers in person, you must be prepared to cope with entries in Latin (until the mid-nineteenth century) and the old German script, plus bad handwriting, and even a style of handwriting that is very different from that of the present day. No one ever said ancestor-hunting was easy!

Illegitimacy was fairly common in some rural areas of Germany. The illegitimate children were always baptized, but often the entry was made upside-down or sideways to emphasize the difference. The entry itself was very specific. The child was a bastard (Hurenkind), the mother a whore (Hure), and the father a fornicator (Hurer) or an adulterer (Ehebrecher).

The entries in the church registers usually include the following information:

BAPTISMS: Name, sex, date, names of parents, father's occupation, place of birth, names and addresses of godparents.

MARRIAGES: Name, age, and address of bride and bridegroom, occupation of groom, names and addresses of parents, occupation of the two fathers.

BURIALS: Name, age, place of death, cause of death, names of parents, name of husband or wife if still alive, date and place of burial.

Usually the above entries were made in three separate registers, but occasionally you will find all three events entered in one register in chronological order as they occurred.

In some parishes, particularly in the eighteenth and nineteenth centuries, you may find Family Books (Familienbücher or Liber de Statu Animarum). These contained complete records of a family and are of great genealogical value. Always check in a particular locality with the Catholic priest or the Lutheran minister as to the existence of a Family Book.

The book showed the name of the head of the household at the time the entry was made, the full names of the various members of the household, their places of birth, their marital status, the dates of death of deceased family members, and the place to which a family member moved if he or she left home (for marriage, work or emigration).

OTHER CHURCH RECORDS

Grave Registers (Grabregister)

These were maintained in the parish church, and although they were a duplicate of the entry of burial in the church register, they often contained additional information such as the date of death and the exact age (i.e., 38 years, 204 days). As the burial entries usually gave the date of *burial* and the age only in years, the grave registers can be of great help.

Church Receipt Books (Einnahmebücher)

These gave details of payments received from church members for such services as bell-tolling for a funeral (with name of deceased and date), and payment for burial plots and funeral cloths (Leichenhemden).

Confirmation Records (Konfirmationbücher)

Most children were between thirteen and twenty when they were confirmed, in both the Catholic and the Lutheran churches. The list gives the child's name and place and date of birth; the name and occupation of the father; and—quite often—the later marriage of the child. These records are either in the original churches or in the church archives.

There is one problem you should consider in connection with church records. If you know the religion of your ancestor but have problems with the location of his or her birthplace because you discover a number of places in Germany with the same name, you may find some help in knowing which religion was predominant in certain areas.

For example, let us suppose you know your Catholic ancestor came from a place named Schwarzenberg. You find there is one place with that name in Hesse (Hessen), one in Brandenburg, one in Prussia (Preussen), and one in Bavaria (Bayern). The odds are that the place you want is in Bavaria, because Brandenburg and Prussia are mainly Lutheran, and Hesse is Protestant but not necessarily Lutheran. This is not an infallible method, but it may help.

The other problem that may cause you difficulty, particularly in Schleswig-Holstein and Friesland, is different naming practices. Farms carried a name, usually the one given to it by the original owner. The name stayed with the farm even when the ownership changed. The trouble is that when a new owner bought the farm he would take its name as his own, or, if a man's wife inherited a farm, he would change his name to her maiden name. This could produce the complication of children bearing different surnames within the same family. If you run into this problem, find out if the confirmation books are available for the particular parish, because these records usually give the original name and the later one.

Another naming problem makes life even more difficult. If you see Wilhelm Brode von Magdeburg, for example, in a list, it does not necessarily mean that Wilhelm was a noble. It could simply be that he was a man named Wilhelm Brode who came from Magdeburg. It could be the case that he had moved from Magdeburg to Hannover and found that Brode was a common name, and so to distinguish himself from all the other Wilhelm Brodes he added the words "von Magdeburg." A generation later it could be shortened by his son to Ernst von Magdeburg.

So the surname may, in fact, be your guide to the actual place of origin of the family. Your next problem will be to discover the original surname, and this you may find if you can trace the baptismal or confirmation record of Ernst, because they are likely to give the true surname.

The final naming problem in this particular area is that of the practice of using patronymics—the naming of a child by giving him a new surname based on the first name of the father. Thus Wilhelm, son of Ernst Borgman, could be christened as Wilhelm Ernst. In instances like this, you must again have recourse to baptismal and confirmation records in order to trace the real surname. If you trace an ancestor back to a particular place and find no one of that name in the place before him, then your most obvious reaction is to assume he must have come there from elsewhere. However, do not make this assumption until you have checked out the possibility of a name change.

Passenger Lists

In most countries these are either non-existent or so few in relation to the whole that they need not be considered as a source of genealogical information. In Germany, however, the story is very different, and that is why I put them second to church registers as a good source of information. In fact, they are equally vital to people whose ancestors came from many other countries in Europe. That is why you will find you are referred to this mother lode of information in the chapters referring to Austria, Bulgaria, The Czech Republic and Slovakia, Hungary, Poland, Romania, Serbia, the Scandinavian countries, and the republics of the former USSR.

Bremen and Hamburg were the main ports for European emigration from 1832 (Bremen) and 1845 (Hamburg) up to 1934. The Bremen lists were destroyed over the years by the authorities to make room for new ones. British bombing in World War II finished the job! However, the Hamburg lists are available and contain the names of five to six million people who emigrated through the port.

The original emigration lists and indexes are housed in the State Archives in Hamburg, and include not only emigrants who sailed overseas directly from Hamburg, but also those who traveled indirectly via Hamburg to other European ports. For example, many emigrants sailed to a British port such as Gravesend or Harwich, crossed the country by train, and then sailed overseas from Liverpool. The period covered by the passenger lists is from 1850 to 1934 (with the exception of January–June 1853 and August 1914– to 1919). However, the lists were only compiled for ships with more than twenty-five passengers. They are indexed on a yearly basis in rough alphabetical order.

The records show the passenger's name, hometown, age, occupation, date of departure, ship, and sometimes his marital status, number of children, and destination. The lists are divided into direct and indirect records. Most emigrants traveled *directly* to a port in their new homeland. For example, the great majority of emigrants to the United States landed in New York; from there they scattered across the country and to Canada and South America.

Microfilm copies of the lists are located in the Historic Emigration Office (c/o Tourist Information am Hafen, Bei den St.-Pauli-Landungsbrücken 3, P.O. Box 102249, 20015 Hamburg). If you know the exact year of emigration, the cost of a search will be (at time of publication) at least thirty dollars per name and year searched. For this you will receive an official certificate which will include all the information that appears in the original passenger list.

The LDS church has also microfilmed and indexed the lists, and I think you will find it cheaper to deal with the LDS Family History Library (35 North West Temple Street, Salt Lake City, UT 84150).

You will not need to search the lists, of course, if you already know the place of origin of your emigrating ancestor, and the details of his or her family. It will be much easier and less expensive to try other sources first (family stories, diaries, Bibles, naturalization records, or letters).

It is important to realize that not all emigrating Germans used Hamburg or Bremen. Some sailed from Le Havre in France (see details of the records in the chapter on France). You must remember, too, that the place of origin shown in the passenger lists is not always the birthplace. However, in that case the odds are that the place of birth was quite near the place of domicile. For example, your ancestor may be shown as coming from Herrenhäusen (a small city), whereas his place of birth may have been Neuburg, a little village a few miles away.

Even if you find no record in the Hamburg lists, all is not lost. Several of the German states kept their own records of emigration from the state, notably Brunswick (Braunschweig), Hesse (Hessen), and Württemberg. Other similar records were kept in many individual cities and towns.

If you are consulting the lists yourself the following glossary may be of help to you:

Alter	Age
Anschrift	Address
Auswanderer	Emigrant
Beruf	Occupation
Bestimmungsort	Destination
Datum	Date
Erwachsen	Adult
Geboren	Born
Geburtsort	Birthplace

Gewerbe	Occupation
Herkunftsort	Place of origin
Kinder	Children
Länder	Provinces or states
Ledig	Single
Namen	Names
Nationalität	Nationality
Ort	Place
Strasse	Street
Verheiraten	Married
Vorname	Given name
Wohin	Destination
Zuname	Surname

INTERNAL MIGRATION

We have talked about German emigration to countries overseas, but we must also give attention to internal migration of Germans within Europe, including immigration of Germans *into* Germany. There are many instances of this; the following provide four major examples:

1. Early in the twelfth century the King of Hungary invited German settlement in the easternmost province of his country, Transylvania, which was underpopulated and open to invasion from warlike tribes to the east. Some five thousand settlers accepted the invitation; mostly they came from the Rhineland, although they later became known as Saxons. They were given as much land as they could cultivate and were granted freedom from taxes and military service, and allowed the right to maintain their own language. Since that time they have been able to preserve their traditions and customs within the area of original settlement, known as the King's land or Königsboden. Of course, many of the settlers found the limited area more than a little confining and some moved out to work for the Hungarian landowners in other parts of Transylvania or to the Banat area to the southwest.

During the period of the Reformation, the "Saxons" became Lutheran, the Magyars were divided between Catholic and Calvinist, and the Szeklers (a race related to the Hungarians) became Catholic, Calvinist, and Unitarian.

2. In 1731–38 some 30,000 German Protestants were expelled from the Salzburg area of Austria by the Catholic prince-bishop. These people, generally speaking, were resettled in Prussia (Preussen). For further information, see the chapter on Austria.

3. Catherine the Great of Russia invited Germans to colonize areas of the fertile Ukraine and the basin of the Volga. This mass migration continued between 1763 and 1862. Most of the emigrants to Russia came from Hesse (Hessen) and the Rhineland, with smaller numbers from other parts of the Germanic area. There were also emigrants from Denmark, France, Sweden and Finland, and Switzerland.

When the German armies invaded the USSR in 1941, they were welcomed by the majority of the Germans living in Ukraine. When the Wehrmacht retreated in 1942, many of the German settlers left, too, fearing reprisals from the Red Army, and they were wise. They made their way back to Germany, the Fatherland their ancestors had left over a century before, and those left behind were killed or imprisoned, or exiled to Kazakhstan.

4. In 1945 Czechoslovakia regained the Sudetenland. This German-speaking area had been taken from Austria in 1919 and awarded to the new country of Czechoslovakia. In 1938 it was re-united with Germany. After 1945 the three and a half million German inhabitants were forcibly expelled and their property and possessions seized.

Note: After the Second World War, thirteen million Germans returned to Germany (most to West Germany). Some of these came voluntarily, but the great majority were given no choice by Czechoslovakia, Poland, and the USSR.

Quite apart from the mass movements of population shown above, there was, of course, a continual movement to and fro between the various states before and after unification in 1871. Most of these movements of individuals were recorded. If a man wished to move from Hannover to Brunswick, for example, he would notify the Hannover police of his impending departure and his destination. On arrival in Brunswick he had to report his arrival to the police within three days. They in turn notified the police in Hannover that he had arrived. Although many of these police records were destroyed in the Second World War, the majority survived and are either in city archives, the local police headquarters, or the provincial archives. Here again you will have to check in the place of your interest to find out if the police records still survive.

Civil Registration (Reichspersonenstandsgesetz)

This started in 1875 following the unification of Germany, but only so far as the main Germanic area was concerned. In some areas the system had started earlier. There is a Register Office (Standesamt) for each particular area. All records of births, marriages, and deaths are kept there, but a duplicate of each entry is sent to the state capital. It should be noted that a registration area can be quite large, covering several towns and villages.

In those areas originally under French control, such as Alsace-Lorraine (Elsass-Lothringen) and a few other small areas west of the Rhine, registration started in 1810; in Frankfurt (once a Free City) it began in 1850, in Lübeck and Oldenburg in 1811, in Hannover in 1809, and in most parts of Prussia in about 1870. The death registers are particularly useful because they very often give not only the place and date of death, but also the names of the parents of the deceased and any surviving children.

Wills (Testamente)

The probate system in Germany is a little complicated. Once a lawyer has drawn up a will, a copy is deposited in the District Court House (Amtsgericht) for the area in which the testator is *living*. The local authorities then notify the Civil Register Office (Standesamt) in the district where the testator was *born*. When he dies, the Standesamt in his place of death notifies the Standesamt in his place of birth, and the latter, in turn, notifies the Court of Law of the location of the will. The court then executes the will. Original wills are either in the district courthouse or in the state archives (Staatsarchiv) in each province.

Censuses (Volkszählungen)

These have been held on a country-wide basis since 1871, but others were held at irregular intervals in various areas. Germany has traditionally conducted the censuses through the states, or provinces, rather than through the central government:

GERMANY: 1871, 1880, 1885, 1890, 1895, 1900, 1905, 1910, 1919, 1925, 1933, 1939

WEST GERMANY: 1946, 1950, 1961, 1970

EAST GERMANY: 1946, 1964

BADEN: 1852, 1855, 1858, 1861, 1867, 1925, 1933, 1946

BADEN-WÜRTTEMBERG: 1946, 1950, 1961, 1970

BAVARIA (BAYERN): 1846, 1849, 1852, 1855, 1858, 1861, 1867, 1946, 1950, 1961, 1970

BERLIN (WEST): 1945, 1946, 1950, 1961, 1970

BERLIN (EAST): 1945, 1946, 1964

BREMEN: 1900, 1905, 1946, 1950, 1961, 1970

COLOGNE: 1961

DRESDEN: 1871

HAMBURG: 1866, 1867, 1871, 1946, 1950, 1961, 1970

HESSE: 1925, 1946, 1950, 1961, 1970

NORTH-RHINE-WESTPHALIA (NORDRHEIN-WESTFALEN): 1946, 1950, 1961, 1970

PRUSSIA: 1895, 1900, 1905, 1910

RHINELAND-PALATINATE (RHEINLAND-PFALZ): 1946, 1950, 1961, 1970
SAARLAND: 1927, 1935, 1961, 1970 (see under France for 1945-57)
SCHLESWIG-HOLSTEIN: 1946, 1950, 1961, 1970
WÜRTTEMBERG: 1821, 1832, 1843, 1846, 1849, 1852, 1855, 1858, 1861,
   1867, 1946, 1950
DEUTSCHES ZOLLVEREIN: 1855 (This was the area included in a Customs
   Union of North German States.)

Note: Some of these returns are only head counts, some name only the head
of the household, some name only men. Do not assume the early returns
(particularly in Prussia) will solve any problems.

The federal government receives the results from the states in order to
make a "national head-count," but the original returns are kept in the individual states and copies can be obtained from the municipal archives
(Stadtarchiv) or the District Registry Office (Standesamt) in each city or
district. East Germany (D.D.R.) destroyed its census returns once they were
counted and so they are not available for research.

In order to consult the census returns or obtain a copy of the original
return, you will, of course, need to have an address in either a city or a
village. For the former you will want a street name but for the latter it is not
so essential. When writing, you should give the full names of your ancestor,
if known, and the names of his or her spouse and children. This will enable
the authorities to distinguish between people of the same name. It will be no
use asking for a copy of the census return of Wilhelm Müller in Neudorf,
Hesse; there might be twenty of them living there at the same time. Wilhelm
Erich Müller would narrow it down, and Wilhelm Erich and his wife Elisabeth
and his sons Erich and Heinrich would pinpoint it.

You must also be prepared to find that some census returns were destroyed by bombing in the Second World War. It may be wise for you to
contact the central census authority and ask if the census returns exist for a
particular location and where they are located. The address is:

   Statistisches Bundesamt
   Gustav Stresemann Ring 11
   Postfach 5528, 65189 Wiesbaden

In addition to the censuses listed above there were others conducted at
irregular intervals over the years by individual cities, for example,
Mecklenburg in 1819. You will have to check on these by writing to the
state and municipal archives for the area in which you are interested.

Police Registration (Einwohnermelderegister)

This started in most of the states in about 1840 and controlled internal
movement. The records included full name, family details, date and place of

birth, and occupation. As I mentioned earlier in this chapter, the records are usually held in local archives, police headquarters, or state archives.

Military Records (Kriegslisten)

These are incomplete and not always easily accessible but they are worth working on because every male was liable for military service in the various state armies. If your ancestors came from the Schleswig-Holstein area, you are luckier than most. The system there involved the registration of every male child at birth and the record was kept up to date as far as addresses were concerned until his call-up date. A good sequence of discoveries can follow: if you find your ancestor's addresses from the military records, you can trace the census returns; if you find the census returns you find the place of birth; if you find the place of birth you find the church records, you lucky people from Schleswig-Holstein! The military lists in general date back to the early 1700s and are in the state archives.

Certificate of Birth (Geburtszeugnis or Geburtsbrief)

When a person wanted to establish citizenship in a city or town, or get married, or join a guild (see below), he or she would have to produce this document. The individual had to produce a letter from the priest or pastor in his or her birthplace and the civil authorities would then issue the certificate.

Guild Records (Gilderbücher)

These can provide valuable information for you. The guild (like the trade union of today) was powerful in the work field. It permitted its members to work only at a particular trade, in a particular place. It made sure that a newcomer in town became a citizen before he joined the guild. Remember that being an inhabitant was not the same as being a citizen. Anyone could be an inhabitant, but you had to earn the right to become a citizen. You had to work hard, not be a charge on the community, not be a bastard, be sober, be a churchgoer, and know the right people.

Then, and only then, the good citizen could apply to join a guild, and the guild records show his name, his trade, the names of his wife and children, the date and place of his birth, the date and place of his marriage, and the date of his arrival in the city and his entry into the guild. The guilds exercised so much control over their members that they could dictate the area of the city in which they lived, and even whom they married (preferably the daughter of another guild member).

The guild records are either in local archives or in state archives, and they date back in many cases to the early seventeenth century, and in a few instances even earlier.

Other Available Records

There are three important sources of information in Germany that are often overlooked. They are, in order of value, Ortssippenbücher (Local Family Books), Geschlechterbücher (Lineage Books), and Leichenpredigten (Funeral Sermons).

These records should be used in conjunction with all the other sources I have listed; none of them, on their own, will provide you with all the answers, but they may well fill gaps, solve relationship puzzles, and give you the place of origin, or marriage, or death of a particular ancestor. Unfortunately, the records I mention are not in any one place, nor are the locations listed. You will have to write to the particular place or general area in which you are interested: to the Mayor (Bürgermeister) for a village, town, or city; or to the local Catholic priest or Lutheran minister; or to the director of the city archives (Stadtsarchiv) or the provincial archives (Landesarchiv or Staatsarchiv). You will have to ferret out the locations for yourself, but I never promised you a Rosengarten!

One final word of warning: be sure to send two International Reply Coupons and a self-addressed airmail envelope, and be prepared for a little resistance in some places to producing the Ortssippenbücher for reasons made clear below.

Local Family Books (Ortssippenbücher)

German genealogists and sociologists have been very interested since the early part of this century in studying the various families living in a particular area. This is partly pure research, partly love of history, and partly the German passion for tidiness, for having everything in its proper place. The Ortssippenbuch for a particular area will list all the members of every family (living and dead) and their relationship with each other. The source of the information was, of course, the church register, both Lutheran and Catholic.

As interest in the projects grew, the organization of them was taken over by a branch of the government, and as each district was completed, the results were published in book form. The ultimate aim was to have a genealogical record of the entire German people.

This was a point where the interests of genealogists in tracing family descent coincided with the National Socialist racial policies for a brief period. After 1933 many German citizens, particularly farmers, government officials, and teachers, were required to provide a certificate proving their Aryan descent—der Ahnennachweis, as it was called—and the existence of a completed Ortssippenbuch for their district simplified their task. The tracing of lineage was required back to the early nineteenth century; only the S.S. demanded lineage back to 1750 for their members.

Publication was suspended in 1940; after the war the task was taken over by the genealogical organizations without regard to any racial purity, and today some 150 books are in print. In addition, very many books were started and never finished, or finished and never printed. You will find the books or manuscripts in local and state archives. The present-day compiling of the books is not being done on a very even basis, since it depends very much on the energy and dedication of the various genealogical organizations. About half of the completed books refer to districts in the Länder of Baden and Hessen-Nassau.

It should be mentioned that some manuscripts are still in the possession of the individuals who worked on them, and if you are referred to a private individual your approach should be a tactful one, since not everyone wishes to be reminded of the original reasons for their genealogical research.

German Lineage Books (Deutsche Geschlechterbücher)

These books date back in some cases to the late eighteenth century when the first known one was published. The contents, of course, go back very much further. They contain the details of descent of bourgeois families, i.e. middle class and lower upper class, not the nobility. Each book contains a number of family trees of various German families. They are on a regional basis in that all the families in the book are from one district.

Some two hundred of the Geschlechterbücher have been published, and more are on the way. Each family section starts with the earliest known member and descends through the years to the date of publication. It also lists occupations and places of baptism, marriage, death, and residence.

Funeral Sermons (Leichenpredigten)

This source of genealogical information is almost unique to Germany but I have found similar records in Hungary. They originated in the sixteenth century for a rather odd reason. When the Reformation reached Germany, it meant the end of a very ornate and impressive funeral mass in the Catholic Church. This was a great occasion in which the deceased was praised at length by a local orator (often a professional, paid for his services), a large choir performed, and a sermon was delivered by the local priest (or by the bishop if the dead man or woman was important enough, or if the remaining spouse was generous to the church).

The end of this kind of ceremony left a gap in the lives of many people, mainly among Lutherans and Calvinists. They had embraced a simple and stark religion, but many of them missed a good funeral mass! So the funeral sermon was born and took the form of a eulogy at the graveside. Some sermons were entirely religious in content, but many were biographical and recounted the whole life of the deceased with details of births, marriages, public or military service, and other events of note.

After the ceremony the sermons were printed and circulated to all the friends of the family. There are well over one hundred thousand of these preserved in various locations and covering the period from about 1550 up to around 1800. Some of them are only a page or two in length, but some, if the deceased was famous, run to a hundred pages or more!

You can usually depend on the information contained in them being accurate; since the sermon was to be circulated among family and friends there was no point in lying or exaggerating the life and accomplishments of the deceased. Obviously, certain events would probably be quietly ignored: a period of insanity, a bastard child, dishonorable discharge from the army, a conviction for theft—that sort of thing would be left unsaid.

You can see that these three sources may well be of great value to you. Remember, though, that two of them are limited in their scope. The Lineage Books are confined to the bourgeois families, the Funeral Sermons to the wealthier Protestants; only the local Family Books record everybody— Catholic and Lutheran, rich and poor, in fact all classes of society.

Because the records I have mentioned are scattered in so many municipal offices, libraries, and archives, the search for one that includes your own family may be long-drawn-out, but if you are successful you may find your family lineage for a good many years, even two or three centuries.

There are still more available records of use to you. In some localities you will find all of them, in others only one or two:

	Approximate starting date
Adressbuch (City Directory)	1750*
Bürgerbuch (Citizenship Record)	1300
Familienregister (Family Registers)	1800
Gerichtsprotokolle (Court Records)	1500*
Grundbücher (Land Records)	1000*
Lehrlingsbücher (Apprentice Records)	1550
Polizeiregister (Police Registers)	1800
Stadtchroniken (City Chronicles)	1600
Steuerbücher (Tax Records)	1400
Zeitungen (Newspapers)	1800*

The dates are approximate because they vary from province to province, and from city to city. Generally speaking, the records marked with an asterisk are in the provincial archives (Staats- und Landesarchiv) and the others in city archives (Stadtarchiv) or district archives (Kreisarchiv), but there are exceptions to this.

One of the major problems about German records of interest to the ancestor-hunter is that they are scattered among church archives, state archives, city, town, and village archives, some government departments and offices, libraries, and museums. To make matters worse, only one attempt has been made to list the location of all genealogical archives and that effort, though praiseworthy, is very incomplete. Make no mistake: the material is there; it is available and informative, and it goes back over the centuries. Even minor local events were recorded and will be of interest to you.

Central Office for Genealogy (Zentralstelle für Genealogie)

This was a department of the East German government. It will continue to exist as part of the National Archive system of Germany, but will concentrate its activities in eastern Germany and—to a lesser degree—on genealogical records in the "lost territories" beyond the Oder-Neisse border with Poland. It is located at Käthe-Kollwitz-Strasse 82, 04109 Leipzig.

The various holdings include the following:

1. A pedigree and ancestor list includes more than 12,000 family trees, including over two million card-indexes of individual names. If you are consulting these cards in person (and you may obtain permission to do so), you must know the system. Because of the variation in the spelling of surnames, it was decided to follow a system of phonetic spelling and file under one spelling variation only. So, for example, under the name Maier you will also find Mayer, Meier, and Meyer.

2. A catalogue of personal writings and eulogies covers the sixteenth to eighteenth centuries and consists of some 700 works. It is being added to on a regular basis and is certainly only in its infancy, and it includes many printed funeral orations and sermons (I have referred to this German custom earlier in this chapter).

3. The Zentralstelle für Genealogie (Z.G.) contains photocopies and microfilms of a number of church registers of all denominations. There is no list available, but this is understandable because the additions are being made constantly and any list would soon be out of date.

4. There are more specialized items in the Z.G. records such as:
   (a) A list of the population of Leipzig before 1800, including the surrounding area.
   (b) Records of the Huguenots who fled from France after the bloody persecution that followed the revocation of the Edict of Nantes in 1685.

5. The library of Z.G. includes 22,000 writings on genealogical subjects, in both published and manuscript form, covering the period from the seventeenth century to the present day.

6. A number of genealogists in eastern Germany have given their research papers to the Z.G., and they have been catalogued and indexed. The Director tells me that the staff are happy to help overseas inquirers with their problems. He does emphasize that requests should include as much

detail as possible—particularly full names, religion, and possible dates and places. The staff will search church registers as well as their own holdings if requested. A fee will be charged and the amount quoted and paid before the search.

The Z.G. can be particularly helpful if you are searching for information about Germans who originated in the areas east of the present German-Polish border.

There are Genealogical Study Groups (Arbeitsgemeinschaften Genealogie) in all the main centers of what was East Germany. The Z.G. will supply you with up-to-date addresses of any groups that exist in your particular area of interest.

ARCHIVES

The many divisions of the Germanic area are the cause of the peculiar distribution of archives. From the fourteenth to the nineteenth century, central power over the Germanic lands was exercised by the Hapsburg dynasty, so the central archives of the old Reich are in Vienna. See the chapter for Austria.

Since then, the various states have preserved their own archives; as a result, there are archives of all kinds scattered throughout Germany, from major cities down to small villages, and there are no central archives with precious genealogical records.

You will find Staatsarchiv (national), Staatsarchiv (provincial), Landesarchiv (provincial), Stadt (city), Bezirk (district), Dorf (village), Familien (family), Dom (cathedral), Pfarr (parish), Gutsarchiv (property), plus many others for individuals, families, professions, manufacturing plants, religious orders, and youth organizations.

In the following pages you will find details of many of the archives of value to the ancestor-hunter. First, the provincial or state archives; then a list of local archives alphabetically by city, town, and village; and finally a list of church archives at a level lower than those included earlier in this chapter. In addition you will find a list of archives devoted to the papers of noble families.

State Archives (Staatsarchiv)

BADEN-WÜRTTEMBERG

Hauptstaatsarchiv
Konrad-Adenauer Strasse 4
70173 Stuttgart

BAYERN	Hauptstaatsarchiv Arcisstrasse 12 80333 Munich 2
BERLIN	Staatsarchiv Archivstrasse 12-14 14195 Berlin
BRANDENBURG	Landeshauptarchiv Sanssouci, Orangerie 14469 Potsdam
BREMEN	Staatsarchiv Präsident Kennedy Platz 2 28203 Bremen
HAMBURG	Staatsarchiv ABC Strasse 19 20354 Hamburg
HESSEN	Hauptstaatsarchiv Mainzerstrasse 80 65189 Wiesbaden
MECKLENBURG-VORPOMMERN	Hauptarchiv Graf Schack Allee 2 19053 Schwerin
NIEDERSACHSEN	Hauptstaatsarchiv Planckstrasse 2 30169 Hannover
NORDRHEIN-WESTFALEN	Hauptstaatsarchiv Prinz Georg Strasse 78 40479 Düsseldorf
RHEINLAND-PFALZ	Staatsarchiv Karmeliterstrasse 1-3 56068 Koblenz
SAARLAND	Landesarchiv Am Ludwigsplatz 7 66117 Saarbrücken
SACHSEN	Hauptarchiv Archivstrasse 14 01097 Dresden

SACHSEN-ANHALT

Hauptarchiv
Hegelstrasse 25
39104 Magdeburg

SCHLESWIG-HOLSTEIN

Landesarchiv
Schloss Gottorf
24837 Schleswig

THÜRINGEN

Hauptarchiv
Marstallstrasse 2
99423 Weimar

Note: In April 1993 the transfer of the Prussian Secret State Archives from Merseburg (Sachsen-Anhalt) to Berlin commenced. It will take a year to complete. The records include property deeds and other records dating back to the twelfth century. They were transferred from Berlin in 1943 and hidden in potassium and salt mines in Sachsen-Anhalt, finally ending up in Merseburg. In Berlin they will be stored temporarily in a converted granary. Information about these records can be obtained from the Prussian Cultural Heritage Foundation, Postfach 3160, 10785 Berlin.

City Archives (Stadtarchiv)

The type of record you will find in local archives includes all or some of the following. It is up to you to write and find out what is available for your particular district. Try to write in German, because even though there may be someone there who understands English, he or she may not read it well enough to understand just what you want to know. I once wrote and asked for the correct name of a book about leading families in a particular city. I had a reply in flawless English telling me they had only one copy of the book, and in any case it would be too heavy to send through the mail! They did not mention the name of the book, either, so I had to write again in German, and then all was well. You may also find that when you write in English you will be answered in German. In this case you can try to find someone who speaks German, a friend or a local teacher, or settle down with a good German-English dictionary in the local library.

At this point let me again remind you to enclose a self-addressed airmail envelope and two International Reply Coupons to cover return postage. If you are planning a great deal of correspondence with Germany, it will save money if you buy German stamps. Write to the post office (Postamt) of any German city, enclose a bank draft for a sum of money (five or ten dollars), and ask them to mail you German stamps of the right value for airmail letters to this country.

The type of records you will find are listed below:

Address books (Adressbücher)
Apprentice Lists (Lehrlingsbücher)
Census Returns (Volkszählungen)
City Chronicles (Stadtchroniken)
City Directories (Adressbücher)
Citizenship Lists (Bürgerbücher)
Court Records (Gerichtsprotokolle)
Emigration Lists (Auswanderungregister)
Family Book (Ortssippenbücher)
Family Register (Familienregister)
Funeral Sermons (Leichenpredigten)
Grave Registers (Grabregister)
Guild Books (Gilderbücher)
Land Records (Grundbücher)
Lineage Books (Geschlechterbücher)
Newspapers (Zeitungen)
Police Registers (Polizeiregister)
Parish Registers (Kirchenbücher)
Probate Records (Testamente)
Tax Records (Steuerbücher)
Wills (Testamente)

The following abbreviations are used in the list of cities, towns, etc., below to show the provinces or Länder in which the places are located:

B	Bayern
BL	Bremen
BR	Brandenburg
BW	Baden-Württemberg
H	Hessen
HL	Hamburg
MV	Mecklenburg-Vorpommern
NS	Niedersachsen
NW	Nordrhein-Westfalen
RP	Rheinland-Pfalz
S	Saarland
SA	Sachsen
SAA	Sachsen-Anhalt
SH	Schleswig-Holstein
T	Thüringen

Aachen (NW)
Aalen (BW)
Abensberg (B)
Ahaus (NW)
Ahrweiler (RP)
Alsfeld (H)
Altdorf (B)
Altena (NW)
Altenburg (SA)
Alt-Wallmoden (NS)
Alzey (RP)
Amlishagen (BW)
Amoneburg (H)
Amstetten (B)
Andernach (RP)
Anklam (MV)
Annaberg-Buckholz
   (SA)
Annweiler (RP)
Ansbach (B)
Apolda (T)
Arnsberg (NW)
Arnstadt (T)
Artern (SAA)
Aschaffenburg (B)
Ascherleben (T)
Aue (SA)
Augsburg (B)
Babenhausen (H)
Bacharach (RP)
Backnang (BW)
Balingen (BW)
Bamberg (B)
Baunatal (H)
Bayreuth (B)
Beeskow (BR)
Bensheim (H)
Bentheim (NS)
Bergisch-Gladbach
   (NW)
Bad Bergzabern (RP)
Berleburg (NW)
Berlin

Bernburg (SAA)
Besighem (BW)
Bevensen (NS)
Biberach (BW)
Bielefeld (NW)
Bingen (RP)
Bischofswerda (SA)
Bitterfeld (SAA)
Blaubeuren (BW)
Blomberg (NW)
Bocholt (NW)
Bochum (NW)
Bonn (NW)
Borken (NW)
Borna (SA)
Bottrop (NW)
Flecken Bovenden
   (NS)
Brafkenheim (BW)
Brakel (NW)
Brandenburg an der
   Havel (BR)
Brandestein bei Elm
   (H)
Braunschweig (NS)
Breckerfeld (NW)
Breisach (BW)
Bremen (BL)
Bremerhaven (BL)
Brilon (NW)
Brühl (NW)
Bad Buchau (BW)
Bühl (BW)
Büren (NW)
Burg auf Fehmarn
   (SH)
Burg bei Magdeburg
   (SAA)
Burgbernheim (B)
Burghausen (B)
Burgkunstadt (B)
Burgsteinfurt (NW)
Burkheim am K (BW)

Butzbach (H)
Buxtehude (NS)
Calbe (SAA)
Calw (BW)
Castrop-Rauxel (NW)
Celle (NS)
Cham (B)
Chemnitz (SA)
Coburg (B)
Coesfeld (NW)
Coswig (SAA)
Cottbus (BR)
Crimmitschau (SA)
Cuxhaven (NS)
Darmstadt (H)
Deggendorf (B)
Deidesheim (RP)
Delitzch (SA)
Demmin (BR)
Dessau (SAA)
Detmold (NW)
Diez (RP)
Dillingen/Donau (B)
Dingolfing (B)
Dinkelsbühl (B)
Dinslaken (NW)
Doberlug-Kirchhain
   (BR)
Donauwörth (B)
Dornburg/Elbe (SAA)
Dorsten (NW)
Dortmund (NW)
Dreieichenhain (H)
Dresden (SA)
Dubeln (SA)
Duderstadt (NS)
Duisburg (NW)
Dulmen (NW)
Düren (NW)
Bad Durkheim (RP)
Düsseldorf (NW)
Eberbach (BW)
Eberswalde (BR)

Ebingen (BW)
Eckernförde (SH)
Edenkoben (RP)
Eggenfelden (B)
Eichstatt (B)
Eilenburg (SA)
Einbeck (NS)
Eisenach (T)
Eisenberg (RP)
Eisenberg (T)
Eisfeld (T)
Eisleben (SAA)
Ellwangen (BW)
Emden (NS)
Emmerich (NW)
Bad Ems (RP)
Endingen (BW)
Engen (BW)
Erding (B)
Erfurt (T)
Erkelenz (NW)
Erlangen (B)
Eschwege (H)
Esslingen/Neckar
  (BW)
Eutin (SH)
Feuchtwangen (B)
Flensburg (SH)
Forchheim (B)
Forst/Lausitz (BR)
Bad Frankenhausen
  (SAA)
Frankenthal (RP)
Frankfurt/Main (H)
Frankfurt/Oder (BR)
Frechen (NW)
Freiberg (SA)
Freiburg/Breisgau
  (BW)
Freising (B)
Freudenstadt (BW)
Friedberg/Hessen (H)
Friedrichshafen (BW)

Fritzlar (H)
Fulda (H)
Furstenau (NS)
Furstenwalde (BR)
Fürth (B)
Füssen (B)
Gaildorf (BW)
Gardelegen (SAA)
Garmisch/
  Partenkirchen (B)
Geislingen (BW)
Geinhausen (H)
Gelsenkirchen (NW)
Gengenbach (BW)
Gera (T)
Gernrode (SAA)
Gerolzhofen (B)
Geseke (NW)
Gevelsberg (NW)
Giengen (BW)
Giessen (H)
Glücksburg (SH)
Glückstadt (SH)
Gnandstein (SA)
Göppingen (BW)
Görlitz (SA)
Goslar (NS)
Gotha (T)
Göttingen (NS)
Greifswald (MV)
Greiz (T)
Greussen (T)
Grimma (SA)
Groitzscg (SA)
Grossbottwar (BW)
Gross-Gerau (B)
Grünberg (H)
Grunstadt (RP)
Guben (BR)
Gudensberg (H)
Güstrow (MV)
Hachenburg (RP)
Hagen (NW)

Halberstadt (SAA)
Halle an der Saale
  (SAA)
Hamburg (HL)
Hameln (NS)
Hanau (H)
Hann-Munden (NS)
Hannover (NS)
Haslach (BW)
Hattingen (NW)
Heidelberg (BW)
Heidenheim/Brenz
  (BW)
Heilbad Heiligenstadt
  (T)
Helmstedt (NS)
Herberg/Elster (BR)
Herford (NW)
Herne (NW)
Herrenberg (BW)
Hersbruck (B)
Bad Hersfeld (H)
Herten (NW)
Hildburghausen (T)
Hilden (NW)
Hildesheim (NS)
Hochstadt (B)
Hof (B)
Hofgeismar (B)
Homberg (H)
Bad Homburg (H)
Horb/Neckar (BW)
Hornburg (NS)
Höxter (NW)
Hüfingen (BW)
Husum (SH)
Ilmenau (T)
Ingelheim (RP)
Ingolstadt (B)
Iserlohn (NW)
Isny (BW)
Itzehoe (SH)
Jena (T)

Jever (NS)
Jülich (NW)
Juterbog (BR)
Kaiserlautern (RP)
Kalkar (NW)
Kamenz (SA)
Kandel (RP)
Karlshafen (H)
Karlsruhe (BW)
Karlstadt (B)
Kassel (H)
Kaufbeuren (B)
Kelheim (B)
Kempen (NW)
Kempten/Aligäu (B)
Kenzingen (BW)
Kiel (SH)
Kirchheim/Teck (BW)
Kirn (RP)
Kirtorf (H)
Kitzingen (B)
Kleve (NW)
Koblenz (RP)
Köln (NW)
Königshofen (B)
Konstanz (BW)
Korbach/Edersee (H)
Köthen/Anhalt (SAA)
Kranenburg (NW)
Krefeld (NW)
Bad Kreuznach (RP)
Kronach (B)
Krönberg (H)
Kulmbach (B)
Kusel (RP)
Lage-Lippe (NW)
Lahnstein (RP)
Lahr (BW)
Landau (RP)
Landsberg (B)
Landshut (B)
Bad Langensalza (T)
Laubach (H)

Lauenburg/Elbe (SH)
Lauf (B)
Laufen (B)
Lauingen/Donau (B)
Lauterbach (H)
Lauterecken (RP)
Leipzig (SA)
Lemgo (NW)
Leutkirch (BW)
Leverkusen (NW)
Lich (H)
Lichtenfels (B)
Limburg-Lahn (H)
Lindau (B)
Linz (RP)
Lippstadt (NW)
Löbau (SA)
Lörrach (BW)
Lubben (BR)
Lübeck (SH)
Luckenwalde (BR)
Lüdenscheid (NW)
Ludwigsburg (BW)
Ludwigshafen (RP)
Ludwigslust (MV)
Lügde (NW)
Lüneburg (NS)
Lünen (NW)
Magdeburg (SAA)
Mainz (RP)
Mannheim (BW)
Marburg (H)
Marienberg (SA)
Markdorf (BW)
Markleeberg (SA)
Marktredwitz (B)
Marl (NW)
Maulbronn (BW)
Mayen (RP)
Meckenheim (NW)
Meersburg (BW)
Meiningen (T)
Meisenheim (RP)

Meissen (SA)
Meldorf (SH)
Melle (NS)
Memmingen (B)
Menden (NW)
Mengen (BW)
Meppen (NS)
Bad Mergentheim
 (BW)
Merseburg (SAA)
Messkirch (BW)
Metelen (NW)
Mettmann (NW)
Meuselwitz (SA)
Michelstadt (H)
Mindelheim (B)
Minden (NW)
Mittweida (SA)
Moers (NW)
Möhringen (BW)
Mönchengladbach
 (NW)
Monschau (NW)
Montabour (RP)
Mühldorf (B)
Mühlhausen/Thur (T)
Munich (München)
 (B)
Münnerstadt (B)
Münster (NW)
Bad Münstereifel
 (NW)
Namedy (RP)
Nassau (RP)
Nauheim (H)
Naumburg/Saale
 (SAA)
Neckarsteinach (H)
Neheim/Hüsten (NW)
Neuburg (B)
Neuenburg (BW)
Neuenhaus (NS)
Neumünster (SH)

Neuötting (B)
Neuss (NW)
Neustadt (B)
Neustadt (SH)
Neustadt/Donau (B)
Nidda (H)
Nideggen (NW)
Nordhausen (T)
Nordhorn (NS)
Nordlingen (B)
Northeim (NS)
Nürnberg (B)
Nürtingen (BW)
Oberhausen (NW)
Obernburg/Main (B)
Oberndorf (BW)
Oberursel/Taunas (H)
Oberviechtach (B)
Ochsenfurt (B)
Oelsnitz im Vogtland
  (SA)
Offenbach/Main (H)
Offenburg (BW)
Ohrdruf (T)
Öhringen (BW)
Oldenburg (SH)
Oldenburg (NS)
Bad Oldesloe (SH)
Olpe (NW)
Opladen (NW)
Oppenheim (RP)
Oranienburg (BR)
Oschatz (SA)
Oschersleben (SAA)
Osnabruck (NS)
Osterburg (SAA)
Osterrode/Harz (NS)
Otterberg (RP)
Otterndorf (NS)
Paderborn (NW)
Paschim (MV)
Pegau (SA)
Perleberg (MV)

Pforzheim (BW)
Pfullendorf (BW)
Pfullingen (BW)
Pirna (SA)
Plauen im Vogtland
  (SA)
Porz (NW)
Pössneck (T)
Prenzlau (MV)
Pritzwalk (BR)
Bad Pyrmont (NS)
Quakenbrück (NS)
Quedlinnburg (SAA)
Radolfzell (BW)
Rain (B)
Rastatt (BW)
Ratingen (NW)
Ratzeburg (SH)
Ravensburg (BW)
Rees (NW)
Regensburg (B)
Reichenbach im
  Vogtland (SA)
Reinheim (H)
Remagen (RP)
Remscheid (MW)
Rendsburg (SH)
Reutlingen (BW)
Rheda/Wiedenbrück
  (NW)
Rheinberg (NW)
Rheine (NW)
Rhein Hausen (NW)
Rheydt (NW)
Rhoden (H)
Riedlingen (BW)
Rieneck (B)
Riesa (SA)
Rinteln (NS)
Rochlitz (SA)
Romrod (H)
Rosberg (NW)
Rosenheim (B)

Rostock (MV)
Rotenburg (NS)
Roth (B)
Rothenburg (B)
Rottwell (BW)
Rudolstadt (T)
Ruhla (T)
Saalfeld (T)
Saarbrücken (S)
Saarlouis (S)
St. Goar (RP)
St. Ingbert (S)
Salzgitter (NS)
Bad Salzuflen (NW)
Bad Salzungen (T)
Salzwedel (SAA)
Sangerhausen (SAA)
Schalkau (SAA)
Schleiz (T)
Schleswig (SH)
Schleusingen (T)
Schlitz (H)
Schmalkalden (T)
Schmölin (SA)
Schneeberg (SA)
Schönebeck (SAA)
Schongau (B)
Schopfheim (BW)
Schorndorf (BW)
Schotten (H)
Schramberg (BW)
Schwabach (B)
Schwäbisch Gmund
  (BW)
Schwäbisch Hall
  (BW)
Schweinfurt (B)
Schwelm (NW)
Schwerin (MV)
Schwetzingen (BW)
Seefeld (B)
Seehausen/Altmark
  (SAA)

Sendenhorst (NW)
Senftenberg (BR)
Siegburg (NW)
Siegen (NW)
Sigmaringen (BW)
Sindelfingen (BW)
Singen (BW)
Sinsheim (BW)
Sondershausen (T)
Sonneberg (T)
Bad Sooden (H)
Speyer (RP)
Sprendlingen (H)
Stade (NS)
Stadthagen (NS)
Stassfurt (SAA)
Stendal (SAA)
Stockach (BW)
Stockum (NW)
Straelen (NW)
Stralsund (MV)
Straubing (B)
Stuttgart (BW)
Suhl (T)
Sulz/Neckar (BW)
Tangermunde (SAA)
Telgte (NW)
Tittmoning (B)
Bad Tolz (B)
Torgau (SA)
Traunstein (B)
Treffurt (T)
Trier (RP)

Tübingen (BW)
Überlingen (BW)
Uelzen (NS)
Ulm (BW)
Ulrichstein (H)
Unna (NW)
Velbert (NW)
Verden/Aller (NS)
Viersen (NW)
Villingen (BW)
Vohburg/Donau (B)
Volklingen (S)
Wachtenheim (RP)
Waiblingen (BW)
Bad Waldsee (BW)
Waldheim (SA)
Waldshut (BW)
Wangen (BW)
Wanne-Eickel (NW)
Warendorf (NW)
Warstein (NW)
Wasserburg am Inn
    (B)
Wattenscheid (NW)
Weiden-Oberpfalz (B)
Weil am Rhein (BW)
Weilburg (H)
Weilheim (B)
Weimar (T)
Weingarten (BW)
Weinheim (BW)
Weismain (B)
Weissenburg (B)

Weissenfels (SAA)
Werl (NW)
Werne an der Lippe
    (NW)
Wernigerode (SAA)
Wertheim (BW)
Wesel (NW)
Wetzlar (H)
Wiedbaden (H)
Wilster (SH)
Bad Wimpfen (BW)
Bad Windsheim (B)
Winsen (S)
Wismar (MV)
Witten (NW)
Wolfach (BW)
Wolfenbüttel (NS)
Wolgast (MV)
Wolmirstedt (SAA)
Wormein (NW)
Worms (RP)
Wulfrath (MW)
Wunsiedel (B)
Wuppertal (NW)
Wurzburg (B)
Xanten (NW)
Zeitz (SAA)
Zelia-Mehlis (T)
Zerbst (SAA)
Zeulenroda (T)
Zittau (SA)
Zweibrücken (RP)
Zwickau (SA)

I do not claim that the above list is complete. It has been put together from a variety of sources, and there will probably be omissions, particularly of smaller places. Correspondence should be sent to the Direktor, Stadtarchiv, followed by the name of the city and the province or Länder.

In addition to the above, there are specialized archives in such places as Jena, for example, where you will find the archives of the Karl Zeiss Company and the Jena Glassworks. If you know your ancestor worked for a large corporation it may be worthwhile to write to the company concerned to ask if it has archival or personnel records available.

There is also the Red Cross Archives in Dresden (Das Zentral Verwaltungsarchiv des Deutschen Roten Kreuzes, Kaitzerstrasse, 01069 Dresden). This may be useful if you are trying to trace someone who was a refugee from the area of Germany now in the Soviet Union.

Parish Archives (Pfarrarchiv)

Many of the city archives shown above also have local church records, but given below are separate church archives known to exist and *not* included in the major church archives previously listed. After the province code, a C or L is given in parentheses to indicate whether the archives hold Catholic or Lutheran records, or both:

Amöneburg (H) (C)
Balingen (BW) (L)
Biberach (BW) (L and C)
Bochum (NW) (L)
Bottrop (NW) (C)
Brakel (NW) (C)
Burgensteinfurt (NW) (L and C)
Duderstadt (NS) (L and C)
Duisburg (NW) (L)
Dulmen (NW) (L)
Emden (NS) (L)
Emmerich (NW) (L and C)
Engelskirchen (NW) (C)
Erfurt (T) (L and C)
Essen (H) (C)
Flensburg (SH) (C)
Göttingen (NS) (L and C)
Gudow (SH) (L)
Hagen (NW) (L and C)
Hattingen (NW) (L)
Herford (NW) (L and C)
Herrenberg (BW) (L)
Hof (B) (L)
Höxter (NW) (C)

Isny (BW) (L)
Karlsruhe (BW) (L)
Kassel (H) (L)
Kulmbach (B) (C)
Leer (NS) (L)
Lich (H) (L)
Lübeck (SH) (L)
Methler (NW) (L)
Molzen (NS) (L)
Munstereifel (NW) (L)
Neuss (NW) (L)
Remagen (RP) (L and C)
Rottwell (BW) (C)
St. Goar (RP) (L)
Schwäbisch Hall (BW) (L)
Siegburg (NW) (C)
Stockum (NW) (C)
Überlingen (BW) (C)
Uelzen (NS) (L)
Viersen (NW) (C)
Wattenscheid (NW) (L and C)
Wetzlar (H) (L and C)
Xanten (NW) (C)
Zweibrücken (RP) (L)

Family Archives (Familienarchiv)

Many of the princely, noble, or prominent German families have either donated the family papers and records to the state, or opened their documents to the general public. Searches can be made without charge—according to local decision. These family archives may be located in the original family residence (often a schloss or castle) or in archives in the state or nearest city or village. You will have to do some letter-writing about this because the variations are infinite. If your ancestors were employed by these families, or were tenant farmers on the estate, the information can be of very great value to you.

The family archives I have been able to discover are listed below, showing the place, the abbreviation for the province or Länder, and the name of the family. (Note: The abbreviations are the same as those given on page 125.)

Adelebsen (NS), Adelebsen
Ahausen (NW), Spee
Alme (NW), Spee zu Alme
Altenhof (SH), Reventlow
Althausen (BW), Württemberg
Amecke (NW), Wrede-Amecke
Amorbach (B), Leiningen
Anholt (NW), Salm
Antfeld (NW), Papen zu Antfeld
Apelern (NS), Münchhausen
Artelshofen (B), Harlach
Aschhausen (BW), Zeppelin
Assenheim (H), Solms-
    Rödelheim
Assumstadt (BW), Waldburg-
    Wolfegg
Aufsess (B), Aufsess
Augsburg (B), Fugger
Aulendorf (BW), Königsegg-
    Aulendorf
Banteln (NS), Benningsen
Beetzendorf (SAA), Von der
    Schulenberg
Beichlingen (T), Werthern-
    Beichlingen
Bentlage (NW), Wittgenstein-
    Berleburg
Berleburg (NW), Wittgenstein-
    Berleburg
Besselich (RP), Barton-Stedman
Bietigheim (BW), Hornstein
Binningen (BW), Hornstein
Birkenau (H), Unstadt

Birstein (H), Isenburg
Bödigheim (BW), Collenberg
Bodman (BW), Bodman
Boltzenburg (MV), Von Arnim
Haus Borg (NW), Kerkerinck
Braunfels (H), Solms-Braunfels
Breitenburg (SH), Rantzau
Breitenhaupt (NW), Kanne
Haus Brinke (NW), Korff-Bilkau
Buchholz (BW), Ow
Budingen (H), Ysenburg
Buldern (NW), Romberg
Burgsteinfurt (NW), Bentheim
Burkeim (BW), Fahnenberg
Caen (NW), Geyr
Calmsweiler (S), Buseck-Weber
Canstein (NW), Elverfeldt
Cappenberg (NW), Stein
Castell (B), Castell
Celle (NS), Lüneberg
Coesfeld (NW), Salm-Horstmar
Corvey (NW), Ratibor
Crassenstein (NW), Ansembourg
Crollage (NW), Ledebur
Dalwigksthal (H), Dalwigk
Darfeld (NW), Vischering
Derneburg (NS), Münster
Deutsch-Nienhof (SH),
    Hedemann-Heespen
Die Poltsdorf (B), Enderndorf
Diersburg (BW), Roeder
Diersfordt (NW), Wernigerode
Dillingen (B), Fuggers

Donaueschingen (BW), Fürstenberg
Donzdorf (BW), Rechberg
Drensteinfurt (NW), Landsberg-Velen
Dresden (SA), Wolkenstein
Bad Driburg (NW), Oeynhausen
Dulmen (NW), Croy
Durbach (BW), Windschläg
Dyck (NW), Reifferscheidt
Ebnet (BW), Gayling
Egelborg (NW), Oer
Eglofs (BW), Syrgenstein
Eichtersheim (BW), Venning
Elbenberg (H), Buttlar
Ellingen (B), Wrede
Eltville (H), Eltz
Erbach (H), Erbach
Erpernburg (NW), Wartenberg-Brenken
Erzelleben (SAA), Alvensleben
Eschenbach (B), Eschenbach
Essingen (BW), Woellwarth
Eybach (BW), Degenfeld-Schonburg
Fachsenfeld (BW), Fachsenfeld
Fischbach (B), Enderndorf
Frankenberg (B), Pöllnitz
Frankisch-Crumbach (H), Gemmingen
Furth-Burgfarrnbach (B), Pückler
Gärtringen (BW), Gärtringen
Gemünd (NW), Harff-Dreiborn
Gemünden (RP), Salis-Soglio
Gersfeld (H), Ebersberg-Froberg
Gödens (NS), Wedel
Göppingen (BW), Liebenstein
Gotha (T), Hohenlohe
Greifenberg (B), Perfall
Grevenburg (NW), Oeynhausen
Gross-Brunsrode (NS), Bülow
Grünsberg (B), Reichenbach
Guttenberg (B), Guttenberg

Burg-Guttenberg (BW), Gemmingen
Hahnstatten (RP), Bieberstein
Haidenburg (B), Aretin
Haimendorf (B), Rehlingen
Harff (NW), Mirbach
Havixbeck (NW), Twikkel
Heimerzheim (NW), Böselager
Heltorf (NW), Spee
Herbern (NW), Merveldt
Herdringen (NW), Fürstenberg
Heroldsberg (B), Geuder
Herrnstein (NW), Reichenstein
Hinnenburg (NW), Asseburg
Hohenstadt (BW), Adelmann
Höllinghofen (NW), Böselager
Hornberg (BW), Gemmingen
Hugstetten (BW), Mentzingen
Irmelshausen (B), Bibra
Jagsthausen (BW), Berlichingen
Jettingen-Eberstall (B), Stauffenberg
Kalbeck (NW), Vittinghoff
Kellenberg (NW), Hoensbroech
Kendenich (NW), Kempis
Kleinbottwar (BW), Schaubek
Königseggwald (BW), Aulendorf
Korschenbroich (NW), Wüllenweber
Kronburg (B), Westernach
Laibach (BW), Racknitz
Langenstein (BW), Douglas
Laubach (H), Solms-Laubach
Lauterbach (H), Riedesel
Lenthe (NS), Lenthe
Lich (H), Solms-Lich
Lipporg (NW), Galen
Loburg (NW), Elverfeldt
Marck (NW), Grüter
Marxwalde (BR), Hardenberg
Massenbach (BW), Massenbach
Merkstein (NW), Brauchitsch
Merlsheim (NW), Mühlen

Mespelbrunn (B), Ingelheim
Meuselwitz (SA), Seckendorff
Mitwitz (B), Würtzburg
Moyland (NW), Steengracht
Nassau (RP), Stein
Neuenburg (B), Gagern
Neuenstein (BW), Hohenlohe
Neunhof (B), Welser
Neuwied (RP), Wied
Niedenstein (BW), Venning
Niederstotzingen (BW),
　Maldegem
Oberbalzheim (BW), Balzheim
Obernzenn (B), Seckendorff
Oberstadion (BW), Schönborn
Öhringen (BW), Hohenlohe
Ostwig (NW), Lüninck
Ottingen (B), Ottingen
Pöttmes (B), Gumppenberg
Rammersdorf (B), Eyb
Ratzenried (BW), Trauchberg
Regensburg (B), Thurn-Taxis
Rentweinsdorf (B), Rotenhan
Rheda-Wiedenbrück (NW),
　Tecklenburg
Rösberg (NW), Weichs
Rotha (SA), Friesen
Rugland (B), Crailsheim
Ruhr (NW), Mühlen
Rust (BW), Böcklinsau
Schatthausen (BW), Ravensburg
Schillingsfürst (B), Hohenlohe
Schlatt (BW), Reischach
Schlitz (H), Görtz
Schönstein (RP), Wildenburg
Schopfheim (BW), Roggenbach
Schwarmstedt (NS), Lenthe
Schwarzenberg (B),
　Schwarzenberg
Schwarzenraben (NW), Ketteler
Schweinsberg (H), Schweinsberg
Sigmaringen (BW), Hohenzollern
Simmelsdorf (B), Simmelsdorf

Singen (BW), Enzenberg
Somborn (H), Savigny
Stapel (NW), Raitz-Frentz-Droste
Steisslingen (BW), Stotzingen
Stetten (BW), Stetten
Sulzfeld (BW), Ravensburg
Surenberg (NW), Heereman-
　Zuydtwyck
Syburg (B), Geyern
Tambach (B), Ortenburg
Tannhausen (BW), Thannhausen
Tannheim (BW), Schaesberg
Thurnau (B), Giech
Trier (RP), Kesselstatt
Trockau (B), Trockau
Ullstadt (B), Frankenstein
Volkershausen (B), Stein-
　Ostheim
Vörden (NW), Haxthausen
Vornholz (NW), Nagel-Doornick
Waake (NS), Wangenheim
Waal (B), Leyen
Wachendorf (BW), Ow-
　Wachendorf
Wallerstein (B), Oettingen
Warthausen (BW), Warthausen
Weeze (NW), Loë
Weissenburg (B), Geyern
Welbergen (NW), Welbergen
Wernstein (B), Künsberg
Wertheim (BW), Löwenstein-
　Wertheim
Westerholt (NW), Westerholt
Westerwinkel (NW), Merveldt
Wewer (NW), Brenken
Wiesentheid (B), Wiesentheid
Wittgenstein (NW), Wittgenstein-
　Hohenstein
Wolfegg (BW), Waldburg-
　Wolfegg
Worms (RP), Hernsheim
Zeil (BW), Waldburg-Zeil

Libraries (Bibliotheken)

The public libraries in cities and towns should not be neglected as a source of information. They usually contain directories, local histories, and newspapers—all of which may date back to the middle or early part of the nineteenth century. In many places names have been abstracted from newspapers and placed on index cards.

Other Records

The LDS Church has some miscellaneous material on microfilm from Neubrandenburg, Rostock, and Schwerin. The Landeshauptarchiv in Dresden has eighty-four volumes of parish registers from former Sachsen Garnisonsorte (military posts in Saxony).

German Archives in the Czech Republic and Poland

The archives of the following cities (originally German) are in the Czech Republic and Poland. The authorities are helpful in answering queries if you can write either in the language of the country or in German or English, preferably the first. Of course, you will remember to cover the return postage by sending two International Reply Coupons and also a self-addressed airmail envelope. You should also offer to pay whatever fees are required. For more information about archives in the two countries, see the chapters on them.

The Czech Republic

Correspondence should be sent to Státní Oblastní Archiv, followed by the street address and new city name, i.e. the names in parentheses below (the German name is given first and the present Czech name is shown in parentheses):

Dominikánsky Kláster
Leitmeritz (Litoměřice)

Semovní ulice 1
Troppau (Opava)

Poland

Correspondence should be sent to Archiwum Państwowe, followed by the street address and new city name, i.e. the names in parentheses below (the German name is given first and the present Polish name is shown in parentheses):

ul. Zamkowa 3
Allenstein (10074 Olsztyn)

ul. Pomorska 2
Breslau (50215 Wrocław)

ul. Dworcowa 65
Bromberg (85009 Bydgoszcz)

ul. Waly Piastowskie 5
Danzig (80958 Gdańsk)

Stary Kiselin 31
Grünberg (66002 Zielona Góra)

ul. Jagiellonska 25
Kattowitz (40950 Katowice)

ul. Zywcięstwa 117
Köslin (75601 Koszalin)

ul. Zamkowa 2
Oppeln (45016 Opole)

ul. Brama Wybranców 2
Pless (43200 Pszczyna)

ul. 23 Lutego 41/43
Posen (61744 Poznań)

ul. Kilinskiego 12
Schneidenmühl (64920 Piła)

ul. sw. Wojciecha 13
Stettin (70410 Szczecin)

pl. Rapackiego 4
Thorn (87100 Toruń)

German Records in Belgium

Under the terms of the Peace Treaty of Versailles the German areas of
Eupen and Malmedy were transferred to Belgium. Church and civil records
relating to that area are in the Belgian Provincial Archives et Liège (Archives de l'État, rue Pouplin 8, 4000 Liège).

Genealogical Associations

There are a number of genealogical associations in Germany. They are all
loosely associated with a national genealogical association: Deutsche
Arbeitsgemeinschaft Genealogischer Verbände or D.A.G.V., Schlosstrasse
12, 50321 Brühl. I list the various associations below. It is important that
you make contact with the one operating in your area of Germany because
(a) they will probably know if someone else has already researched your
family; (b) many of them have their own libraries and archives, which may

contain items of vital interest to you; (c) many of them publish magazines at regular intervals and will publish small ads or queries, either free or for a small charge. Some of them only accept queries for their own members, so you might consider joining.

The D.A.G.V. issues good advice in English to people sending inquiries to them, or to the individual associations. It is worthwhile giving you a précis of the advice.

1. There is no connection between the church records of the two major denominations. If you want a search made in a church archive or register, you must know the actual religion.

2. There can be no answer to questions about an ancestor unless you know a place of origin, birth, or marriage. Inquiries based on "Germany," or "Pruessen," or "near Stuttgart" cannot be answered.

3. Do all the research you possibly can in your own country through family papers, wills, obituary notices, and family Bibles.

4. If you are asking questions about several people who came from different locations, write each query on a separate sheet of paper.

5. If you have already done some research, give all the details.

6. Good English is better than bad German. Use a typewriter, or print all names of persons and places.

7. Send *four* International Reply Coupons to cover postage and expenses. Donations are appreciated.

The list of associations I mentioned is given below. It is as complete as I can make it, but bear in mind addresses can change, and there can always be additions or deletions. If you do not find one that covers your area of interest, write to the D.A.G.V. for further information:

BADEN-WÜRTTEMBERG
Verein für Familien- und Wappenkunde
Konrad-Adenauer Strasse 8, 70173 Stuttgart

(Has a good family card index)

BAYERN
Bayerischer Landsverein für Familienkunde
Winzererstrasse 68, 80797 Munich

Gesellschaft für Familienforschung in Franken
Archivstrasse 17, 90408 Nürnberg

(Only concerned with the Franken [Franconia] area)

Schwabische Forschungsmeinschaft
Universität Augsburg
Universitätstrasse 10, 86159 Augsburg

BREMEN

Gesellschaft für Familienkunde

Präsident Kennedy Platz 2, 28203 Bremen

(Covers the area of Bremen and district)

HAMBURG

Genealogische Gesellschaft

Postfach 302042, 20307 Hamburg

(Concerned with Hamburg, Niedersachsen, Mecklenburg, Schleswig-Holstein)

HESSEN

Hessische Familiengeschichtliche Vereinigung

Staatsarchiv, 64283 Darmstadt

(Primary concern is the former Duchy of Hessen-Darmstadt—very helpful to overseas inquirers if International Reply Coupons are enclosed)

Familienkundliche Gesellschaft für Nassau und Frankfurt

Niederwaldstrasse 5, 65187 Wiesbaden

(Area of Nassau and Frankfurt only)

Gesellschaft für Familienkunde in Kurhessen und Walde

Postfach 410328, 34131 Kassel-Wilhelmshöhe

(Interested in the two districts only)

Vereinigung für Familien- und Wappenkunde Fulda

Taunusstrasse 4, 36043 Fulda-Edelzell

(Concerned with the Fulda area)

NIEDERSACHSEN

Familienkundliche Kommission für Niedersachsen und Bremen sowie
  angrenzende ostfälische Gebiete

Appelstrasse 9, 30167 Hannover

(Concerned with Niedersachsen, Bremen, and east Westfalen)

Familienkundlicher Verein Hildesheim

Wallmodenweg 2, 31141 Hildesheim

(Only concerned with the Hildesheim area)

Landsverein für Familienkunde

Köbelinger Strasse 159, 30159 Hannover

Genealogisch-Heraldische Gesellschaft

Theaterplatz 5, Stadtarchiv, 37073 Göttingen

(Only interested in this one area)

Oldenburgische Gesellschaft für Familienkunde
Lerigauweg 14, 26131 Oldenburg

(Concerned with the area of the old Duchy of Oldenburg)

Ostfriesische Landschaft-Aurich
Postfach 1580, 26603 Aurich

(Only interested in the Ost Friesland area and the city of Aurich)

NORDRHEIN-WESTFALEN
Westfälische Gesellschaft für Genealogie und Familienforschung
Warendorfer Strasse 25, 48145 Münster

(Concerned with the old province of Westfalen)

Lippischer Heimatsbund
Bismarckstrasse 8, 32756 Detmold

(The main area of interest is in the old State of Lippe)

Düsseldorfer Verein für Familienkunde
Erich Klausener Strasse 42, 40474 Düsseldorf

RHEINLAND-PFALZ
Arbeitsgemeinschaft für Pfälzisch-Rheinische Familienkunde
Rottstrasse 17, 67061 Ludwigshafen am Rhein

Pfalzische Geschichte und Folkskunde Bensinoring
Postfach 2860, 67657 Kaiserslautern

SAARLAND
Arbeitsgemeinschaft für Saarländische Familienkunde
Kohlweg 54, 66123 Saarbrücken

(Covers the Saarland area)

SCHLESWIG-HOLSTEIN
Schleswig-Holsteinische Gesellschaft für Familienforschung
    und Wappenkunde
Gartenstrasse 12, 24103 Kiel

(Only concerned with the Free City of Lübeck)

BERLIN
Verein zur Forderung der Zentralstelle für Personen- und Familien-geschichte
Archivstrasse 12-14, 14195 Berlin-Dahlem

There are also several organizations concerned with more general areas, or with more specific subjects:

OST UND WEST PREUSSEN
Familienforschung in Ost und West Preussen
Eichstrasse 6, 25336 Elmshorn

OST DEUTSCHLAND (EASTERN GERMANY)
Arbeitsgemeinschaft für Ostdeutsche Familienforscher
Ernst-Moritz-Arndt Strasse 25, 53225 Bonn

Berlin and Brandenburg:
Interessengemeinschaft Genealogie Berlin
z.H. Frau Gabriele v. Griesheim
Heinrich-Heine-Strasse 11, 10179 Berlin

Mecklenburg-Vorpommern:
Arbeitsgemeinschaft Genealogie (Rostock)
W.-Schlaak-Strasse 8, 17489 Greifswald

Arbeitsgemeinschaft Genealogie und Heraldik
Zum Netzboden 14, 23966 Wismar

Sachsen:
Arbeitsgemeinschaft Genealogie Annaberg-Buchholz
Hauptstrasse 118, 09477 Arnsfeld

Arbeitsgemeinschaft Genealogie Chemnitz
Usti nad Labem 23, 09119 Chemnitz

Arbeitskreis vogtländischer Familienforscher
Forststrasse 37, 01099 Dresden

Arbeitskreis vogtländischer Familienforscher
Genealogische Gruppe Plauen
Auguststrasse 18, 08523 Plauen

Arbeitskreis vogtländischer Familienforscher
Genealogische Gruppe Reichenbach
Zwickauer Strasse 95, 08468 Reichenbach

Arbeitskreis vogtländischer Familienforscher
Genealogische Gruppe Treuen-Auerbach
Poststrasse 4, 08233 Treuen

Interessengemeinschaft Genealogie Dresden
Krenkelstrasse 9, 01309 Dresden

Leipziger Genealogische Gesellschaft e.V.
Bahnhofstrasse 95, PF 3708, 04448 Wideritzsch

Sachsen-Anhalt:
Arbeitsgruppe Genealogie
Kultur- und Heimatverein Magdeburg e.V.
Schillerstrasse 48, 39108 Magdeburg

Thüringen:
Arbeitsgemeinschaft Genealogie Thüringen
Otto-Schwarzstrasse 58, 07745 Jena-Winzerla

(Branches in Erfurt, Gera, and Weimar)

There is also an organization in the western area of Germany that is mainly interested in eastern Germany. It is: Arbeitsgemeinschaft für Mitteldeutsche Familienkunde Eythstrasse 5, 91058 Erlangen.

MITTEL DEUTSCHLAND (CENTRAL GERMANY)
Arbeitsgemeinschaft für Mitteldeutsche Familienforschung
Emilienstrasse 1, 34121 Kassel, Hessen

WEST DEUTSCHLAND (WEST GERMANY)
Westdeutsche Gesellschaft für Familienkunde
Rotdornstrasse 6, 50996 Köln

BERLIN
Herold Verein für Heraldik
Archivstrasse 12-14, 14195 Berlin

(This organization is concerned with heraldry and noble families)

HUGENOTTEN (HUGUENOTS)
Deutschen Hugenott Vereins
Hafenplatz 9a, 34385 Bad Karlshafen

(This association researches families of Huguenot descent)

There is another method of ancestor-hunting in Germany—a paid ad in the genealogical magazine *Familienkundliche Nachrichten* (known as FANA). This is published every two months by Verlag Degener and Co., Postfach 1340, 91413 Neustadt (Aisch). The cost (at the time of this writing) is about $15.

GERMAN SETTLERS IN RUSSIA

Perhaps, even though you are of pure German ancestry, your family is descended from the Germans who emigrated to Russia between the mid-1700s and the mid-1800s. In that case you may have assumed there is no chance of tracing your forebears back to their place of origin in the area that is now Germany. In fact there is a very good chance that records exist which will give you some vital information.

In 1763 the Empress Catherine II of Russia invited all foreigners who possessed skills of some kind to come to her country as settlers and colonists. In cases of financial hardship the cost of transportation was paid. In addition, all settlers received a loan of money toward the costs of building a house and buying livestock and farm or trade equipment, with repayment required in ten years.

The proclamation of the Empress was distributed throughout Europe but did not meet with any great response except in the Germanic area. Most of the colonists came from Hessen and the Rhineland, but many other German-speaking areas were represented to a lesser extent.

Purely as an aside, and with nothing to do with your ancestry, I want to share with you the extraordinary number of titles held by the Empress and included in her proclamation of 1763: "Empress and Autocrat of all the Russians at Moscow, Kiev, Vladimir, Novgorod, Czarina of Kasan, Czarina of Astrachan, Czarina of Siberia, Lady of Plaskow, Grand Duchess of Smolensko, Duchess of Estonia and Livland, Carelia, Twer, Yogoria, Permia, Viatka, and Bulgaria, and others; Lady and Grand Duchess of Novgorod in the Netherland of Chernigov, Resan, Rostov, Yaroslav, Belooseria, Udoria, Obdoria, Condonia, and Ruler of the entire North Region and Lady of the Yurish, of the Cartalinian and Grusinian czars, and the Cabardinian land, of the Cherkessian and Gorisian princes, and the lady of the manor and sovereign of many others."

The areas opened up for settlement by the Empress were underpopulated, and open to frequent attack by the Ottoman Turks. The Germans, for their part, were eager to settle for many different reasons, among them religious persecution, starvation, high taxes, civil disorders and foreign wars, compulsory military service, and a high population density.

Between 1804 and 1842 over 72,000 people emigrated, and total estimates for the entire period range as high as 150,000 from the German area alone. It was one of the great mass movements of history. For a century Germans poured into Russia and established themselves in fairly close areas of settlement in the Volga region, the Black Sea area, and the Caucasus.

The whole story is documented in a remarkable book by Dr. Karl Stumpp entitled *The Emigration from Germany to Russia, 1763-1862* and published in 1978 by the American Historical Society of Germans from Russia, 631 D Street, Lincoln, NE 68502. It lists the names of some 50,000 German settlers, with their places of origin and settlement.

It may be helpful to quote the areas of origin and settlement over the century:

Period of Emigration	Place of Origin	Area of Settlement
1763-68	Hessen, Rheinland, Pfalz, Sachsen, Württemberg, Switzerland	Volga (Evan.[1] and Luth.[2])
1765	Sulzfeld, Württemberg	Reibensdorf (Evan.)
1766	Hessen, Württemberg, Brandenburg	Petersburg, Black Sea
1766	Hessen	Belowesh (Evan. and Cath.[3])
1780	Preussen, Württemberg, Bayern	Josefstal, Fischerdorf, Jamburg, in Dnieper area
1782	Sweden	Schwedendorf (Evan.)
1786	Preussen	Alt-Danzig
1789-90	Danzig, West Preussen	Chortitza (Menn.[4])
1804-6	Alsace, Pfalz, Baden	Franzfeld, Mariental, Josefstal, by Odessa (Cath.)
1804-6	Württemberg, Alsace, Pfalz, Baden, Hungary	Grossliebental, Neuburg, Alexanderhilf
1804-6	Danzig, West Preussen	Halbstadt, Molotschna (Menn.)
1804-6	Württemberg, Baden, Hessen	Prischib, Molotschna (Evan. and Cath.)
1804-6	Württemberg, Switzerland	Neusatz, Zürichtal, in the Crimea (Evan. and Cath.)
1808-10	Württemberg, Alsace, Pfalz	Bergdorf, Glückstal, Kassel, Neudorf, area of Odessa (Evan.)
1808-10	Alsace, Baden, Poland	Baden, Elsass, Kandel, Selz, Mannheim, Strassburg (Cath.)
1808-10	Alsace, Baden, Pfalz, Württemberg	Beresan and Odessa (Cath.)

Period of Emigration	Place of Origin	Area of Settlement
1812-27	Württemberg, Baden, Hessen	Prischib, Molotschna (Evan.)
1814-16	Württemberg, Preussen, Bayern, and Poland	Bessarabia, and near Odessa
1817-18	Württemberg	South Caucasus (Evan.)
1821-34	Württemberg, Preussen, Bayern, and Poland	Bessarabia, and near Odessa
1822-31	Württemberg	Swabian colonies near Berdjansk (Evan.)
1823-42	Danzig, West Preussen, Baden, Hessen, Rheinland	Grunau area (Evan. and Cath.)
1853 and 1859-62	Danzig, West Preussen	Samara (Menn.)

This was the last emigration from Germany.

[1]Evangelical, [2]Lutheran, [3]Catholic, [4]Mennonite.

GREECE

After the Roman Empire was divided into eastern and western sections in 395, the history of Greece was tied to that of the eastern section, the Byzantine Empire. There were invasions by Visigoths, Huns, Slavs, and Bulgars, and finally in the fifteenth century by the Turks. A few parts remained unconquered. Genoa ruled Chios until 1566, and Venice controlled Crete until 1669. In addition, a continuing series of wars between Venice and the Turks meant that several islands and even Athens itself were occupied by the Venetians on various occasions. Greece itself became a poor and neglected province of the Ottoman Empire, although many Greeks made their peace with the conquerors and held high administrative positions in the empire.

The long period of darkness ended in the early nineteenth century with a sudden resurgence of Greek nationalism. In 1821 a struggle for independence started and soon involved Great Britain, France, and Russia. Turkey gave Greece local autonomy in 1829, and in 1832 the country declared its complete independence. Crete remained under Turkish control until 1898, then it became independent, but it finally joined Greece in 1913.

Greece became involved in the Balkan Wars in 1912–13, and then in the First World War in 1917. As a result of these wars and the later peace conferences, Greece added to her territory with the inclusion of parts of Macedonia, the whole of Thrace, and the islands of the Dodecanese. In 1921 she invaded Turkey but was defeated in the following year.

In 1923 there was a massive interchange of populations, organized by the League of Nations. One and a half million Greeks left Asia Minor (where there had been Greek settlements for centuries) for Greece, and 800,000 Turks and 80,000 Bulgarians from areas transferred to Greece went back to their homelands. The wounds left by this great exodus of people have never healed.

In 1940 Italy, and later Germany and Bulgaria, invaded Greece and occupied it until the end of the Second World War. There was constant guerrilla warfare, and many churches and local government offices and their records were destroyed.

Archives

The main archives are the General State Archives (Genika Archeia Toù Kratous, Eleftheriou Venizelou 28, Athens). Records there are available for research after a period of fifty years; however, the genealogical information in the archives is confined to records brought from Asia Minor after the evacuation of 1922. This collection, which was brought to Athens by Greek officials and refugees, contains church registers, family papers, wills, and many other documents covering the period from 1800 to 1922.

There are also genealogical records of various kinds in the Historical Archives of Crete (Historika Archeia Kritis, Odos I. Sfakianaki 20, Khanea, Kriti). Other small archives are in some of the Ionian Islands—Corfù, Cefalonia, Paxi, Levkas, Zakynthos, Ithaki, and Kythera.

Church Registers

There are no central records of church registers or even information about their whereabouts. Basically, the records are in the individual churches (if they have not been destroyed), but they are fairly recent, since the keeping of records was a very chancy affair before 1800. His Grace Maximos Xydas, the Archimandrite of the Greek Orthodox Church, told me with regret that it is impossible to provide ancestor-hunters of Greek descent with addresses of churches, indexes to records, or even any information as to whether parish records exist or not.

The country is divided into "Metropolis" areas (each under a metropolitan, or bishop) and these include very many individual parishes. If you know the village from which your Greek ancestors came you should write directly to the priest there. Do try to get your letter translated into Greek, because it is most unlikely that a village priest will read any English, or that anyone else in the village will read it. If you receive no reply, you should write to the headquarters of the Orthodox Church, Aghias Filotheis 21, Athens, and ask for the address of the metropolitan whose territory includes your particular village. Then write to him for information.

Civil Registration

This started on a local basis in 1831. The records are kept in the municipal offices, but many have been destroyed. In 1925 it was organized on a national basis; registration bureaus were set up in Athens, Piraeus, and Thessaloniki. In other cities, and in villages, the mayor or an official appointed by him acts as registrar. Marriage certificates are also issued by the local priest. If you know the exact place of origin, you can write to the mayor for information about the specific vital event. My advice above about writing in Greek will apply here, too. If you have difficulties you should write to the Civil Registration Division, Ministry of the Interior, Panepistimiou Street 57, Athens.

Censuses

These started in 1907 and have been held at intervals of about ten years since then. However, most of the earlier ones have been destroyed. Access to recent ones is restricted, but special permission can be given by the Director, National Statistical Service, Lycourgou Street, Athens, providing that you can prove descent or relationship, and explain that the information is needed for genealogical research into your own family.

Wills

These date back to 1843 and are located in the Court of the First Instance, Panepistimiou Street 47, Athens.

Genealogical Research

It is not wise to be optimistic about your genealogical research in Greece. It all depends on whether your ancestral village was destroyed or damaged; on your ability to get your letters written in Greek; on the ability of the local priest to reply; and on your own persistence. You are more likely to succeed if your ancestor came from one of the three big cities, but all the odds are that he or she came from a small village. If your area is the Aegean Sea and its islands, you may be luckier than if it were on the mainland because there was less destruction of records.

HUNGARY

The Magyars, or Hungarian people, originated in an area of present-day Russia, between the Volga River and the Ural Mountains. There are slight similarities between Hungarian, Finnish, and the dialect in use in the Baskir autonomous area. It is thought that in about 2000 B.C. the Hungarians moved east into the Urals, and the Finns and the Estonians moved west toward the Baltic Sea. By the year 600 the Hungarians, under pressure from Asiatic nomadic peoples, also moved west, and by 896 they had occupied most of present-day Hungary. The Hungarian language is among the purest in Europe in that it resembles most closely its original form of 3000 years ago (apart from a few Bulgarian and German words picked up during the great migration of the seventh century).

The Hungarian alphabet has 38 letters, consisting of 22 of our 26 (Q, W, X, and Y are missing) and 16 additional letters:

á   cs   é   gy   í   ly   ny   ó   ö   ő   sz   ty   ú   ü   ű   zs

By 1000 Hungary had become a unified kingdom, but by 1541 it had collapsed, owing to invasion by the Ottoman Turks from the east and the southeast. The western section of the country fell under Hapsburg control for the next four centuries; the central plains were occupied by the Turks; and the eastern part, or Transylvania, was ruled by Hungarian princes who accepted the suzerainty of the Ottoman Empire and paid an annual tribute. In 1686 Budapest was captured by the Hapsburgs, and in the following year the Turks withdrew from Transylvania. There was an unsuccessful revolt by the Hungarians, which ended in 1711, and another attempt at independence was not made until 1849. This was partially successful in that it led to reforms in the administration of the country.

In 1867, after Austria had been defeated in war by Prussia, it became more amenable, and the Austro-Hungarian Empire was created, with Hungary as an equal partner. At this time Hungary included Transylvania, Croatia-Slavonia, Ruthenia, Slovakia, the Burgenland, and the Banat. If your ancestors came from these areas it is vital for you to understand that the genealogical records you need may still be in Hungary, or they may be in one or more of the so-called "Successor States."

In 1919, after the First World War, Hungary paid the price of being on the losing side (not that it had any choice in the matter), and when the Austro-Hungarian Empire disintegrated Hungary lost two-thirds of its territory under the harsh terms of the peace treaty. The Burgenland was transferred to Austria; Slovakia formed part of the new country of Czechoslovakia; Yugoslavia took Croatia, Slavonia, and part of the Banat; and Romania took the rest of the Banat and the whole of the province, and ancient principality, of Transylvania.

There are twenty counties (Megye), apart from the capital (Budapest), and they each have their own archives. These come under the control of the National Archives (Magyar Országos Levéltár, Bécskapu tér 4, 1014 Budapest). However, you are quite welcome to correspond directly with the archive for the place in which you are interested.

The Consular Section of your nearest Hungarian Embassy will provide school reports and certificates of births, marriages, deaths, and divorces for a fee. The address of the U.S. embassy is 3910 Shoemaker Street, N.W., Washington, DC 20008; the Canadian embassy is located at 7 Delaware Avenue, Ottawa, ON K2P OZ2. Be prepared to wait six months!

Archives (Levéltárak)

I list the counties and their archives below, together with their addresses. I also list, for your guidance, the main towns within each archival area. In addition, you will also see a list of the original Hungarian counties, since there have been considerable changes in county names and areas since 1919.

A county is a *megye*, a district a *járás*, a county town a *megyei város*, a town a *város*, and a town district a *kerület*. The archives listed below, then, are Megyei Levéltár:

BÁCS-KISKUN   Kossuth tér 1
6001 Kecskemét
(Covering Baja, Kalocsa, Kecskemét
Kiskörös,Kiskunfélegyháza, Kiskunhalas)

BARANYA   Kossuth u. 11
7621 Pécs
(Covering Komlo, Mohács, Szigetvár)

BÉKÉS   Petőfi tér 3
5701 Gyula
(Covering Békés, Békéscsaba, Gyula,
Orosháza, Szarvas)

BORSOD-ABAÚJ-ZEMPLÉN	Tanácsház tér 1 3525 Miskolc (Covering Kazincbarcika, Leninváros, Mezőkővesd, Ozd, Sárospatak, Sátoraljaújhely)
CSONGRÁD	Honvéd tér 5-6 6701 Szeged (Covering Csongrád, Hódmezóvásárhely, Makó, Szentes)
FEJÉR	István tér 9 8001 Székesfehérvár (Covering Dunaújváros, Székesfehérvár)
GYŐR-MOSON-SOPRON	Liszt Ferenc u. 12 9022 Győr (Covering Csorna, Győr, Mosonmagyaróvár, Kapuvár, Sopron)
HAJDÚ-BIHAR	Vöröshadsereg ut 20 4024 Debrecen (Covering Debrecen, Hajdúböszörmény, Hajdúnánás, Hajdúszoboszló)
HEVES	Kossuth Lajos ut 9 3301 Eger (Covering Eger, Győngyös, Hatvan)
KOMÁROM-ESZTERGOM	Vorosmarty u. 7 2500 Esztergom (Covering Esztergom, Komárom, Oroszlány, Tata, Tatabánya)
NÓGRÁD	Bajcsy-Zsilinszky ut 1 3100 Salgótarján (Covering Balassagyarmat, Salgótarján)
PEST	Városház ut 5-7 1052 Budapest (Covering Buda, Cegléd, Gödöllő, Nagykőrös, Százhalombatta, Szentendre, Vác)
SOMOGY	Rippl Ronai tér 1 7400 Kaposvár (Covering Kaposvár, Nagyatád, Siófok)

SZABOLCS-SZATMÁR	Benczur tér 1
	4400 Nyiregyháza
	(Covering Kisvárda, Mátészalka, Nyirbátor, Nyiregyháza)
SZOLNOK	Kossuth Lajos ut 1
	5000 Szolnok
	(Covering Jászberény, Karcag, Kisújszállás, Mazőtúr, Szolnok, Törökszentmiklós, Túrkeve)
TOLNA	Béla tér 1
	7100 Szekszárd
	(Covering Dombóvár, Szekszárd)
VAS	Hefele Menyhért ut 1
	9700 Szombathely
	(Covering Kőszeg, Sárvár, Szombathely)
VESZPRÉM	Pf 152
	8200 Veszprém
	(Covering Ajka, Balatonfűred, Keszthely, Pápa, Tapolca, Várpalota, Veszprém)
ZALA	Széchnyi tér 3
	8900 Zalaegerszeg
	(Covering Nagykanizsa, Zalaegerszeg)

In addition, there is a Capital City Archive (Főváros Levéltár) in Budapest: Városház u. 9-11, 1350 Budapest.

The original counties of Hungary (before the Treaty of Trianon in 1919) are as shown below. However, it must be realized that many of these old counties are now in Austria, Croatia, Czech Republic, Romania, Slovakia, Ukraine, and Yugoslavia under quite different names. Some counties were transferred in their entirety, others were split between two or more countries, and others were merged with the remnants of old counties to form some of the new ones already listed earlier in this chapter:

Abaúj-Torna, Alsó-Fehér, Arad, Árva, Bács-Bodrog, Baranya, Bars, Békés, Bereg, Besztercze-Naszód, Bihar, Borsod, Brassó, Csanád, Csik, Csongrád, Esztergom, Fejér, Fogaras, Gömör, Győr, Hajdú, Háromszék, Heves, Hont, Hunyad, Jász-Nagy-Kun-Szolnok, Kis-Küküllö, Kolozs, Komárom, Krassó-Szörény, Liptó, Máramaros, Maros-Torda, Moson, Nagy-Küküllö, Nógrád, Nyitra, Pest- Pilis-Solt-Kiskun, Pozsony, Sáros, Somogy, Sopron, Szabolcs, Szatmár, Szeben, Szepes, Szilágy, Szolnok-Doboka, Temes, Tolna, Torda-Aranyos, Torontál, Trencsén, Turócz, Udvarhely, Ugocsa, Ung, Vas, Veszprém, Zala, Zemplén, and Zólyom.

Before we start talking about the various sources of information in Hungary, and there are plenty, let me deal with some of the problems first:

1. Just because your grandfather's immigration or naturalization papers state he came from "Hungary," do not assume that this means within the boundaries of present-day Hungary. The records you need may well be in Austria, Croatia, Czech Republic, Romania, Slovakia, Ukraine, or Yugoslavia, because the place in which he was born may have become part of one of these countries.

2. If your ancestor's nationality appears as "Austrian," this may simply mean he was born within the boundaries of the Austro-Hungarian Empire, and he might have been born in Hungary, or in any one of a dozen other countries.

3. Allow for the fact that he may have changed or simplified his original name, or even that an immigration officer may have anglicized his name out of kindness (or malice).

4. If the present generation of your family no longer speaks Hungarian, try to find someone to translate your letters of inquiry, and the subsequent reply. You will find practically no Hungarians in the smaller towns or villages who speak English.

5. Be patient. Your letters will not be answered quickly. Remember you are not the only ancestor-hunter of Hungarian descent who is writing to the archives or the village priest or pastor!

6. Finally, don't be too demanding; be polite and friendly. No one is required to answer your letter.

Civil Registration (Állami Nyilvántartó)

This started in 1895; before that date the only records of vital events were the entries of baptism, marriage, and burial in the church registers. The original entries of registration since 1895 are kept in registration offices (Állami Nyilvántartási Hivatal) in each municipality, with copies in the county archives (Megyei Levéltár). Access is normally restricted to recent records, but special application can be made, giving the reason the information is required and proving descent from the person named in the entry. The churches still maintain their own registers as they did before 1895, but only civil registration is compulsory and of legal value.

If you have problems obtaining civil registration certificates, you should complain directly to the main administrative office of the National Archives (Magyar Országos Levéltárak Központja, Uri Utca 54, 1250 Budapest).

Church Registers (Köszégi Anyakőnyv)

Hungary is mainly Catholic, but other religions include the Reformed Church, Lutheran, Greek Orthodox, Greek Catholic, and Jewish. All the church registers up to 1895 are in the original churches, but microfilm copies are in the county archives (Megyei Levéltár). Registers since 1895 (the first year of civil registration) are also in the churches, of course, but are not on microfilm in the various archives. The registers for the churches located in those parts of Hungary "lost" after the First World War are no longer within the boundaries of Hungary, although some of them have been microfilmed and copies are in the county archives. Fuller details about these are given later in this chapter.

Although the keeping of church registers was ordained at the Council of Trent in the middle 1500s, the early Hungarian church registers were nearly all destroyed by the invading Ottoman Turks and not many exist before 1700. To take random examples, you will find earlier ones for Hédervár (1673), Ágfalva (1661), Győr (Győrsziget) (1642), Magyarfalva (1636).

The early registers were in Latin, but by the middle nineteenth century the entries were in Hungarian.

Baptisms (Keresztelő)

These registers for all the denominations (except Jewish) include the full names of the children, address and occupation of parents, and names of godparents or witnesses.

Marriages (Házasság)

These include names, addresses, places of birth, occupations, names and addresses of parents, and names of witnesses.

Burials (Temetés)

These show the name and age of the deceased, place of birth and death, cause of death, and quite often, occupation and names of survivors and/or next of kin.

The Hungarian names of the major denominations are:

> Catholic (Katholikus)
> Reformed (Református)
> Greek Orthodox (Görög Keleti)
> Greek Catholic (Görög Katholikus)
> Lutheran (Evangelikus)
> Jewish (Izraelita)

The number of church registers of all denominations held on microfilm in the National Archives or elsewhere is too great to list by name—there are over 3500 of them. The actual figures are: Catholic, 1679; Reformed, 1033; Greek Orthodox, 84; Greek Catholic, 101; Lutheran, 297; and Jewish, 314. The National Archives of Hungary (Magyar Országos Levéltár) has published a complete list of these microfilmed registers (Egyházi Anyakönyvek Mikrofilm-Másolatai), which you can purchase.

It is possible, however, to list the microfilmed registers available for those areas ceded to Austria, Czechoslovakia, Romania, and Yugoslavia, and they are given below with their present location:

Austria

Microfilms of the Burgenland parishes originally part of Hungary (until 1919) are located in two of the county archives (Megyei Levéltár):

Vas Megyei Levéltár

Catholic. Alsóbeled, Alsóőr, Arokszállas, Badafalva, Baksafalva, Bándol, Barátfalva, Borostyánkő, Burgóhegy, Csém, Egyházasfüzes, Felsókethely, Felsőőr, Felsőszénégető, Gyanafalva, Incéd, Karácsfa, Kicléd, Királyfalva, Kukmér, Kupfalva, Léka, Lödös, Magashegy, Máriafalva, Nagyfalva, Nagysároslak, Nagyszentmihály, Németcsencs, Németlövő, Németszentgrót, Németújvár, Óbér, Óriszentmárton, Pásztorháza, Pinkafő, Pinkakertes, Pinkamiske, Pörgölény, Posaszentkatalin, Pusztaszentmihály, Rábakeresztúr, Rábaszentmárton, Rohonc, Rótfalva, Sámfalva, Strém, Szentelek, Szentkút, Újhegy, Városszalónak, Várszentmiklós, Vasdobra, Vasfarkasfalva, Vasjobbágyi, Vaskomját, Vasvörösvár, and Vörthegy.

Reformed. Felsőőr.

Lutheran. Alhó, Alsólövő, Borostyánkő, Felsőlövő, Felsőőr, Kukmér, Nagyszentmihály, Némethidegkút, Őrisziget, Pinkafő, Rohonc, Ujkörtvélyes, Vágod, Városszalónak, Vasdobra.

Győr-Sopron Megye 2 sz Levéltár

Catholic. Alsópulya, Alsórámóc, Barátudvar, Boldogasszony, Borbolya, Borsmonostor, Büdöskút, Cinfalva, Császárfalu, Császárkőbánya, Csáva, Darázsfalu, Darufalva, Feketeváros, Felsőkismartonhegy, Felsőlászló, Felsőrámóc, Féltorony, Fertőfehéregyháza, Fertőmeggyes, Fertőszéleskút, Frakno, Fraknónádasd, Füles, Gálos, Gyirót, Harácsony, Illmic, Kabold, Kelénpatak, Királyhida, Kisboldogasszony, Kishöflány, Kismarton, Kisostoros, Köpcsény, Középpula, Lajtafalu, Lajtakáta, Lajtakörtvélyes, Lajtapordány, Lajtaszék, Lajtaszentgyörgy, Lajtaszentmiklós, Lajtaújfalu, Lánzsér, Ligvánd, Locsmánd, Lók, Loretto, Malomháza, Márcfalva, Miklóshalma, Mosonbánfalva, Mosonszentandrás, Mosontarcsa, Mosontétény, Mosonújfalu, Nagyhöflány, Nagymarton, Nemesvölgy, Némethidegkút, Németjárfalu, Nezsider, Nyulas, Oka, Oszlop, Pandorfalu, Pátfalu, Pecsenyéd, Pomogy, Récény, Répcebónya, Répcekethely, Répcekőhalom, Répcesarud, Rétfalu, Ruszt, Sásony, Selegszántó, Sérc, Siklósd, Somfalva, Sopronkeresztúr, Sopronkertes, Sopronnyék, Sopronszentmárton, Szabadbáránd, Szárazvám, Szarvkő, Szentmargitbánya, Szikra, Tormafalu, Valla, Vámosderecske, Védeny, Veperd, Vimpac, Völgyfalu, Vulkapordány, Zárány, and Zurány.

Czechoslovakia

Microfilms of the parish registers in areas ceded to this country by Hungary in 1919 are in the following archives, which are now located in Slovakia, with copies also in the Hungarian National Archives:

Slovenska Archívní Správa, Bratislava (Pozsonyi Állami Levéltár)

Catholic. Bazin, Modor, Nagyszombat, Pozsony (Szent Márton), Pozsony (Blumenthal), Szentgyörgy.

Lutheran. Bazin, Modor, Nagyszombat, Pozsony (Német), Pozsony (Szlovák-Magyar), Selmecbánya.

Slovenska Archívní Správa, Bánská-Bystrica (Besztercebányai Állami Levéltár)

Catholic. Besztercebánya, Selmecbánya.

Lutheran. Besztercebánya.

Slovenska Archívní Správa, Košice (Kassai Állami Levéltár)

Catholic. Abaújnádasd, Jánok, Kassa, Királyhelmec, Nagykázmér, Nagykövesd, Nagytárkány.

Romania

Microfilms exist for a very few of the churches in the Kolozsvár area of Romania (ceded in 1919). There are copies in the Hungarian National Archives, but otherwise they are in the Romanian State Archives at Cluj (originally Kolozsvár):

Catholic. Kolozsvár (Főtér), Kolozsvár (Monostor).

Greek Catholic. Kolozsvár.

Reformed. Beszterce, Kolozsvár.

Lutheran. Kolozsvár.

Greek Orthodox. Kolozsvár.

Unitarian. Kolozsvár.

Yugoslavia

Microfilms of the registers of the parishes ceded to this country by Hungary in 1919 are located in the following Hungarian Archives, with additional copies in the National Archives in Budapest:

Vas Megyei Levéltár, Szombathely

Catholic. Alsószentbenedek, Csendlak, Felsőlendva, Mártonhely, Muraszombat, Nagydolány, Perestó, Péterhegy, Szentsebestyén, Vashidegkút, Vizlendva.

Zala Megyei Levéltár, Zalaegerszeg

Catholic. Alsólendva, Bagonya, Belatinc, Cserföld, Lendvavásárhely.

Kalocsai Érseki Levéltár (Archdiocese of Kalocsa), Kalocsa

Catholic. Ada, Adorján, Apatin, Bács, Bácsföldvar, Bácsgyulafalva, Bácskertes, Bácskossuthfalva, Bácsordas, BácsSzentiván, Bácstóváros, Bácsújfalu, Bácsújlak, Bajmok, Bajsa, Béreg, Bezdán, Borócz, Csantavér, Csonoplya, Csurop, Dernye, Doroszló, Dunabökény, Dunacséb, Gádor, Gombos, Hódság, Horgos, Kerény, Kishegyes, Körtés, Kucora, Kula, Kullöd, Ludas, Magyarkanizsa, Martonos, Militics, Mohol, Monostorszeg, Nemesmilitics, Óbecse, Okér,Ószivac, Őrszallás, Pacsér, Palánka, Palona, Paripás, Péterréve, Regőce, Sándor, Szabadka, Szabadka (Szent György), Szabadka (Szent Rókus), Szentfülöp, Szenttamás, Szépliget, Szilberek, Szond, Temerin, Tiszakálmánfalva, Titel, Topolya, Újfutak, Újverbász, Újvidék, Vajszka, Veprőd, Zenta, Zenta (Felsőnegy), Zombor, Zzablya.

Catholic Church Archives (Katholikus Levéltár)

Archdioceses (Főegyházmegye)

EGER	Szechenyi ut 1 3301 Eger
ESZTERGOM	Berényi Zsigmond ut 2 2500 Esztergom
KALOCSA	Szabadság tér 1 6300 Kalocsa

Dioceses (Egyházmegye)

CSANAD	Aradi Vértanúk tér 2 6701 Szeged
GYŐR	Káptalan-domb 1 9002 Győr
PÉCS	István tér 23 7624 Pécs
SZÉKESFEHÉRVÁR	Szabadság tér 10 8000 Székesfehérvár
SZOMBATHELY	Berzsenyi Dániel tér 3 9701 Szombathely
VÁC:	Vak Bottyán tér 1 2600 Vác
VESZPRÉM	Tolbuhin ut 16 8020 Veszprém

Greek Catholic or Uniate (Hajdúdorogi Görög Katholikus Egyházmegye)

HIVATAL   Bethlen ut 5
4401 Nyiregyháza

Reformed Church Archives (Calvinist)

Magyar Reformatus Levéltár
Kálvin tér 8, 1091 Budapest IX

Evangelical Church Archives

Evangelikus Levéltár
Űllői ut 24, 1085 Budapest VIII

Censuses (Népszámlálások)

Although censuses are held at regular intervals, they are only used for statistical purposes, and the returns are later destroyed. However, a number of local or regional censuses have been held over the centuries and you should check with the appropriate county archives (Megyei Levéltár) about these. Some fragments also remain of national censuses held in 1527, 1715, 1720, and 1828 and these are in the National Archives. If, by any chance, your Hungarian ancestor was living in the old county of Zemplén (now in Slovakia), you are lucky. The 1869 census for that county is practically complete and gives names, birthplaces, relationships, ages, occupations, and an exact address. It is in the National Archives in Budapest.

Wills (Végrendeletek)

These date back to the mid-1600s and give much detail about family relationships, apart from details of property involved. In the main they are in the National Archives, but more recent ones are in local municipal offices or archives (Tanacsi Levéltár).

Land Records and Deeds (Telekkönyvek-Telekkönyvezés)

These started in the early 1700s, with the departure of the Turks from various areas, but basically only refer to large estates of the old noble families. They are in the National Archives, as well as county archives. There are also Land Registration records in the county archives and in local courthouses. You will often find details of family relationships spelled out in these records.

Nobility Records (Nemesi Jegyzék)

These records are of use if your ancestors were members of the nobility from the fifteenth century up to the late 1800s. They are in the National Archives and local archives and refer in the main to court or political appointments of members of noble families.

Muster-Rolls (Katonai Anyakönyv or Létszámellenőrzö Ivek)

These are in the National Archives and include personal records of men serving in both regular and local militia units. However, there are many gaps, there is rather inadequate indexing, and in most cases the muster-rolls are only usable if you can specify the particular regiment and the approximate date of your ancestor's service.

So much for the genealogical records of Hungary. You can be very successful in your hunt but you will need patience. It may be of some guidance to note that between 1870 and 1910 over two million Hungarians emigrated, most of them from the northern areas of the country, and mostly through the port of Hamburg, in Germany. I have mentioned the detailed Hamburg Passenger Lists in the chapter on Germany, and if you do not know the exact place from which your family came, a search of the lists may give you that information.

ICELAND

Iceland was settled by Norsemen in the ninth century, and in 930 a Parliament, or Althing, was established. In the mid-1300s the island came under Norwegian control, and in 1380 it passed with Norway to the Danish Crown. During the next two centuries Iceland suffered a series of disasters, both manmade and natural. Her coasts were devastated by the raids of pirates from Algeria, England, and Spain; epidemics and volcanic eruptions killed off a third of the people; and Danish economic policies brought the island to bankruptcy and starvation. In 1874 limited autonomy was granted. Iceland got home rule from Denmark in 1904, and in 1918 it became an independent state under the King of Denmark. In 1944 it chose to become an independent republic.

The country is divided into various municipal units. There are some two hundred counties (hreppur), and several of these are grouped together into a region (sýsla), of which there are nineteen. The sixteen major towns are excluded from this system and each forms a separate unit. The ecclesiastical divisions consist of parishes (each of which may include several churches) and all are administered by a bishop.

In Iceland, as in most other countries, there has been a great movement of population from the country to the capital. Over thirty-four percent of the population now lives in Reykjavík.

Civil Registration (Skráning)

This started in 1735 when Lutheran pastors recorded the vital events of each parish and supplied the bishop with a copy. This system was replaced by the National Register in 1953. Church records are still maintained in the original churches.

Censuses (Manntal)

Many of the censuses have been indexed and published. The first took place in 1703 as part of a Danish government investigation of economic conditions in Iceland. The returns are complete for the year and are in the National Archives (Thjódskjalasafn), Safnahúsid, Hverfisgata, 101 Reykjavík.

Names and ages were recorded, as well as relationships to the head of the household, occupations, and full addresses. There was another census in 1729 but most of the returns have been lost; only those for three of the counties have survived: Árnessýsla, Hnappadalssýsla, and Rangárvallasýsla. Other censuses were taken in 1762, 1801, 1835, 1840, 1845, 1855, 1860, and every ten years to 1901, then every ten years from 1910 to 1960. The information requested in each of these censuses varies considerably. In addition there were local censuses in various places over the centuries. They are all in the National Archives. The census of 1950 and the special one in 1952 were the basis for the original roster of the National Register. This has replaced the holding of regular censuses.

The National Register (Thjódskrá)

This was started in 1953 with the object of providing a central registration of the population for administrative and statistical purposes. It meant that civil registration and the holding of regular censuses were no longer necessary. Regular updating of the register is effected by the reporting of vital events, and the details of immigration and emigration that are maintained by government departments. The register is brought up to date every four months with regard to changes of address and internal or external migration, in addition to the annual check each December 1. Changes of address are reported to the local municipality to which the individual moves, and it in turn passes on the information to the National Register.

The Lutheran pastors (and any other clergymen) must report births, baptisms, marriages, deaths, and burials as they occur. The Ministry of Justice reports naturalization, adoption, and divorce. Local magistrates report details of separation orders granted to husbands and wives.

The information contained in the National Register is the name, address or temporary address, sex, marital status, religion, nationality, place of birth, date of birth, and a personal eight-digit number. Every individual over the age of thirteen receives an identity card. The records are kept in the Statistical Bureau of Iceland (Hagstofa Íslands), Hverfisgata, 101 Reykjavík.

Church Registers (Kirkjubaekur)

These are kept in the National Archives but more recent ones are still in the churches. They date from 1664 in some cases, but generally do not start much before 1750. The information contained in the registers is of the usual type:

BAPTISMS: Name, date, parents, occupations, addresses, godparents or witnesses.

MARRIAGES: Names, ages, addresses, and names of parents and witnesses.

BURIALS: Names, ages, addresses, occupation, cause and place of death.

The address of the headquarters of the Evangelical Lutheran Church is Biskup Íslands, Klapparstig 27, 101 Reykjavik. In actual fact the President of Iceland is head of the church, but he delegates his authority. The church is governed by the Bishop and a Church Assembly. In 1982, 93.2 percent of the population belonged to the Lutheran Church.

Other church records include the following:

Confirmations (Fermingarskýrslur)

These date from 1830 to the present and list the names, addresses, and ages of the persons confirmed. More recent records also give the date and place of birth. Records up to 1958 are in the National Archives; more recent records are in the church.

Church Censuses (Sóknarmanntal)

These were held at irregular intervals from about 1790 onward, although in some places they were started later. Earlier ones are now in the National Archives. Apart from the usual personal information you would expect to find in any census, these also give details of people who have left the parish, or are about to leave, and their destination in Iceland or overseas. In fact, there is a double-check available on emigration details because apart from these church records of departures, there are also Emigration Lists in the offices of the regional municipalities (sýslur).

Ministerial Biographies (Prestaaefir)

Since the Lutheran Church is so prominent in the life of Iceland, it is perhaps logical that the personal history of the ministers is recorded. Many details about them date back as far as the year 1000, it is claimed. All this information is also in the National Archives.

Surnames

One major problem in researching your Icelandic ancestry is the continued use of patronymics. For example, according to the Personal Names Act of 1925, every Icelandic citizen is entitled to "one or two" Icelandic names. People in Iceland with a surname, as we understand the meaning of the word, are in a small minority. In the telephone directory of Reykjavík, for example, all people are listed under the first letter of their Christian name, and people with a family or surname may be listed under the first letter, too, so Tryggvi Thoroddsen could be listed under T or TH.

Wills (Skiptabaekur)

The National Archives contain wills from about 1717 up to 1937; later wills are in the custody of the local courts.

Mortgages (Vedmalabaekur)

These date from the late 1700s and give details of property; real estate transactions; and sale, transfer, or leasing of property. In many cases these records give details of family relationships. The records are in the National Archives up to the end of the last century, and in the local courts since then.

Court Records (Thingbaekur)

These start in 1619 and, of course, cover not only criminal cases, but also a wide variety of civil proceedings—marriage settlements, disputes between executors, differences over property settlements, real estate transactions, and land disputes. Here again the usual pattern is followed—early records are in the National Archives and more recent ones in the local court.

Other Records

The National Archives also contain a mass of more specialized information: genealogical collections of family trees and family histories; stories from Icelandic history (both imagined and real); biographies; family details of sheriffs (very prominent local officials), and similar details about members of the Althing (Parliament). If your ancestors were at all prominent in their locality, these records, which are indexed, may give you a great deal of information.

One final word of warning about Icelandic ancestor-hunting: the National Archives are very bad about answering requests for information, let alone supplying an answer. The LDS Family History Library has many Icelandic records on microfilm and you should use their resources first before attempting to pry information out of the National Archives.

ITALY

Italy was, of course, the core of the Roman Empire until its end in 476. Then waves of invasion by Goths, Byzantines, Lombards, Franks, Magyars, Arabs, Carthaginians, and Germans followed in the area that we now know as Italy. These invasions were followed by a union of Italy and Germany and the beginning of the Holy Roman Empire.

By 1250 the Papacy had become the predominant power in the Italian peninsula, but it existed side by side with the great princely and ducal families of Visconti, Sforza, Gonzaga, and Este, and the powerful republics of Venice, Florence, and Genoa. At the end of the fifteenth century the Kingdom of Naples and Sicily was established in the south, the Papal States controlled the central part, and in the north power was possessed by the great duchies of Ferrara, Mantua, Milan, Modena, and Savoy, and by the republics of Venice and Genoa.

At the end of the century the invasions began again, this time by France, Spain, and Austria. By 1748 Naples, Sicily, Parma, and Piacenza were under Spanish control, and the Austrians then occupied Milan, Mantua, Modena, and Tuscany. The only independent areas left were the Papal States, and Venice, Genoa, Lucca, and Sardinia.

When Napoleon defeated the Austrians in 1796 he redrew the map of the peninsula. A puppet kingdom was set up under his brother Joseph as king, and other areas were included in France. These were Savoy, Piedmont, Parma, Liguria, Tuscany, and the Papal States. The Congress of Vienna in 1814–15 restored the status quo, except that Venetia and Lombardy became Austrian, and Naples and Sicily were united in a separate kingdom.

In 1848 rebellions broke out, ending in 1861 when the kingdom of Italy was established. In 1866 Venetia was included, and in 1870 Rome was annexed. Austria retained the South Tirol and Trieste until 1919. After the Second World War, Italy lost several small Alpine districts to France (mainly Brigue and Tende) and several islands and part of Venezia Giulia to Yugoslavia. In 1954 Trieste, and the surrounding area which had been under United Nations supervision, were returned to Italy.

It is important to understand Italy's unfortunate history over the centuries. Before 1861 it was a most extraordinary collection of kingdoms, principalities, dukedoms, Papal States, republics, city-states, personal fiefdoms. You name it; Italy had it! The result is that there is very little centralization of genealogical records. Oh, the records are there, but the problem is finding them, and then fighting your way through the almost impenetrable bureaucratic jungle that surrounds them! With all due respect to my archivist friends in Italy, the staff of the state archives are not renowned for their speed in answering questions, and their answers (when you eventually receive them) will probably be long on charm and politeness and loquacity and short on hard information. In fact, you may find you have to start all over and repeat your original letter but use different words.

One major problem, of course, is that Italians are not fluent in English, and you must really try to find someone locally who can translate your letter into Italian, and then interpret the answer for you when it arrives. A letter written in English will produce any one of three results: (a) you will receive a reply in Italian; (b) you will receive a reply in a form of English that will be difficult to understand (but at least they were kind enough to try); (c) you will receive no answer at all (even though you have sent two International Reply Coupons and a self-addressed airmail envelope). So far as (a) is concerned, you may find that the letter is friendly and polite but does not answer a single question!

A letter written in Italian is ninety percent certain to produce a reply, and this applies particularly when writing to a local priest. As far as the latter is concerned, gamble by enclosing a ten dollar (U.S.) bill. The average priest is underpaid and overworked. The donation will ensure an answer as he is very likely to have been caught before by overseas inquirers who obtain information and send no payment. The same remarks apply to local municipal officials. You can't pour out money without results but I think this advice will work for you!

You may find all he can tell you is the location of the parish registers, because they may now be in the custody of the diocesan archives (archivio diocesano). These archives seem a little reluctant to reply to inquiries and here, again, an advance donation should help. Unfortunately, there is no central source of information that gives you the location of church registers, nor is there any particular law setting down when registers should be deposited in the archives, either civil or ecclesiastical. In many places the registers are kept in the church under appalling conditions and are subject to flooding, benign neglect, dampness, carelessness, and theft. When the Arno overflowed its banks in Florence a few years ago, a number of church registers were last seen floating down the river.

There are 103 state archives in Italy. The country is divided into 19 regions (Regioni) and within these regions are 102 provinces, each with a state archive. The 103rd archive is in Rome (Roma) and is the Central State Archives (Archivio Centrale di Stato, Piazzale degli Archivi 40, 10144 Rome). This should not be confused with the State Archives of the Province of Roma (Archivio di Stato, Corso Rinascimento 40, 00186 Rome).

Because of Italy's piecemeal development it is impossible to generalize and say that parish registers began in 1545 or that notarial records started in 1456. Nearly every region is based on an ancient independent state with its own laws and records and systems of record-keeping.

The regions and the provinces within them are set out below. Each province is named after the chief city in that province, so when writing to the state archives, all you need to do is to address the envelope to Direttore, Archivio di Stato, and then the name of the city and that of the region:

ABRUZZO: Chieti, L'Aquila, Pescara, Teramo.

BASILICATA: Matera and Potenza (Basilicata was formerly Lucania).

CALABRIA: Catanzaro, Cosenza, Crotone, Reggio di Calabria, Vibo Valentia.

CAMPANIA: Avellino, Benevento, Caserta, Napoli, Salerno.

EMILIA-ROMAGNA: Bologna, Ferrara, Forli-Cesena, Modena, Parma, Piacenza, Ravenna, Reggio Emilia, Rimini.

FRIULI-VENEZIA GIULIA: Gorizia, Pordenone, Trieste, Udine.

LAZIO: Frosinone, Latina (Littoria), Rieti, Roma, Viterbo.

LIGURIA: Genova, Imperia, La Spezia, Savona.

LOMBARDY (LOMBARDIA): Bergamo, Brescia, Como, Cremona, Lecco, Lodi, Mantova, Milano, Pavia, Sondrio, Varese.

MARCHE: Ancona, Ascoli-Piceno, Macerata, Pesaro-Urbino.

PIEDMONT (PIEMONTE): Alessandria, Asti, Biella, Cuneo, Novara, Torino, Vercelli.

PUGLIA: Bari, Brindisi, Foggia, Lecce, Taranto (Ionio).

SARDINIA (SARDEGNA): Cagliari, Nuoro, Oristano, Sassari.

SICILY (SICILIA): Agrigento, Caltanisetta, Catania, Enna, Messina, Palermo, Ragusa, Siracusa, Trapani.

TRENTINO-ALTO ADIGE: Bolzano and Trento.

TUSCANY (TOSCANA): Arezzo, Firenze, Grosseto, Livorno, Lucca, Massa Carrara, Pisa, Pistoia, Prato, Siena.

UMBRIA: Perugia and Terni.

VALLE D'AOSTA: Aosta.

VENETO: Belluno, Padova, Rovigo, Treviso, Venezia, Verona, Vicenza.

There are also sub-archives at Anagni Guarcino, Barletta, Caltagirone, Camerino, Castrovillari, Este, Fabriano, Faenza, Fano, Fermo, Foligno, Gubbio, Imola, Lamezia Terme, Lanciano, Locri, Lucera, Modica, Noto, Orvieto, Palmi, Pescia, Pontremoli, Sanremo, Sciacca, Spoleto, Sulmona, Termini Imerese, Trani, Urbino, Varallo, Ventimiglia, and Verbania.

Civil Registration (Stato Civile)

This began in 1869 for the whole country but the system was not centralized. So, to obtain details from these records, you need to know where your ancestor was born, was married, or died. In some parts of Italy a form of registration came into force much earlier, a beneficial result of so many different states and laws. In the state archives in Florence (Firenze) there is a complete collection of civil registration records for the whole of Tuscany (Toscana) for 1808–66; in the state archives in Napoli there are records for Napoli and Sicily (Sicilia) for 1806–70; in parts of northern Italy civil registration started in 1803–15; in the south, in Abruzzo, Campania, Puglia, Basilicata, and Calabria, it started in 1820. You must check with the nearest archive for more information. In Trentino (South Tirol) civil registration started in the sixteenth century, but there are gaps.

Details contained in the records for births, marriages, and deaths are as follows:

Births

Birth records contain name, date and place of birth, names of parents with mother's maiden name, and father's occupation. From 1900 on you will also find a marginal entry (similar to those in France) containing later information about eventual marriage with date, place, and name, and finally, date and place of death.

Marriages

Marriage records include name and age of bride and groom; marriage date and place; marital status; place of birth of each; names of parents and maiden name of mother; names of witnesses; occupation and addresses of all concerned (bride and groom, their parents, and witnesses); and date of consent of parents or guardians.

Deaths

Death records contain name of the deceased and date and place of death, date and place of birth, names of parents and address if they are still alive, name of the spouse of the deceased, occupation and address of the deceased.

The above records are in the Civil Registry Office (Ufficio di Stato Civile) in the city, town, village, or commune where the event took place. Be sure you request a full certificate. This way you will get all the details on the original entry, for otherwise the information will be just the bare essentials. You will certainly want the names of parents, both as a check and also to take you further back, and the magic sentence is "Favorisca inviare estratti con nomi dei genitori" or "Please send extracts with names of parents." If you run into any difficulties over civil registration (you cannot trace the location of a place, or the local office does not reply) write, explaining your difficulties, to the Central Statistical Institute (Istituto Centrale di Statistica, Via Cesare Balbo 16, 00100 Rome).

Certificate of Family Genealogy (Certificato dello Stato di Famiglia)

This kind of record is unique to Italy. It started in about 1869 and although there are gaps, and even places that did not begin recording information until this century, it can be of great value. Basically, it is an attempt by the authorities to have a complete record of each family in each locality. It contains names, relationships, birth dates, and birthplaces of all living family members at the time it was put on record. The office that undertakes the task and preserves the information in each municipality is the Ufficio Anagrafe.

Emigration Records (Registri dell' Emigrazione)

These records are in the various state archives, and also in the Ministry of the Interior (Ministero dell' Interno, Rome). They are not open for inspection, even though they date back as far as 1869, but the authorities have been known to give some details to overseas inquirers, provided that the relationship is proved, and the reason for the research given.

Conscription Records (Ufficio Matricola e Centro Documentale)

These started in 1869 and continue to the present day. They include name, birth date, town of residence, and whether the draftee served, was refused, was exempted, died, or emigrated before the call-up age of eighteen. The records are in the custody of the local Military District (Distretto Militare). The address for the area in which you are interested can be obtained from your nearest Italian Embassy or Consulate. The state archives can supply records from 1870–1920.

Clerical Survey (Status Animarum)

These records were kept from the early 1700s until about 1860 and list all persons under the jurisdiction of the parish church. Many have disappeared or been damaged, and not all parishes bothered to maintain them. Certainly it is worth checking to see if they exist if you are writing to the local priest, because they might just solve a problem, but it is very unlikely.

Notarial Records (Atti Notarili)

Never omit a check on these frequently ignored records. They can date back to as early as 1340 and they come right up to the present day. Generally speaking, any record older than one hundred years is in the state archives, and since then is either in the notarial offices or in the local notarial archives. The information recorded can cover an endless list of items, but the main ones are marriage contracts and settlements, dowries, contracts of sale and purchase of land or houses, wills, lawsuits, inheritance, and property inventory and division. However, if your ancestors did not own land or property, it is unlikely their names will appear in such records. A poor Italian scratching a precarious living on his fazzoletto (handkerchief) of soil was not likely to have any reason or money to consult a notary. The entries were in Latin until 1725 and since then have been in Italian.

Passports (Passaporti)

These were issued by the various state governments between 1800 and 1869, and then the issuance was taken over by the local police headquarters (Questura). Passports up to 1920–30 (depending on the region) are in the state archives; later passports are in the local Questura.

Wills (Testamenti)

These can date back to the 1300s in certain areas and are either in the state archives or in the local notarial archives (depending on the date), or in the local registry office (Ufficio del Registro) in the particular town.

If you have any problem tracing the location of a notarial archive, or obtaining an answer, you should get in touch with the head of the notarial archives (Ispettore Generale, Archivio Notarile, Via Flaminia 160, Rome).

University Records (Registri delle Università)

If your ancestor attended one of the very ancient universities in Italy, you will find the registers of students dating back to 1267, giving not only age and address and graduation date, but also much more detailed biographical information. The records are either in the state archives or in the actual university, sometimes half in one and half in the other.

Genealogical Collections (Archivi Genealogici)

These can be found in both published and manuscript form in the various state and municipal archives, and also in many university libraries. However, in the main they are about noble families or leading members of the clergy.

Censuses (Censimenti)

These have been held every ten years from 1861 to 1931, then in 1936, and again every ten years from 1951 to 1991. Not all the census returns are open for public search, and since some changes are being contemplated in the law governing this, I suggest you write for information about availability to the Direzione Generale dei Servizi Tecnici, Istituto Centrale di Statistica, Via Cesare Balbo 16, Rome.

Tax Assessments (Catasti)

As you may imagine, there are a variety of tax records: taxes on land, taxes on houses, taxes on land sales, taxes on heads, special taxes and imposts. It is no wonder that Italians are famed for tax-avoidance—they have been doing it successfully for many centuries. I am not going to even try to list the various tax records, but basically you will find records of taxes paid to the national or provincial governments in the state archives and those of municipal taxes in the town or village offices. They are generally not indexed and are certainly not easy to consult. Keep your knowledge of them in the back of your mind and do not use them unless you really need them.

Church Registers (Registri Parrocchiali)

So far as the Catholic Church is concerned, the parish registers started in 1545, but very few exist before the beginning of the seventeenth century. The earliest known ones are those of Guardiagrele (Chieti), 1325; Cava dei Tirreni (Salerno), 1350 (for baptisms only); Lucca, Pisa, Siena, baptisms and deaths from 1360, and Florence (Firenze) from 1423. Registers of baptism were called Liber Baptizatorum, those of marriages Liber Matrimoniorum, and those of burials Liber Defunctorum. They were kept with great care by the priests, as until the introduction of civil registration in 1869 they were the only records of the vital events of a family.

Many parishes have been abolished or merged with a neighboring one, and in these cases, where a church no longer stands or is closed, you will usually find the church registers lodged in the Diocesan Curia, or office of the Bishop of the Diocese in which the church is located.

The parish church may have other records as well as the usual baptisms, marriages, and burials. These may include land records of the parish (cadastral), confirmations, and church accounts including records of donations, payments for masses for the dead, payments for bell-tolling, and payments for the purchase or rental of burial vaults. All of these records are likely to be of value to you. You may find that they have been transferred to the Diocesan Archives (Archivio Vescovile della Diocesi). If the local priest replies to your letter, he will certainly give you the address of this archive if his records have been transferred there.

This whole question of transfer of registers to other archives creates problems for an ancestor-hunter in Italy. For example, in Umbria all the parish registers, except for the most recent years, are in the Diocesan Archives; in Rome itself eighty percent of the registers are deposited in the Sacred Archives of the Vatican (Archivio Segreto del Vaticano) and, very unfortunately, it seems impossible to obtain any reply even with the inclusion of the usual two International Reply Coupons and self-addressed envelope. I have reported this on several occasions, and even my complaints have been unanswered. You may, perhaps, be able to obtain some help from your own parish priest.

The information you will find entered in the average parish register is as follows:

Baptismal Records (Atti di Battesimo)

These include date and place of birth and/or baptism; sex; name; name of father; maiden name of mother; often, names and addresses of godparents, their fathers' names, and their relationship to the child; names of proxies standing in for the godparents if they were absent.

Marriage Records (Atti di Matrimonio)

These contain name and address of the bride and groom; age and place of birth; names of the fathers of the bride and the groom; names (and maiden names) of the mothers of the bride and the groom; names of other parishes where the banns were also published (since a marriage usually took place in the commune where the bride lived, this will give you the place of origin of the groom); marital status; and letters of consent of parents or guardian.

Burial Records (Atti di Sepoltura)

Burial records contain date and place of death; name and age of deceased; often, the cause of death; address at the time of death; names of parents and surviving spouse, or next of kin; and place and date of burial.

Confirmation (Cresima)

These also date back to 1545 and include the personal details of the child and witnesses' names and addresses. They are usually in the Diocesan Archives, together with records of Excommunication (Scomunica), special dispensations (dispensa), and details of tenants of church property and land.

In addition, the Secret Archives of the Vatican have the tax and census records of the Papal States from the mid-1300s. These states included the modern provinces of Ancona, Ascoli Piceno, Macerata, Pesaro-Urbino, Perugia, Terni, Frosinone, Latina, Rieti, Roma, and Viterbo.

Waldensian Registers

This small Protestant sect is confined to a few remote valleys in the Piedmont area on the border with France. Its history began in Lyons, France, in 1179, when Pierre Valdes started to preach a gospel of extreme simplicity within the Catholic Church. His followers were called "the poor men of Christ." After much persecution (12,000 of them were in prison in 1686) they became Protestants and established relations with Calvinists and Lutherans in Switzerland and Germany. On at least two occasions there were mass flights to safety into Switzerland and Germany, and even as far away as the Netherlands, England, and Ireland. Most of the refugees eventually returned and were granted complete freedom of religion by Napoleon.

Their registers start in 1685 and are still in the local churches. Some of the records in the Pinerolo district have been microfilmed by the LDS Church.

Genealogical Organizations

If you write to one of the following genealogical organizations, be sure you enclose a self-addressed airmail envelope and the usual two International Reply Coupons.

Instituto di Genealogica et Araldica
Via Antonio Cerasi 5a, 00100 Rome

Instituto Genealogico
Via S. Spirito 27, 50125 Florence

There are also two very helpful and reputable North American organizations: Italian Genealogy and Heraldry Society of Canada, 2951 St. Clair Avenue, Windsor, Ontario N9E 4A1, Canada; and POINT (Pursuing Our Italian Names Together), P.O. Box 2977, Palos Verdes Peninsula, California 90274. The former is the typical Family History Society, with an enthusiastic membership and is a non-profit organization. It can provide form letters, written in Italian, and a wide variety of other services. If you have lost the language of your Italian ancestors, you will find this society is vital to the success of your search. POINT is a commercial organization with a database of 6,000 Italian surnames and a close connection with archival authorities in Italy.

You can obtain further information from both these organizations by sending a No. 9, self-addressed envelope, and including return postage.

So much for the genealogical records of Italy. I hope I have not discouraged you from tracing your Italian ancestors, but I always try to be honest about the quality and location of records and the helpfulness of the people who look after them.

As I told you earlier, all the records are there, but you must have infinite patience in tracing their whereabouts. In the past in Italy there were no major movements of population within the country, as there were in so many other European areas. Once you know your ancestor's point of departure and date of birth, you should be able to go back a considerable way.

LATVIA

Latvia was formed from four historic areas—Latgale and Vidzeme, which were part of Livonia, and Kurzeme and Zemgale which belonged to the Duchy of Courland. Its population is Lett, but there are Lithuanian, Russian, Belarussian, Polish, German, and Jewish minorities.

The Letts were conquered and Christianized by the Livonian Knights in the thirteenth century. Latvia was part of Livonia until 1561. It then passed to Poland, to Sweden in 1629, and to Russia in 1721. During this whole period, German remained the official language until it was supplanted by Russian in 1885. There were many uprisings over the years until Latvia became independent in 1918 after World War I. Its freedom only lasted until 1940. In that year the German-Soviet Pact transferred it to the USSR, while nearly all the German inhabitants were returned to Germany. It declared its independence again in 1991, and this fact was recognized by the former Soviet Union and the United Nations. The three main religions are Catholic, Lutheran, and Orthodox.

There are three state archives in the capital (Riga) and all are of interest to genealogists. They will undertake research for overseas inquirers for a fee. You may also visit the country and do your own research. There is no charge for this at the moment, but you must make prior arrangements before your visit.

The archives (Valsts arhīvs) are in the following locations:

The Central State History Archives
(Centrālais Valsts vēstures arhīvs)
Slokas ielā 16, 226007 Riga

Here you will find records of the pre-Soviet period.

The Central State Archives
(Centrālais Valsts vēstures arhīvs)
Bezdeligu ielā 1, 226007 Riga

Documents of the Soviet period are here.

The Central State Cine-phono-photo Documents Archives
(Centrālais Valsts Kino-Foto-dono-dokumentu arhīvs)
Skuni ielā 11, 226007 Riga

The archives will undertake research of church registers (baznīcu grāmatas) and wills (testamenti). They will also search census returns and land records where they exist. Accounts will be payable in hard currency.

If you wish to deal directly with the three main religions the addresses are:

LUTHERAN: Latvijas ev.lt. baznīcas konsistorija
Laćpleśa ielā 4-4, 226010 Riga

CATHOLIC: Katolu baznīcas metropolijas Kurija
M.Pils ielā 2a, 226047 Riga

ORTHODOX: Krieuva pareizticigp baznīcas eparhijas parvalde
M. Pils ielā 11, 226047 Riga

The public libraries of Boston, San Francisco, and Seattle hold some records of Latvians settlers in their areas.

LIECHTENSTEIN

The Principality of Liechtenstein was formed in 1719 by joining the county of Vaduz and the barony of Schellenberg. The area was owned by the family of the same name, which also owned vast estates in Austria. It was a member of the German Confederation from 1815 to 1866, but became independent in that year. Liechtenstein is represented abroad by Switzerland.

Civil Registration

This started in 1878 and the registry books were kept by the local Catholic priests, acting as representatives of the government. Before that year the records were part of the parish registers and are still in the local churches or in the church archives. Since 1878 they have been in the Civil Registry Bureau in Vaduz, the capital. Copies of the records can be obtained for a small fee, or free, depending on the searching to be done and the staff available at the time.

All inquiries concerning government records or documents should be sent to the Chancellery of the Government of Liechtenstein (Kanzlei der Regierung des Fürstentums Liechtenstein), Vaduz 9490.

Church Registers

These date back to 1640. The population is predominantly Catholic and there are ten parishes within the country.

Wills

These date back to 1690 and are in the custody of the local courts in each district.

Archives

There are village and church archives in the following places: Balzers, Bendern, Eschen, Gamprin, Mauren, Schaan, Schellenberg, Triesen, Triesenberg, and Vaduz. Also in the latter place are the Government Archives and the House Archives of the ruling family.

LITHUANIA

The Liths are thought to have settled in the area as far back as 1500 B.C., although there is some dispute about this. In the thirteenth century the German military order—the Livonian Brothers of the Sword (also known as the Livonian Knights) occupied part of the country. Later an independent state under a Grand Duke was established; Lithuania became a great and powerful nation in the fourteenth century, including all of Belarus, a large part of Ukraine, and part of Russia itself.

In 1386 a dynastic marriage joined the country with Poland. In 1410 the joint forces of the two countries defeated the Livonian Knights at Tannenberg. In 1569 there was a complete merger with Poland, but during the two partitions of Poland Lithuania disappeared from the map as an independent state and became part of Russia.

After World War I Lithuania proclaimed its independence. In 1920 the capital, Vilnius, was seized by Poland, and in 1923 the Lithuanians took Memel from Germany. In 1939 Vilnius was returned by Poland and Memel returned to Germany. In 1940 the Red Army occupied the country and Lithuania became part of the Soviet Union.

In 1991 Lithuania declared its independence once again and this was recognized by the former Soviet Union and the United Nations.

There are three state archives in Vilnius:

The Historical State Archives
(Lietuvos valstybinis istorijos archyvas)
10 Gerosios Vilites, Vilnius

The State Parish Register Archives
(Lietuvos valstybinis metriku archyvas)
21 Kalinausko, Vilnius

The State Archives
(Lietuvos valstybinis archyvas)
Kareiviu 21, Vilnius

The latter archives contain birth, marriage, and death registers, wills, land records, and all other records of genealogical interest (except for the parish registers, which are in the State Parish Register Archives mentioned above).

During the brief period of independence between 1918 and 1940 the church registers were in the churches, but were later transferred to the archives. Original present-day registers are still in the churches, but copies are sent to the State Parish Register Archives.

You may search in the archives yourself, but must pay for any photocopies you require. At present there is no charge made for personal searches. If you do plan a visit it would be wise to write beforehand to make sure the registers or records you need do, in fact, exist.

The State Archives will also search the records for people unable to visit the country. There is an initial, non-returnable fee ($50 at the time of this writing), as you are paying for the search and not for the results. How soon they learn of the benefits of capitalism! The amount deposited may not be enough to cover the costs of a prolonged search, and in such a case you will be told of the additional sum required. Your payment may be made to the archives by personal certified check, or to the Vneshekonombank in Vilnius (Account No. 676305137).

So far as the records of the Catholic Church are concerned, these may be retained in churches using the Polish language. The addresses of the headquarters of the three main religions in the country are:

CATHOLIC
Valanciaus, Kaunas

ORTHODOX
Ausros Vartu, Vilnius

LUTHERAN
68 Laisves, Tauragė

The Belzekas Museum (4012 Arches Avenue, Chicago, IL 60632) and the Chicago Public Library have records of Lithuanian settlers in that state.

LUXEMBOURG

Luxembourg was originally a county that included the present Belgian province of Luxembourg. It first came to prominence in 1308 when its count was elected Holy Roman Emperor. His grandson, the emperor Charles IV, made Luxembourg a duchy in 1354. In 1445 it became part of the Duchy of Burgundy, and in 1482 it became part of the vast Hapsburg domains. For the next three centuries its history was that of the south Netherlands as it passed from Spain to Austria to France, and back again to Spain and France, the inevitable fate of a small country in that part of Europe.

The Congress of Vienna (1814–15) made Luxembourg a grand duchy in personal union with the King of the Netherlands. At the same time it joined the German Confederation, and the capital (which is also named Luxembourg) was garrisoned by Prussian troops. When Belgium rebelled against the Netherlands in 1830, Luxembourg joined in on the Belgian side. As soon as Belgium gained its independence it rewarded Luxembourg by claiming the whole country. In 1839 Luxembourg was forced to cede the territory that is now the Belgian province of the same name. The remainder became autonomous, though still a member of the German Confederation and in personal union with the King of the Netherlands.

In 1866 the King decided to sell the country to France and nearly brought about a war between France and Prussia. In 1867 the European powers declared Luxembourg a neutral country. It was occupied by Germany during the First and Second World Wars. Now Luxembourg is a member of Benelux, the economic union of Belgium, the Netherlands, and Luxembourg. The official language is French but German is widely spoken, as is Letzeburgesch (a Low German dialect). The country is divided into two administrative regions, Luxembourg and Diekirch, basically the north and south areas of the country.

The National Archives (Archives de l'État) are on the Plateau du Saint Esprit, BP 6, 2010 Luxembourg. There are also municipal archives in the

Hôtel de Ville, Place Guillaume, Luxembourg. The Catholic Church archives are in the office of the bishop (Évêché de Luxembourg, BP 419, 2010 Luxembourg).

Civil Registration (Enregistrement Civil)

This started in 1796 and the records are in the local municipal offices throughout the country. A copy remains there and a duplicate is lodged in the Courts of Justice in Luxembourg and Diekirch. Every ten years all entries are indexed, and the indexes placed in the National Archives.

Censuses (Recensements)

These have been held every ten years since 1793 and the returns are in the National Archives.

Church Registers (Registres Paroissiaux)

These are still in the original churches, but microfilm copies of them all are in the same archives. The earliest registers for the city of Luxembourg date back to 1601, but there are many gaps. There were about 150 parishes in the country in the eighteenth century, but it is probable that the number has been reduced since then.

Notarial Records (Les Protocoles Notariaux)

These are details of court cases over property rights, executors' disputes, and the drawing up of marriage settlements, dating from 1612. More recent records are in the offices of local notaries, but any documents more than sixty years old must be lodged in the National Archives.

Scholarships (Bourses d'Études)

This is a record that I have not found in any other country. The scholarships started in 1882 and there is a great deal of information about the family background of successful entrants. The records are indexed in a very useful book entitled *Fondations de Bourses d'Études Instituées en Faveur des Luxembourgeois, 1882–1907.*

I am fairly sure there is a wealth of genealogical information in the National Archives. Unfortunately, they do not have enough help to attend to written requests about Luxembourg ancestry. If you have a query or need more detailed information, I suggest you write directly to Le Directeur des Archives de l'État, Archives de l'État, at the address above.

MACEDONIA

Macedonia was a republic of Yugoslavia until it declared independence in 1992, which has now been recognized by the United Nations and the European Community (EC). Because of this, you should also read the chapter in this book on Yugoslavia for information about records that cannot be separated easily.

Macedonia's ancient territories included areas of Bulgaria and Greece. It has always been the victim of warring nations, and at various times in its long history the region has been under the control of Romans, Byzantines, Goths, Huns, Slavs, Bulgarians, and Turks. In more recent times Bulgaria, Greece, and Serbia have all laid claim to the Macedonian area.

After the two Balkan wars of 1912 and 1913 the Treaty of Bucharest awarded a small portion of Macedonia to Bulgaria and divided the rest between Greece and Yugoslavia more or less along present boundary lines. In the Second World War the whole of the Macedonian area was occupied by Bulgaria, but a peace treaty in 1947 restored the original boundaries between the three countries. The capital city of Macedonia is Skopje.

Religions
Macedonia is mainly Orthodox, but there is a very large Muslim minority.

Language
Although Macedonia was part of Yugoslavia until recently, the Macedonians do not speak Serbo-Croatian but have their own separate language.

It should also be mentioned that there are more than 400,000 Albanians in Macedonia.

Archives

The National Archives of Macedonia are in Skopje (Kej Dimitar Vlahov, 91001 Skopje). The addresses of the various historical archives are given below:

Moskovska 1
91000 Skopje

Bulevar 1 maja 55
97000 Bitola

Moše Pijade 134
97500 Prilep

27 Marta 2
92400 Strumica

Cvetan Dimitrov 1
91220 Tetovo

Nikola Karev 1
97300 Ohrid

Sane Georgiev 35
92400 Štip

Goce Delčev 25
91300 Kumanova

Maršala Tita 53
91400 Titov Veles

MALTA

Malta, like many other places in the world located on trade routes or in key strategic areas, has had more than its share of foreign occupation. Over the centuries it has been occupied by Phoenicians, Greeks, Carthaginians, Romans, Saracens, Byzantines, Arabs, Normans, Franks, Knights of Malta (the Knights Hospitallers), French, and British. Malta became independent in 1964, and a republic in 1974.

Great damage was done to government offices and churches and their records by Italian and German bombing during the Second World War. Malta consists of three islands: Malta, Gozo, and Comino, plus a few uninhabited rocklets. The capital is Valletta, on the main island of Malta.

Civil Registration
This started in 1863 and the records are in the Public Registry Office (L'Insinua), 197 Merchants Street, Valletta, for the island of Malta, and in the Public Registry Office, Victoria, Gozo, for the island of that name. A small charge is made for a photocopy of a certificate.

Church Registers
Church registers date back to 1537 for the cathedral in Valletta, and to about 1550 in the various parishes. Some, of course, are partially or wholly missing as the result of the bombing in the last war. Generally speaking, the parish churches hold recent registers and the early ones are in the Cathedral Museum, Archbishop Square, Mdina, or in the Archbishop's Curia, St. Calcedonious Square, Floriana. However, there are still many parish churches that have retained their early registers in their own possession. Each parish has its own Archivium, which may contain useful information for you about tombstones, confirmation records, and so on.

Censuses

These were first held on the islands in 1842, and then in 1851 and every ten years until 1931, and then again in 1948, 1957, 1967, 1977, and 1987. The returns are open for inspection in the Public Library in Valletta, and also in Victoria, Gozo, for that island. The staff will probably look up a specific entry without charge provided that you can give an exact address on the island, and also send them two International Reply Coupons and a self-addressed airmail envelope.

Wills

Wills dating back to the fourteenth century are in the Public Registry Offices in Valletta, Malta, and Victoria, Gozo. However, it was not essential to deposit a will before 1863. Wills since then are either in the Registry of the Civil Courts in Valletta for the island of Malta, or in the similar office in Victoria, Gozo, for that island. Wills may also be found in the Public Registry Offices in Valletta and Victoria. Photocopies may be ordered by mail for a small fee. You must also send a photocopy of the death certificate of the person concerned if he or she died within the past hundred years. For wills before then, no death certificate is needed.

Notarial Archives

These are located at 3 M.A. Vassalli Street, Valletta, and may contain information about wills, probate, and disputes over property. The records date back to 1465. The archives for the island of Gozo are located on Republic Street in Victoria.

There is no genealogical information in the State Library or in the National Library, except that the latter does hold the archives of the Knights of Malta, and these contain information about some of the knights and their families.

There is no genealogical organization in Malta, but there are at least two genealogical researchers, and their names and addresses can be obtained from the National Library or the Archbishop's Curia.

MONACO

This tiny independent principality of 150 hectares consists of the districts of La Condamine, Monte Carlo, and Monaco-Ville (the capital). It has been successively part of the kingdom of the Lombards, part of the kingdom of Arles, under Turkish rule for five centuries, and ruled by the Grimaldi dynasty since the thirteenth century. It was under Spanish protection from 1542 to 1641; under French control from 1641 to 1793; included in France from 1793 to 1815; and under Sardinian protection from 1815 to 1861. Since 1861 it has been under French protection again.

Civil Registration (Enregistrement Civil)
This commenced in 1792 and the records are in the Mayor's Office (Bureau de l'État-Civil), Mairie de Monaco. From 1546 to 1792 the recording of vital events was done by the Catholic Church. The civil registers are not open to public inspection, but information can be given if a relationship can be proved and the object of the inquiry is acceptable.

Church Registers (Registres Paroissiaux)
As mentioned, these started in 1546 and all of them up to the end of the last century are located in the Chancellery of the Bishop's Palace (l'Évêché).

There are five parishes in Monaco: Immaculée-Conception (Cathédrale de Monaco), St. Jean-Baptiste, Ste. Dévote, St. Charles, St. Martin. They have the registers going back to approximately 1900.

Censuses (Recensements)
These started in 1757 and have been held at intervals of between three and seven years ever since. Those held before 1873 are open to public search, and information can be divulged from later ones under the conditions men-

tioned above under Civil Registration. The census returns are also in the custody of the mayor.

Wills (Testaments)

These date back some three hundred years and are in the custody of l'État-Civil.

There are no genealogical organizations in Monaco and it is suggested that initial inquiries by ancestor-hunters of Monégasque descent be sent to the Bureau de l'État-Civil.

THE NETHERLANDS (HOLLAND)

The Low Countries (what is now the Netherlands and Belgium) have had a very checkered history. Because of their strategic position they were almost constantly in a state of war for many centuries. Originally they belonged to the empire of Charlemagne, and later the major part of them came under the control of one of the minor German kings. After 1384 the various provinces were ruled by the Dukes of Burgundy, who acquired them by purchase, blackmail, cession, theft, and marriage (just normal real estate transactions in the Middles Ages)! In 1548 they passed by marriage into the ownership of Spain.

From 1568 to 1648 there was a succession of rebellions in the northern provinces (what is now called the Netherlands), and these were followed by similar revolts in the southern provinces (now Belgium). In 1581 the northern provinces proclaimed their independence and William of Orange became the Statthalter. Spain did not recognize this independence until the Treaty of Westphalia in 1648. From 1810 to 1814 the Netherlands were incorporated into France by Napoleon. In 1815, at the Congress of Vienna, the Netherlands and Belgium (now known as the Austrian Netherlands) were united in one country. In 1831 Belgium seceded and became an independent country.

In view of the constant turbulence in the area over the centuries, it is surprising that genealogical records exist at all. However, they do, and they are well organized and easily accessible. The major drawback to ancestor-hunting in the Netherlands is that there is no central registration of births, marriages, and deaths. Civil registration was started by the French in 1811 and each of the approximately one thousand municipalities kept its own records. From 1811 to 1892 duplicate records were kept in the various provincial archives, but these are not indexed, and so, without knowledge of the city, town, or village from which your ancestor came, it is almost impossible to trace him or her. To make matters worse, before the nineteenth century, births, marriages, and deaths were registered according to religion. So even if you know the exact place, you will still have to check the records of each church unless you are sure about the original religion of your family.

Fifty percent of the inhabitants were Catholic; the remainder were Protestant, divided among Evangelical Lutheran, Restored Evangelical Lutheran, and Netherlands Dutch Reformed (Nederlandse Hervormde Kerk).

Other sects (Mennonite, Huguenot, Walloon) will be considered later in this chapter. Regardless of your family religion, you will be searching the registers of the Dutch Reformed Church, because from 1588 to 1795 it was the official state church, and non-members had to marry in that church, or before a magistrate, as well as in their own churches. So the marriages of Catholics, Jews, and all other religions and sects will be found in the Reformed Church registers.

Archives

The archives in the Netherlands are as follows:

National Archives (Algemeen Rijksarchief)

Algemeen Rijksarchief
Prins Willem-Alexanderhof 20-30
2595 BE The Hague ('s-Gravenhage)

Provincial Archives (Rijksarchief)

DRENTHE	Brink 4, Postbus 595
	9400 AN Assen
FLEVOLAND	See Overijssel below
FRIESLAND	Boterhoch 3, Postbus 97
	8900 AB Leeuwarden
GELDERLAND	Markt 1
	6811 CG Arnhem
GRONINGEN	St. Jansstraat 2
	9712 JN Groningen
LIMBURG	St. Pietersstraat 7
	6200 AV Maastricht
NOORD-BRABANT	Waterstraat 20
	5211 JD 's-Hertogenbosch
NOORD-HOLLAND	Kleine Houtweg 18
	2012 CH Haarlem
OVERIJSSEL	Eikarstraat 20, Postbus 1227
	8001 BE Zwolle

UTRECHT	Alexander Numankade 201
	3572 KW Utrecht
ZEELAND	St. Pietersstraat 38
	4311 EW Middelburg
ZUID-HOLLAND	Bleyenburg 7, Postbus 90520
	2509 LM The Hague

In addition to the above archives there is also the Central Bureau for Genealogy (Centraal Bureau voor Genealogie), Postbus 11755, 2502 AT The Hague. This is not exactly an archive, nor is it exactly a genealogical organization. It is a superb combination of both. There will be more about this helpful organization later.

Generally speaking, the National Archives contain records from the whole country, while the provincial archives contain the records of the particular province, plus many records deposited by local municipalities because of lack of local storage space.

The city or municipal archives (Stadsarchief or Gemeentearchief) hold local records from either a city or a municipality. Bear in mind that the latter (Gemeente) can be a city, or it can be a district covering a city and its surrounding villages, or it can be a large district that may include twenty or thirty villages. There are also regional archives (Streekarchieven), which have been established by a group of several municipalities working together to save costs. In addition to the archives there are, of course, city or municipal registry offices (Stads- or Gemeentesecretarie) and city and town halls (Stadhuis and Gemeentehuis) which may contain civil registration. After all this, I must also tell you that there are church archives, which may contain church registers that have not been lodged with the various provincial archives.

Unfortunately, there is no infallible central listing of all archives, and I can only advise you to tread with care through this Low Country morass. If you inquire about a particular record in one archive and are told it does not exist, don't take that as the final answer. Check with another archive—municipal, regional, provincial, or national. Of course, you should also seek guidance from one of the genealogical organizations, or the Central Bureau (see below), or your nearest LDS family history center.

The Central Bureau for Genealogy
The Central Bureau for Genealogy was established in 1945 under government supervision. The original collections included many documents acquired by the government, including a collection of 66,000 surnames from 1795 to 1932 of the Fund for Biographical Documentation (Fonds voor Biografische Documentatie); the genealogical manuscripts of the Associa-

tion for Genealogy (Verbond voor Sibbekunde); and the collection of identity cards of the Office of National Security (Bureau voor Nationale Veiligheid).

After 1945 the bureau acquired a number of private genealogical collections, and the government donated the identity cards of people dying after 1938. The bureau also acquired many microfilms of church registers.

The bureau now has all the genealogical collections in the Netherlands *except* those of the Royal Dutch Society for Genealogy and Heraldry (Koninklijk Nederlandsch Genootschap voor Geslacht-en Wapenkunde), and the Dutch Genealogical Society (Nederlandse Genealogische Vereniging). However, the directorate of the bureau does include representatives of the two societies just mentioned, and it is probable that a full merger will eventually take place. The bureau is eighty percent state-financed, the remainder being made up by donations and membership fees. It deals with over 7,500 queries a year, so if you write, please don't expect a quick answer! They are very efficient and helpful, but the staff is limited and you must have patience. Briefly, here is a rundown of the holdings of the bureau:

Library
This contains nearly everything written in Dutch or in other languages about Dutch families—personal papers, obituaries, military lists, telephone books, local and family histories, and inventories of government archives.

Heraldry
There is an index of families entitled to a coat of arms, and if you wish to register a new one for your family it can be arranged for a fee.

Publications
The bureau has a number of publications, mostly in Dutch, of course, but some in English.

The Gelderland Marriages
This is a list of all marriages entered in the registers of the Calvinist churches in this province. It is indexed under the names of both bride and groom.

Military Marriages
These contain details of marriages of military men in the garrison towns of most of the provinces.

Walloon Card Index
This contains over a million cards reproduced on microfiche giving abstracts from baptism, marriage, and burial registers of Walloon churches in the Netherlands, plus a number from Belgium, France, and Germany.

Manuscript Collections

These are donated or acquired by purchase and list 60,000 surnames, including many family trees. They are indexed.

Advertisements

This collection includes several million announcements of births, marriages, and deaths from newspapers dating back to 1795.

Church Registers

Nearly all of these are on microfilm in the bureau.

Civil Registration

This started in most of the Netherlands in 1811 and some of the records are open for public inspection in the bureau.

Red Cross Collections

A card index file is here with the names of people who died and were buried in Germany and other countries during the Second World War, including those in slave labor and concentration camps.

Emigrants Lists

There are some records on cards and computer printouts but, of course, only a fraction of the total number.

Identity Cards

In 1938 a new system was introduced for the Netherlands. Every inhabitant was issued with a card that has the first and family names, date and place of birth, religion, occupation, names of parents and their dates and places of birth, date and place of the card-holder's marriage (when it occurs), name of the husband or wife with date and place of birth, and in the event of divorce, date, place, and reason. It also gives the names, addresses, and dates and places of birth of the children of the card-holder. If a person leaves the Netherlands permanently, the card must be sent to the Central Population Register and it is kept there. If the card-holder moves within the country, his or her card is sent to the new municipality to be recorded and returned to the holder. A copy is kept in the original municipality.

If a person dies, his or her card is sent to the Central Bureau of Statistics. Once a year all the cards of deceased persons are sent to the Central Bureau for Genealogy, where they are retained and indexed. This means that the bureau has a complete card index of all persons who have died in the Netherlands since 1939. The cards are arranged alphabetically for the whole country and the information on a card can cover quite a period of time. For example, if a man died in 1940, aged 80, his card would give the birth dates of his parents, and this could mean information for the period from 1820 to 1940.

The cards are not available for public inspection but a copy will be issued for a fee. Here is one way in which these records can be useful. Let us suppose you know that your father came from the Netherlands but you don't know the place. However, you know he left a brother behind who died in 1940 in Haarlem and you know his name. By obtaining a copy of his card you will know where he was born (and probably where your father was born, too) and, even more important, you will have the names of his parents and details of their marriage!

Now let us talk about genealogical records in the Netherlands in more detail, leaving the most important ones, the church registers, to the end; they are a little complicated, and I would like to talk to you about them after we have solved some other record problems.

Emigration Records

The story of passenger lists is the same in the Netherlands as in almost all countries: the records were destroyed. Some more recent emigrants from Rotterdam are recorded in the existing lists of various shipping companies in that port city but only from about 1914. If you can find details among your family papers of the name of the ship on which your emigrant ancestor sailed, or at least the name of the company, you may find information about him.

The government kept Emigration Registers (Emigratieregisters) from 1847 to 1878 and these are in the central and provincial archives. For these, of course, you need to know the province of residence of your ancestor. The lists give names, ages, occupations, religion, financial state, number of children, name of ship, destination, and date of departure.

From 1875 to 1934 there were similar lists kept and these are in the city archives (Stadsarchief) of Amsterdam and Harlingen.

Population Registers (Bevolkingsregisters)

These started in 1810 and are still maintained. Up until 1850 these records were kept in some localities and not in others. Check with the appropriate provincial archive as to the existence of registers for the 1810–50 period in your area of interest. The registers, like a census, are rechecked at ten-year intervals. You will find the names, ages, religion, relationship, occupation, former residences, and date of arrival in the locality, plus name of previous town or village. You will find copies for a particular area in the local archives as well as in the provincial ones.

Civil Registration (Burgerlijke Stand)

This started in a few places in 1795 but became nationwide only in 1811. Up until about 1900 you will find the registers in the provincial archives, and since then in local registry offices or district courthouses. The registers include rather more items than you will find in similar records in this country.

Because the French introduced the system, the early entries, up to about 1815, are in French. The original system of recording vital events has hardly changed over the years. The entries are in duplicate, both signed by the registrar, the informant, and two witnesses. One copy is kept by the registrar of the city or other municipality and the duplicate is sent to the county court. These duplicates, bound in a volume for each year, are then deposited in the provincial archives. Up to 1892 they are public property and information from them is given quite easily. Every register has an alphabetical index, and for every ten-year period there is an alphabetical index for each municipality.

In the same department of the archives are all the original documents submitted when a marriage was recorded: copies of birth or baptism records, death records of parents, death record of any earlier husband or wife, and details of the groom's army service.

For the period after 1892 the records may not be inspected, but a copy can be obtained by written application and payment of a fee to the local registrar in each municipality (Ambtenaar van de Burgerlijke Stand). Be sure you ask for a full copy and then you will get all the information on the original registration documents. Otherwise an abridged version will be sent to you.

If you want information about a living person, you will have difficulty in obtaining it. This restriction, of course, is a justifiable one designed to protect the privacy of the individual. Imagine if you had quietly shed a few years off your admitted age and then a friend (or enemy) could get a copy of your birth certificate and confront you with it! On the other hand, if the information was needed to prove your right to an inheritance, or to enable an elderly person to be given a pension, a letter of application from a lawyer will either produce a copy of the original certificate or an official letter providing the equivalent information.

Quite apart from the usual records of births, marriages, and deaths, plus names and addresses of parents, witnesses, and so on, you will also find more arcane records in connection with the custom of marriage. For example:

Marriage Intentions and Proclamations (Aankondigiging and Huwelijksaf)

These were in use from 1811–1935 and give personal details about the bride and groom.

Marriage Consents (Huwelijkstoestemming)

These include the above details but also the details of the parents or guardians on both sides and the date of their consent to the marriage. The records started in 1913 and are still in use today.

Marriage Supplements (Huwelijksbijlagen)

These records (dating from 1811) are important if you know the marriage date and place but nothing about birth date or parents. They include birth records of both spouses, and in some cases names of grandparents and great-grandparents. They may also include death dates of parents. These records are not indexed but are in chronological order.

Divorces (Echtscheidingen)

These started in 1811 and are only recorded in the municipality where the marriage took place.

Indexes

There are indexes to the registers of births, marriages, divorces, and deaths. In the early years after 1811 various methods of indexing were tried, both alphabetical and chronological. Sometimes the indexing was exact to the second letter of the family name, sometimes only within each letter and in no other order, so that the B names, for example, could be Br, Ba, Bl, Bo, Be. In the northern provinces, where patronymics (naming after the father's first name) were used, the births and deaths are entered in sequence of first names, followed by patronymics in alphabetical order, then the first and family names of the parents.

Census Records (Volkstellingen)

Some of the earliest censuses date back to 1580, and from then to 1829 they were taken in various parts of the country at various times in various ways. All these early local censuses can be found in local archives, with some duplicates in the provincial archives. After 1829 they were national in scope but only until 1850, when the population registers commenced. Since then a number of the bigger towns have held local censuses at irregular intervals and these are in local archives.

Military Records (Militaire Registers)

These can also be found in all the different levels of archives—except, of course, that those in local archives only refer to that particular area. In 1795 a national militia was established and service in it is still required. Full personal details, including next of kin, are included.

Other military records commence in about 1700 and include length of service, personal descriptions, wounds, location of service, character references, and date of discharge.

Civil Marriages and Divorces (Burgerlijke Huwelijken-Echtscheidingen)

These registers date from 1575 to 1811 and are located in all the different levels of archives. They contain details of the marriages of people who were not members of the Netherlands or French Reformed Churches, and include dates of intention, publication of banns, names of former husband or wife, and names, dates of birth, and addresses. Before 1795 civil marriages were not permitted in the provinces of Groningen, Drenthe, and Friesland; in the latter province, the district court was required to grant permission before the marriage could be performed in a Reformed Church, if one or both parties were not church members.

The College of Law (College van de Wet) had the authority to dissolve civil and church marriages and the decisions are recorded in the Keur Boeken (church books), along with details of the names and ages of any children, and the causes of the divorce. These records are in the various archives and in the Central Bureau for Genealogy.

Notarial Records (Notariële Protocollen)
These date from as far back as 1530. They include wills and codicils, marriage contracts and settlements, divisions of estates, deeds, contracts, mortgages, appointments of guardians, letters of apprenticeship, and civil-court notes and documents. They are partially indexed from 1803 and are in all archives and municipal registry offices.

Tax Rolls and Registers (Belasting Registers)
As you can imagine, these records date back into the mists of time, tax collecting being the second-oldest profession! The registers start, in fact, in 1240 and continue without a break until the present. They are located in all types of archives and cover all kinds of taxes: national and local taxes, head taxes, poll taxes, land taxes, water taxes, trade taxes, and so on. They generally give individual names and addresses, occupations, valuations, and tax assessments. Where inheritance or transfer of property is involved, they may be of great genealogical value.

Guild Records (Gilde Registers)
These date back to 1578 and can be a great source of information. If any of your ancestors were craftsmen in one of the cities, they would have to join a guild in order to set up in business. For example, if your ancestor had served his apprenticeship as a diamond-cutter in Amsterdam, he could not start his own business without applying to join the guild. He would have to produce evidence of his successful apprenticeship, a letter of reference from the master cutter to whom he had been apprenticed, a letter of reference from the priest or minister of his church, other character references from well-known people, evidence of his financial stability, details of his parentage and of his wife and children (if any), and possibly, an offer of employment from a craftsman aware of his ability. All such items are in the guild records in the provincial or city archives.

The guild was all-powerful, and unless the craftsman was accepted for membership he could never be in business for himself. The organization was the closed-shop trade union of the Middle Ages, and its power lasted until the early part of the nineteenth century.

Citizen Books (Burgerboeken)

It was not sufficient to be an inhabitant of a city if you wished to succeed in life, or even to join a guild. You had to be accepted as a citizen, and for this you needed the highest references, both civil and ecclesiastical, and to be financially secure. The records of those granted citizenship in the cities cover the period from 1240 to 1811. The records are in the provincial and municipal archives.

Land Registers (Land Registers)

These are in the archives at all levels and cover the period from 1200 to the present. They give full details of transactions involving land: the buyers and sellers, the lessors and lessees, together with names, addresses, and payments made.

Many of the records I have mentioned in this chapter as being in the various archives are indexed, or are in the process of being indexed. Any information I gave you on this score would be out-of-date by publication day.

So much for all the miscellaneous records in the Netherlands. Now for the church registers. There are a large number of different sects and religions that have developed and faded away over the years, but since many of them were either short-lived or of very minor importance, we will concentrate on the three major denominations: Catholic, Dutch Reformed, and Evangelical Lutheran. The Dutch Reformed Church records are the most valuable because for a period they also included the vital events of other religions not recognized by the state.

Catholic Church (Katholiek Kerk)

As in other European countries, the Catholic Church was the only recognized religion until the Reformation started in 1517. The Netherlands came under its influence and Protestantism developed, particularly in the northern provinces. In 1548 the country came under the rule of Spain and the King attempted to eradicate Protestantism. In 1568 a rebellion against Spanish rule broke out, but Spain quickly subdued the southern provinces, which were, generally speaking, Catholic. The northern provinces continued their resistance, uniting in 1579. Two years later they formed the Republic of the United Netherlands.

A few years earlier the cities of the Netherlands had closed their gates against Spanish troops and confiscated the properties of the Catholic Church, which were then given to the Calvinists (later named the Dutch Reformed Church). Mass was not celebrated in public for twenty years, nor were baptisms or marriages performed by Catholic priests. In 1648 the independence of the northern provinces was accepted by Spain and the Dutch Reformed Church became the state religion. The Reformed Church was quite tolerant toward the Catholics; the civil laws against them were abolished and the mass could again be read. Catholic church registers and records in the north date from this year. In the south, still controlled by Spain, the Catholic records are nearly complete from about 1580.

In the early eighteenth century a split occurred in the Catholic Church and by 1724 the Old Catholic Church was well established in fifty-one parishes in the provinces of Utrecht and Holland. If you are interested in that area and your ancestors were Catholic, remember this split, because it means that the fifty-one parishes still hold all records of the Catholic Church before the division of the church.

In 1853 the Catholic Church was officially re-established in the Netherlands with all its original rights and privileges. At the present time the Netherlands are about equally divided between Catholics and Protestants.

The earliest Catholic records (the documents of the Bishop of Utrecht) date back to 723. Apart from the registers, the churches have confirmation and communion records, and records of graves, of payments for bell-tolling, of donations to priests, and of the provision of mort-cloths for burial.

It was the Council of Trent (1545–63) that ordered the Catholic priests throughout the world to record baptisms, marriages, and burials, but very few registers in the Netherlands date back to that time. Deventer has some dated 1542, Utrecht 1559, and Amsterdam 1564, to name a few.

The entries in the registers were mostly in Latin. Before 1775 it was only the date of baptism and not of birth that was recorded. The children-naming pattern in common usage up until the latter part of the last century was that the first two boys were named after the grandfathers, the first two girls after the grandmothers, and the next boy and girl after the father and mother.

Confirmations

These usually took place between the ages of seven and nineteen and the lists date back in some places to 1542. The names of the child and parents, the places of birth and residence, and the names of witnesses were included.

First Communion Lists (Neocommunicaites)

This event took place between the ages of seven and eight and these lists contain the same personal details as for confirmations.

Marriage Records (Huwelijksregisters)

The laws of 1571–78 allowed marriages to be performed in the Dutch Reformed Church, and in 1584 a law gave non-Catholics a choice of either the Dutch Reformed Church or a civil marriage before an alderman or a sheriff. In 1795 it was ordained that only civil marriages could be performed, but the marriage could be blessed afterwards in a church. All these changes and variations are important for you to understand if your ancestors were Catholic, because you may find the record of their marriage in a Dutch Reformed Church or in the local municipal office.

Since 1811 civil registration of marriage has been compulsory, but the Catholic Church continues to record vital events. These records often give you an extra check on accuracy of the civil records. The early Catholic registers are nearly all in the provincial archives, but some originals and many duplicates are in the individual churches, or in various Catholic Archives:

ARCHBISHOP OF UTRECHT: Utrecht

BISHOP OF BREDA: Veemarktstraat 48
4811 ZH Breda

BISHOP OF GRONINGEN: Markstraat 9
9712 BP Groningen

BISHOP OF HAARLEM: Nieuwe Gracht 80
2011 NJ Haarlem

BISHOP OF 'S-HERTOGENBOSCH: Postbus 1070
5200 BC 's-Hertogenbosch

BISHOP OF ROERMOND: Paredisstraat 10
6041 JW Roermond

BISHOP OF ROTTERDAM: Koningin Emmaplein 3–4
3016 AA Rotterdam

The Archives of the Dutch Reformed Church (Carnegielaan 9, 2502 LS The Hague) also has some details of Catholic records.

It should also be noted that various laws against the Catholic Church resulted in variations in record-keeping in two provinces:

Overijssel. Anti-Catholic laws did not apply in the town of Twenthe (under Spanish control) from 1580 to 1630. Also, in the years 1625–48 all baptisms had to take place in a Dutch Reformed church.

Noord-Brabant. Because of several wars in the province in the sixteenth and seventeenth centuries, many people in Brabant had their children baptized in 's-Hertogenbosch. In addition, from 1609 to 1621, for the same reason, many children were taken to Antwerp, in Belgium, for baptism.

From 1625 to 1648 Catholics were banned, and although baptisms and marriages were often performed in secret by a priest, no records exist.

Early records in Catholic churches were in Latin. I give below some words you will come across in the registers in Latin, English, and Dutch:

Latin	English	Dutch
Acatholicus	Non-Catholic	Niet-Katholiek
Aetas	Age	Ouderdom
Amita	Aunt on father's side	Tante van vader's zijde
An, anno	Year	Jaar
Arbiter	Witness	Getuige
Avia	Grandmother	Grootmoeder
Avunculus	Uncle on mother's side	Oom van moeder's zijde
Baptisatus	Baptism	Gedoopt
Caelebs	Bachelor	Vrijgezel
Cippus	Gravestone	Grafsteen
Coelebs	Single	Vrijgezel
Compater	Godfather	Peetoom
Conjux	Spouse	Echtgenoot, echtgenote
Copulatio	Marriage	Trouwen
Cuis suspectories	Godparents	Peetouders
Defunctus	Dead	Gestorven
Dununciatio	Banns	Huwelijks- afkondigingen
Domus	House	Huis
Filia	Daughter	Dochter
Filius	Son	Zoon
Frater	Brother	Broeder
Genitores	Parents	Ouders
Germana	Sister	Zuster
Germanus	Brother	Broeder
Illegitimus	Illegitimate	Buitenechtelijk
Levans	Godfather	Peetvader
Ligatus	Husband	Echtgenoot
Marita	Wife	Echtgenote
Mater	Mother	Moeder
Matrina	Godmother	Peetmoeder
Mors	Death	Dood
Novercus	Stepfather	Stiefvader
Noverca	Stepmother	Stiefmoeder

Latin	English	Dutch
Orbus	Orphan	Weeskind
Pater	Father	Vader
Patruus	Uncle on father's side	Oom van vader's zijde
Pontificius	Catholic	Katholiek
Puer	Son	Zoon
Puera	Daughter	Dochter
Relicta	Widow	Weduwe
Renatus	Baptized	Gedoopt
Sepultus	Buried	Begraven
Sexus	Sex	Geslacht
Soror	Sister	Zuster
Testes	Witnesses	Getuigen
Vedovus	Widower	Weduwnaar
Vidua	Widow	Weduwe
Virgo	Maiden	Meisje
Xped	Baptized	Gedoopt

The Dutch Reformed Church (Nederlandse Hervormde Kerk)

As mentioned above, the records and registers of this church are important to members of other churches too, because over various periods Catholics, Jews, Mennonites, and so on, were compelled to have their children baptized and married in a Dutch Reformed Church. These mainly anti-Catholic laws affected periods in the sixteenth and early seventeenth centuries.

The registers of the Dutch Reformed Church began at different times in the various provinces. You will recall that the Protestant provinces were the seven northern ones and the approximate starting date for records was: Holland (1573), Zeeland (1578), Groningen (1580), Utrecht (1583), Gelderland (1587), Friesland (1590), Overijssel (1638).

However, having given you these dates, I must also tell you that in very many places the starting date was much later, even a century later. Once the registers did start, the baptism and marriage entries are accurate and quite comprehensive in their information, with two exceptions: first, in the baptismal registers the name of the mother is not always given, and, second, in the big cities there are many gaps in the burial records. These were caused by the frequent epidemics of the plague and the heavy death toll. The ministers of the church were just too busy with burials to spend time making entries in the registers.

If your ancestors came from Zeeland you may run into some additional difficulties because the provincial archives were destroyed during the Second World War and many church registers were lost. Fortunately, some duplicates did exist, and you should check with the Rijksarchief in Zeeland for more detailed information.

Baptisms

As mentioned, the early entries (before 1792) did not always give the date of birth. You will find great variation in the spelling of surnames and even first names owing to the changes in ministers and their inability to spell. If you are in doubt as to whether, for example, Klaas van der Kist who had a son Henrick is the same man as the Claes van Derkes who had a son Cornelis two years later, you should check the names of the witnesses or sponsors at both baptisms. They were nearly always close relatives, and if the same names appear in both entries you may be certain that the same father is concerned in the two baptisms. Of course, you will also get variations in the spelling of the witnesses' names, but let's not get into that as well!

Marriages

Remember that civil marriages have been permitted since 1584, and if your ancestor was marrying a member of another denomination, or of no denomination at all, the marriage may well have been a civil one in the local town hall. It may, or may not, have been blessed in the Dutch Reformed Church after the civil ceremony. The only exception to this permission to hold civil marriages appears to have been in the small town of Bommenede, in Zeeland. The marriage records also include the Intentions to Marry, and these announcements were usually made from the pulpit for three successive Sundays before the ceremony, and afterward a note was made in the registers.

Burials

These records gave date and, often, the cause of death. They also show whether the burial took place in a family vault within the church, or in the churchyard outside.

Although civil registration has existed since 1811, the Dutch Reformed Church has continued to enter vital events in its registers. (The headquarters of the church is Nederlandse Hervormde Kerk, Carnegielaan 9, 2502 LS The Hague.)

Evangelical Lutheran and Restored Evangelical Lutheran

These two churches, which split in 1791 and became whole again in 1952, form only a small part of the religions of the Netherlands. However, the Lutheran movement was powerful and influential far beyond its small membership. Many of the Dutch Reformed Church members showed interest in the doctrines and eventually transferred their allegiance. For that reason, if you are of Dutch Protestant stock you should know about the Lutheran movement and its records.

The Lutherans, then mostly of German and Scandinavian origin, established their first church in Amsterdam in 1633 and the faith spread quickly into the other main cities and towns. By the end of the century there were thirty-four churches in the Netherlands, all in urban areas.

As in nearly all Protestant religions that came into being after the Reformation, there were disputes over doctrine and many splits and schisms. Probably the very strong characters of the early Protestant dissenters led to the fierce arguments that spawned the many different sects. In 1791 a breakaway group founded the Restored Evangelical Lutheran Church Society, and congregations in Enkhuizen, Gorinchem, Harlingen, Hoorn, Medemblik, and Zwolle joined the new church. The schism continued, as I mentioned above, to as recently as 1952.

Lutheran ministers were allowed to perform marriages in the province of Holland, but in Zeeland Lutheran marriages had to be solemnized in the Dutch Reformed churches. In Gelderland and Utrecht they could have civil marriages. In Overijssel the Lutherans were totally banned until 1653. After that date they were tolerated and could either have civil marriages or be wed in the Dutch Reformed Church. Lutherans in Groningen province also had this choice until 1735, but after that they could be married in their own church.

Generally speaking, the Lutherans were treated by the Dutch Reformed Church as misguided friends, whereas the Catholics were the enemy. Certainly they did not operate under major restrictions or difficulties for very long, and by the early eighteenth century their ministers were officiating at Lutheran baptisms, marriages, and burials.

The Lutheran records are basically the same as those of the other two religions we talked about. The entries in the early dates were usually in German and in either the German or the Dutch script, neither of which is easy to read.

Registers for the following Lutheran parishes are in the various archives (provincial, regional, and municipal). Some are for baptisms, marriages, and burials, while others are for only one or two of these three categories. The starting dates vary considerably. For example, Amsterdam 1590, Delft 1617, Groningen 1695, Leerdam 1737, Vlissingen 1809:

FRIESLAND: Harlingen, Leeuwarden.

GELDERLAND: Arnhem, Culemborg, Doesburg, Doetinchem, Nijmegen, Zutphen.

GRONINGEN: Groningen, Nieuwe Pekela, Sappemeer (Hoogezand-Sappemeer), Wildervank, Winschoten, Winschoterzijl.

LIMBURG: Maastricht, Vaals.

NOORD-BRABANT: Bergen op Zoom, Breda, 's-Hertogenbosch.

NOORD-HOLLAND: Alkmaar, Amsterdam, Beverwijk, Edam, Enkhuizen, Haarlem, Hoorn, Medemblik, Monnikendam, Naarden, Purmerend, De Rijp, Weesp, West-Zaandam, Zaandijk.

OVERIJSSEL: Deventer, Kampen, Zwolle.

UTRECHT: Amersfoort, Utrecht.

ZEELAND: Middelburg (destroyed 1940), Vlissingen, Zierikzee. The latter two are in the National Archives (Rijksarchief).

ZUID-HOLLAND: Bodegraven, Delft, Dordrecht, Gorinchem, Gouda, 's-Gravenhage, Hellevoetsluis, Leerdam, Leiden, Rotterdam, Schiedam, Woerden.

Finally, the headquarters of the Evangelical Lutheran Church is Amsterdamseweg 311, 1182 HA Amstelveen.

Genealogical Organizations

By far the most important and valuable after the Central Bureau described earlier is the following:

Nederlandse Genealogische Vereniging
Postbus 976
1000 AZ, Amsterdam

It has over 5,500 members and is the second-largest genealogical organization in Europe. Staffed entirely by volunteers, it does not undertake research but will send you a list of members willing to do work for you for an agreed fee. If you become a member yourself, you will receive a monthly magazine (in Dutch) and will be able, when you visit the Netherlands, to use the facilities of the Genealogical Center. This is located at Adr. Dortsmanplein 3a, 1411 RC Naarden (about 20 miles southeast of Amsterdam). It contains (1) a large library, (2) a collection of press clippings, (3) a central card-index, and (4) a collection of manuscripts.

Other organizations are listed below:

Koninklijk Nederlandsche Genootschap voor Geslacht-en Wapenkunde
Prins Willem-Alexanderhof 24, 2595 BE The Hague

Sectie voor Geslacht-naam-en wapenkunde van het Prov. Genootschap van Kunsten en Wetenschappen
Maasbandijk 30, Kerkdriel
(Area of interest: North Brabant)

Zuidhollandse Vereniging voor Genealogie
Postbus 404, Rotterdam
(Area of interest: South Holland)

Kommissie voor Westfries Genealogie
Hemmerbuurt 135, Hem
(Area of interest: Friesland)

Gruoninga
Postbus 1127, Groningen
(Area of interest: Province of Groningen)

Genealogysk Wurkforbân de Fryske Akademy
Doelestraat 8, Leeuwarden
(Area of interest: Friesland)

It is possible there are other smaller local organizations, and you should check with either the provincial archives or the local city or town hall.

While the records in the Netherlands are not as good as those in the Scandinavian countries, they are still among the best in Europe. Because of the decentralization of records among the various archives (not only the twelve main ones, but the seventy-five local ones), it will take you longer to track down sources of information. However, the records are there, and you must have the dogged determination of your Netherlands ancestors!

NORWAY

If you have already read the chapters on Denmark and Sweden, you will know most of Norway's history, since the three Scandinavian countries were linked, willingly or unwillingly, over the centuries. If you have not read those chapters, I suggest you do so, because as you get further back in your ancestor-hunting you may well find useful genealogical information in their records as well as in those of Norway itself.

Up until the ninth century the country was divided into a number of petty kingdoms. Then there was a brief period of unity under Harold I, followed by two centuries of Norse raids on the coasts of western Europe and Britain, the establishment of the Norse Duchy of Normandy, and then a long period of civil war. In 1397 the three Scandinavian countries were united under the queen of Denmark. Although Sweden soon withdrew from the union, Norway remained as a part of Denmark until 1814, when it was ceded to Sweden. However, Norway was soon recognized by Sweden as a separate country in personal union with Sweden, and given its own Parliament and constitution. In 1905 Norway declared its complete independence, and this was accepted by Sweden after a plebiscite showed the Norwegians to be overwhelmingly in favor of separation. A son of the king of Denmark was elected king of Norway.

There are two forms of language in use in Norway, both Norwegian, but Bokmål is the book language and Nynorsk the so-called country language. Recent grammar reforms have brought the two languages nearer and there is hope that one language (Samnorsk, or common Norwegian) will eventually emerge. Meanwhile, though you will only encounter Bokmål in books, records, and correspondence, you will undoubtedly encounter Nynorsk if you visit the country. The alphabet of both languages is the same as that used for English, with the addition of three extra letters: æ, ø, and å. The country is divided into eighteen counties (fylker), plus the capital district of Oslo. There are, of course, smaller administrative areas, such as kommuner (townships) and prestegjeld and sokn (parishes).

Before 1919 the counties (fylker) were named "amt." The singular of fylker is fylke. This change of name is important for you as you trace back.

Quite apart from this change of description for a county, you must also know that a number of counties have changed their names. I give below the name of each of the fylker and in parentheses the old name. Where no name appears in parentheses, it means that the county name has not changed:

Akershus

Aust-Agder (Nedenes)

Buskerud

Finnmark

Hedemark

Hordaland (Søndre Bergenhus, including Bergen)

Møre og Romsdal (part of Søndre Trondheim)

Nordland

Nord-Trøndelag (Nordre Trondheim)

Oppland (Christian)

Oslo (Christiania)

Østfold (Smaalenene)

Rogaland (Ryfylke, also Stavanger)

Sogn og Fjordane (Nordre Bergenhus)

Sør-Trøndelag (part of Søndre Trondheim)

Telemark (Bratsberg)

Troms (Tromsø)

Vest-Agder (Lister og Mandal)

Vestfold (Jarlsberg og Larvik)

Archives

The National Archives of Norway are called Riksarkivet and are located at Folke Bernadottes vei 21, Postboks 20, Kingsjå, Oslo. In addition there are six regional archives (Statsarkivet) and one sub-archive (Statsarkivets Kontor i Tromsø):

STATSARKIVET I OSLO

Folke Bernadottes vei 21, Postboks 8

Kingsjå, Oslo

(Covers Østfold, Akershus, Oslo, Buskerud, Vestfold, and Telemark fylker)

STATSARKIVET I HAMAR

Strandgaten 71, 2300 Hamar

(For the fylker of Hedemark and Oppland)

STATSARKIVET I KRISTIANSUND

Vesterveien 4, 4600 Kristiansund S

(For Aust-Agder and Vest-Agder fylker)

STATSARKIVET I STAVANGER
Domkirkeplassen 3, 4000 Stavanger

(For Rogaland fylke)

STATSARKIVET I BERGEN
Årstadveien 22, 5000 Bergen

(For the fylker of Hordaland, including Bergen, and Sogn og Fjordane)

STATSARKIVET I TRONDHEIM
Høgskoleveien 12, 7001 Trondheim

(For the fylker of Møre og Romsdal, Sør-Trøndelag, Nord-Trøndelag, Nordland, Troms, and Finnmark [see below])

STATSARKIVKONTORET I TROMSØ
Petersborggaten 21-29, 9000 Tromsø

(Although the principal records of the Troms and Finnmark fylker come under the control of the Statsarkivet i Trondheim, they are, in fact, kept in Tromsø.)

In Norway, even more than in many countries, it is vital that you do your homework before you start your search. Try to find out what your emigrant ancestor did for a living in the old country, whether he was a farmer or a farmhand, a clerk or a merchant, a watchmaker or a wheelwright. This could affect the type of records you may be searching. Find out his religion and be sure he did not change it after his arrival in his new country. Find out the correct family name; check to see if the spelling was changed in any way. Bear in mind that surnames could come from three different sources: the family, the father, or the farm. When a farmer sold one farm and bought another, he often changed his name from the name of the old farm to that of the new. If he took a farm laborer with him, the latter might change his name too. Family names, as we know them today, only developed four or five generations ago. This did not apply to the nobility or people of prominent families.

You will be helped in overcoming these difficulties in various ways. Church records often joined the name of a family and a farm together with a hyphen; children baptized or confirmed were often described in the same way. Until the early years of this century there was a pattern of naming children that was widely observed, i.e., oldest son after father's father, second son after mother's father, third son after father, and the same with daughters on the female side. After the first three names were used up in this way, the pattern followed the next generation back, that of the great-grandparents.

There is a complication to this naming pattern. Nowadays, if we have a child who dies in infancy, we do not usually use the same first name again for a later child. In earlier days this did not apply. The naming pattern was too rigid to disregard and so you may find, in days of high infant mortality, that a first name would be repeated and repeated until eventually a child survived. So, in a birth register you may find three successive sons named Olav, but if you turn to the death entries you will find out what happened to the first two.

Finally, while we are on the subject of names, remember that a name may have been simplified by your emigrant ancestor to make it more easily understood and spelled in his or her new country.

So far as the place of origin is concerned, it is almost essential you produce this from within your own family records. There are a limited number of Norwegian surnames and no one is going to be able, for example, to tell you the birthplace of Olav Andersen who left Norway for overseas in 1855 except someone within your own family. Even then, make sure it is the name of a place and not a farm. There are a limited number of immigration and emigration records, and also passenger lists, but they are a small percentage of the whole and you should not expect too much of them. Once you know the place, a great many records are open to you.

On this side of the Atlantic there are a number of sources that may either help you to pin down a place of origin or let you know if a history of your family has already been written:

The Norwegian-American Historical Association (St. Olaf College, Northfield, Minnesota 55057) has published a number of books about Norwegian ancestry. If you get a list from the association, you will be able to borrow them through your local library.

The Supreme Lodge of the Sons of Norway (1312 West Lake Street, Minneapolis, Minnesota 55408) also has various publications.

Other sources worth checking are the following:

The University of Minnesota Library, Minneapolis
The Memorial Library of the University of Wisconsin, Madison
The Preus Library, Luther College, Decorah, Iowa
The Library of the Lutheran Theological Seminary, St. Paul, Minnesota

In Norway there are a number of places where you may find local histories for the area in which you are interested, or family histories either already published or in manuscript form about many Norwegian families (and not only the prominent ones):

Universitets Biblioteket i Oslo (University Library), Oslo 2.
Universitets Biblioteket i Bergen, 5000 Bergen.
Videnskabsselskabets Bibliotek, 7000 Trondheim.
Deichmanske Bibliotek, Oslo 1.
Norsk Slektshistorisk Forening (Norwegian Genealogical Society), Postboks 9562, Egertorget, Oslo 1.
Aust-Agder-Arkivet, 4800 Arendal (for Aust-Agder fylke only).

Parish Records

Many localities in Norway have village books (Bygdebøker) that give very detailed information about farms and families in the parish. The Statsarkiv will be able to tell you what is available for your particular area of interest. The genealogical society mentioned above can also put you in touch with any local genealogical organization that may be operating in a particular fylke that is of interest to you.

Church Records

There is no civil registration of births, marriages, and deaths as we know it in this country. The Lutheran Church is charged with the responsibility of recording vital events and it is with the church that you must deal. Since 1903 the Central Bureau of Statistics (Statistisk Sentralbyrå) has kept copies of the entries in the church registers (Kirkebøker), but these are kept for statistical purposes only and are not available for public search.

The church records are transferred to the regional archives (Statsarkivet) eighty years after the recorded event, so that only the last eighty years are in the individual churches. However, in rural districts a duplicate register is maintained by the deacons of the church and sent to the archives as soon as it is completed.

Registers less than sixty years old are not available for public search without special permission from the regional archivist. However, a copy of a specific entry is supplied on application. It may save delay if, when writing, you enclose your proof of descent from the person for whose certificate of baptism, marriage, or burial you are applying. This is unlikely to cause you any problem because you will probably only be interested in register entries older than sixty years, anyway.

The church registers (Kirkebøker) may contain information about confirmations, vaccinations, engagements, maternal introductions (see p. 208), and movements in and out of the parish, depending on the date. The records start about 1700, but some are much earlier and some much later. Andebu, in Vestfold, for example, started in 1623, while Kvam, in Hordaland, began in 1843.

The vast majority of Norwegians are members of the Lutheran Church, which is the state religion, and it was not until 1891 that any recognition was given to any other denomination. Consequently, *all* vital events had to be recorded in the Lutheran registers, even though the parties concerned were nonconformists. In 1891 the latter were allowed to perform marriages in their churches, and in 1896 Unitarians and Jews were included in these provisions. Even so, the events had still to be recorded in the Lutheran registers by the local Lutheran minister. Those with no religion at all had to report the event to a local magistrate, bailiff, or the chief of police, and the official concerned then passed on the information to the Lutheran minister.

Early entries are in Danish (since, as you know, Norway was originally part of Denmark), and written in the Germanic script. This does not make personal searching very easy. The contents of the registers vary over the years according to the church laws. From 1623 to 1735 they included only details of baptisms, marriages, and burials. From 1736 to 1814 they also included intentions to marry (to 1799 only), introductions, and confirmations (these latter took place when the child was at least fourteen). From 1814 to 1876, possibly key years for you, the registers listed arrivals in the parish and departures. They also included all vaccinations. Details of these various records are as follows:

Births

The information in the registers varies; some give the date of birth, some the date of baptism, and some give both dates. Sometimes, too, only the name of the father is given (no one having told the minister the facts of life!). However, if you are lucky you will find the full name of the child, names of both parents, ages, occupations, addresses, and witnesses and their relationship to the child. Sometimes, if a child was sickly at birth and his or her survival was in doubt, the baptism would take place in the home as soon as possible after birth, and the entry was then made in the church register. Usually, the baptism took place on the first or second Sunday following the birth.

Marriages

The records show the names of both parties, their status (if previously married), occupations, addresses, and since 1830, their places of birth and the names of the two fathers, and whether they were alive at the time of the marriage. The engagement or betrothal of the couple was also entered in the church records and an announcement made from the pulpit. This was the equivalent of publishing the banns.

Deaths

The date, place, and cause of death are given, as well as the address, occupation, and full name. Since about 1890 the place of birth is also shown. Often, the name of the survivor (wife or husband) is given, and also that of the person reporting the death.

Confirmations

This record gives name, age, address, names of parents, and since 1814, date of baptism.

Introductions

This referred to the practice of the mother of a child being "introduced" to the congregation at her first appearance in church after the birth, and being formally "cleansed." Her name and that of her husband are given, together with the date of the birth and the date of the introduction.

Arrivals and Removals (Tilgangslister and Avgangslister)

These records can be of tremendous help to you if the minister of the day was conscientious in keeping these records. The period covered was from 1814 to 1876 and listed people arriving in and leaving the parish. The place from which they came and, in the case of departures, their intended destination are shown. Full names, ages, and parish address are also given.

Vaccinations

During the last century great encouragement was given to the vaccination of children, and the ministers were handed the job of urging that it be done, and of recording the event afterward. The name and address of the child is given, and usually the ages and the names of the parents. The period covered is from 1814 to 1876.

The year 1814 is important for church records because from then on greater care was taken in keeping the records, and much more detail appeared.

The nonconformist churches continue to maintain their own registers in the individual churches; a few have been transferred to the regional archives, but only a few. I suppose that because it took so long to get permission to keep their own records they are reluctant to surrender them to anyone else!

Remember that in rural areas the farm where people lived (as either owners or tenants) was nearly always included in the entry in the registers. Be sure you note this, because the information may help you in other areas. For instance, many land, mortgage, and probate records are indexed by farm name and not by a personal name.

Census Returns (Folketellinger)

We are luckier with census records in Norway than in most other countries. Norway started the censuses earlier, they were more widespread, and in many cases there are records that, while not technically census returns, are similar and predate church registers in many instances. Before the official censuses were started, a head-tax list (Manntall) was started in 1664–66. This covered the rural areas and listed men and boys over the age of twelve. Names and ages were recorded. Copies are in the National Archives, as well as regional archives. In 1701 a similar list was compiled and this, too, is in the same archives. Unfortunately the list is missing for the eastern part of the country, except for Rygge, Odal, part of the Larvik district, and six areas of Romerike.

Another early source of "census-like" information is the county and bailiwick accounts (lens og fogedregnskaper) now in the National Archives. These started in the sixteenth century and include tax lists and real estate registers, and may make it easy for you to trace ownership of a particular farm or estate. There are also similar records for the towns called byreg-nskaper, and these, too, are in the National Archives.

The first census to list complete families was that of 1769, but it did not apply to the whole country. Check with the regional archives to find out if they have one for your area of Norway. The 1801 census is very good genealogically as it is complete, in both the National Archives and regional archives, and lists farm names, and name, age, occupation, and marital status of everyone in the house. From 1815 a census was taken every tenth year to 1875, but again was not complete for the whole country. The records are in the National Archives (1865 and 1875 are almost complete), and since the returns listed farm names, personal names, places of birth, occupations, religion, marital status, and in the cities, street names and house numbers, they are well worth checking. Copies for 1865 are in the National Archives and for 1875 in the regional archives. The 1870 and 1885 censuses were for towns only and are in both.

From 1890 a census for the whole country has been taken every ten years. They are in the National Archives and regional archives. Only those before 1900 are open to public inspection, but under special circumstances (e.g., inheritance), information from a later census may be divulged by the National Archivist to a notary.

Probate Registers (Skifteprotokoller)

These show the registration, valuation, and division of real estate and property left by the deceased person, and also give the names and addresses of heirs. The registers started in 1660 and were kept by the probate court in the country districts and by magistrates in the towns. They are now in the regional archives. A program of indexing the registers has been started but it will be many a long year before it is completed. Quite often the information from the register is clearer and more accurate than that in a church register or a census.

Registers of Conveyances and Mortgages (Skjøte og pantebøker)

These registers list real estate transactions, mortgages, liens on property, bills of sale, and contracts. They date from about 1700 or later and are either in the regional archives or in the custody of the local town clerk.

Real Estate Books (Matrikler)

These date from 1665 and are in the National Archives. Many have been printed and indexed. They list the names of owners and tenants of farmland.

Court Records (Justisprotokoller)

Don't be afraid to use these records. It is unlikely that you will find great-great-grandfather was a criminal! The courts are more concerned with civil actions than with criminal cases and you will find references to property, probate, marriage contracts, real estate, and sometimes, very detailed information about a family and its land holdings.

Tax Lists (Skattelister)

As you may imagine, there are a variety of these dating from about 1645. They are in the National Archives and regional archives.

Lists of Emigrants

Your first source of information, as mentioned above, is in the parish records. In addition, since about 1858 the police in many districts have kept lists of emigrants with name, home address, date of sailing, destination, and name of ship. You should not assume that your ancestor sailed from a Norwegian port. He or she may well have sailed from Hamburg, in Germany, and the Hamburg Passenger Lists may be of use to you (see the chapter on Germany). The police lists are in the local police station, but the earliest ones for Oslo, Kristiansund, Bergen, Ålesund, Molde, and Trondheim are in the various regional archives. The regional archives in Oslo have the White Star Line's emigrant lists for 1883–1923. The Stavanger emigrant lists were destroyed in a fire.

Other things to bear in mind about the emigrant lists: the address given by the emigrant may be the place in which he is living temporarily while waiting passage, and not his actual place of birth or domicile. Not many of the lists have been indexed, and you will probably need the help of a professional researcher suggested by the archives to check them for you.

Military Records (Militaerprotokoller)

These date from 1643 up to the present. The muster-rolls, as they are called, are not very reliable for the first fifty years or so, but are very detailed since then. Recent ones are in the various military headquarters, but the earlier ones in which you may be interested are in the National Archives and regional archives. Useful genealogical information can be found, as the records show next of kin, wife and family, and home address. Military service in Norway has been compulsory on various occasions over the years, and so the great majority of males will be listed in these records. Unfortunately there are gaps. Oddly enough, you may be told by the regional archives that the muster-roll for a particular district is missing and later you will find it in the local fylke records, or in a town hall.

Guild Records

If your ancestor was a craftsman belonging to a guild in one of the big cities, you may find out a great deal about him and his family in the local city archives, particularly in Oslo. The trade guilds were the ancient version of the trade unions, except that they were more powerful and, because they represented a skilled craft, more exclusive. The guild records give full details of applicants for membership, their qualifications, where they served an apprenticeship, and their address, children, and marital status. Once a man was accepted into a guild, his success in life was assured, he was protected against competition, and he was looked up to by his friends and neighbors. In short, he had arrived!

Other Records

These include citizenship records, school lists, newspapers, card-index biographies in local libraries, trade indexes, land commissions, and deeds.

As you will now have seen, the records in Norway are exceptionally good, but your success in your search is very dependent on knowing your ancestor's place of origin. When you do know it, write a short letter to the local newspaper (a Norwegian embassy or consulate will give you its name) and ask if there are any relatives of your emigrant ancestor still in the neighborhood. You never know how many distant cousins you will discover and what stories they will be able to tell you about your family history.

There is one fairly new source of information. The Norwegian Historical Date Archives were started by the University of Tromsø in 1981 to computerize eighteenth- and nineteenth-century genealogical material. They can offer information to overseas inquirers who are tracing their Norwegian ancestors. You should write to the Data Arkivet, Universitet i Tromsø, 9001 Tromsø.

POLAND

The country is divided into forty-nine provinces (the equivalent of our counties) and the city-provinces of Warszawa, Łódź, and Kraków. The capital of the country is Warsaw (Warszawa). The present boundaries were established in 1945 after the end of the Second World War and are now recognized by all her neighbors.

It is doubtful that any country in Europe has had such an unfortunate and tragic history as Poland. The combination of geography, the rapacity of its neighbors, and the lack of realism of the Poles themselves has been almost fatal. The area called Poland has varied in size and shape over the centuries. The initial expansion of the country started in the tenth century, and from then on, the Poles fought wars with the Holy Roman Empire, Bohemia, Pomerania, Kiev, Denmark, Hungary, Moldavia, the Ottoman Turks, the Tatars, the Russians, the Austrians, and the Prussians. In addition, there were internal disputes between the Catholic and Greek Orthodox churches, troubles between the kings and the nobles, dynastic changes, and peasant revolts.

The astounding thing is that Poland survived. Poland disappeared from the map of Europe in 1795 and did not reappear until 1918. In 1772, 1793, and 1795 the country was partitioned among Austria, Prussia, and Russia. Rebellions followed (1830–63) in the Russian-held territory where the treatment of the Poles was particularly severe. Only in the Austrian-held area of Galicia were the Poles allowed any kind of autonomy.

In 1919 Poland was reconstituted, but even then some of her eastern areas were lost to the USSR as the result of a short war in 1921. There were also disputes and minor adjustments of some territories with Czechoslovakia and Lithuania. In 1939 a fourth partition took place, the country being divided between Germany and the USSR. In 1945 the areas held by Germany became Polish again but the eastern territories remained in the hands of the USSR. These lands are now divided among Russia, Belarus, and Ukraine.

The destruction of records during the centuries was on an immense scale, and for this reason any genealogical research in Poland is complicated and, in some instances, impossible.

A major complication in ancestor-hunting in Poland is the question of names—both names of families and names of places. Names of families were changed because, after emigration, many people found that their Polish names were virtually unpronounceable to non-Poles, and so Prszybyslawski became Price, and Szawlowski became Shaw. Names of places were altered because during the partition period Polish place-names were changed from Polish to German or Russian and then back again. Thus Olsztyn became Allenstein, and Zielona Gorá became Grünberg. In a further complication when Polish territory was ceded to Czechoslovakia, Troppau became Opava and Leitmeritz became Litoměřice. There is also considerable duplication of place-names in Poland. So, tread carefully, and check and double-check both family names and place-names.

There is also the further complication that the Polish alphabet contains nine more letters than ours and, believe me, full use is made of these extra letters! They are as follows:

ą, ć ę Ɫ, ń, ó, ś, ź, ż

Anyway, try it by yourself and see how it goes. You may find eventually that you need some help from an expert in Polish genealogy.

Archives (Archiwa)

The National Archives are located in Warsaw at the following address:

National Archives
(Naczelna Dyrekcja Archiwów Państwowych)
ul. Dɫuga 6, skrytka pocztowa 1005
00950 Warsaw

There are also other archives of genealogical importance:

Main Archive of Ancient Documents
(Archiwum Gɫówne Akt Dawnych)
ul. Dɫuga 7, 00263 Warsaw

Older historical records are housed here.

Archive of New Documents
(Archiwum Akt Nowych)
ul. Niepodlegɫości 162, 02554 Warsaw

This is the Polish national center for newer historical records.

Archive of the Main Statistical Office
(Archiwum Gɫównego Urzędu Statystycznego)
ul. Niepodlegɫości 208, 00925 Warsaw

Central Military Archive
(Centralne Archiwum Wojskowe)
00910 Warsaw 72

The country is divided into voivods, the equivalent of our counties. They each have archives (some have branches) and a good amount of genealogical research material, but allow for many gaps because of war damage.

These archives are called Archiwa Wojewódzkie and mail should be addressed to Archiwum Państwowe, followed by the postal code and city or town names show below. The cities marked with an asterisk (*) also have subsidiary archives in neighboring locations.

15950 Białystok
85009 Bydgoszcz*
42200 Częstochowa
80958 Gdańsk*
58500 Jelenia Góra
62800 Kalisz
40950 Katowice*
25953 Kielce
75601 Koszalin*
31041 Kraków
64100 Leszno
91415 Łodź
20950 Lublin
34400 Nowy Targ
10074 Olsztyn*
45016 Opole*
97300 Piotrków

09402 Płock
61744 Poznań*
37700 Przemyśl
26600 Radom
35064 Rzeszów
27600 Sandomierz
08100 Siedlce
76200 Słupsk
16400 Suwałki
70410 Szczecin*
87100 Toruń*
00270 Warsaw
50215 Wrocław*
22400 Zamość
66002 Zielona Góra (Stary Kisielin)*
05730 Żyrardów

The archives of the following cities (originally German) are now in Polish archives in the various voivods. The German name is given first and the present Polish name is shown in parentheses. Except for the two cities marked with an asterisk—Pless and Schneidemühl—the Polish name can be found listed in the archives above. The records of Pless (Pszczyna) are in a department (Oddzialy) of the Katowice Archives, and the records of Schneidemühl (Piła) are in a department of the Poznań Archives.

Allenstein (Olsztyn)
Breslau (Wrocław)
Bromberg (Bydgoszcz)
Danzig (Gdańsk)

Grünberg (Zielona Góra)
Kattowitz (Katowice)
Köslin (Koszalin)
Oppeln (Opole)

Pless (Pszczyna)*   Stettin (Szcezcin)
Posen (Poznań)   Thorn (Toruń)
Schneidemühl (Piła)*

Note: Two other cities from the German-held area of Poland are now in the Czech Republic: Leitmeritz (Litoměřice) and Troppau (Opava). In these two cases the German name is shown first and the Czechoslovak name is in parentheses. Mail should be sent to Státní Oblastní Archiv, followed by the street address, and the Czechoslovak place-name:

Státní Oblastí Archiv
Dominikánsky Kláster, Litoměřice

Státní Oblastí Archiv
Semovní ulice 1, Opava

The Polish government is not exactly enthusiastic about giving non-Poles permission to search records in the various archives. They prefer you deal by correspondence with the National Archives or with overseas Polish embassies. However, various archivists have told me that an application to do personal research will be considered if you prove your descent from a particular Polish ancestor and give the names of the archives you wish to visit, together with at least three months' advance notice. I have also been told that the result of your application often depends on whether your ancestor left Poland before or after 1945 (the earlier the better)!

Civil Registration (Akta Stanu Cywilnego)

These records commenced in 1809 and were organized originally by priests or ministers of the various churches. It was officially organized by the state in 1946. Generally speaking, you are likely to find that the pre-1919 records are in municipal offices in the German-held areas, the part originally included in Prussia (Preussen). In the areas occupied by the Austrians and the Russians, the churches maintained the records and in some areas still retain them.

So far as modern records are concerned, a copy of a certificate of birth, marriage, or death may be obtained for a small fee from the local Vital Statistics Office (Urząd Stanu Cywilnego) for the town or village. As for Warsaw (Warszawa), there are two different offices serving two halves of the city. Your application should be made to the above office in either Warszawa-Praga or Warszawa-Śródmieście, depending on the particular area in the city in which your ancestor lived. If you don't know, write to either one, giving the address of the individual and the date of the event. There are also copies in state archives and district courts. If you run into any difficulty, you should write to the Archive of the Main Statistical Office (Archiwum Głównego Urzędu Statystycznego, ul. Niepodległości 208, 00925 Warsaw).

Church Records

Many church records and registers of all denominations have been destroyed over the centuries in wars and revolutions. You may also find the register or record but there will be many pages missing. You may be lucky or you may be completely frustrated—be prepared!

It is impossible to be precise about the location of the registers of the various churches in Poland. Some are in the Main Archive of Ancient Documents, some in the provincial archives, some in church archives, and some still in the original churches. The National Archives cannot always give you the location of a church register. Your best plan is to start at the level of the local church and work up the archival scale from there.

For those registers from what was East Prussia (Ostpreussen), see the chapter on Germany. Most of them were saved.

Bear in mind, too, that after 1808 the various clergymen kept civil registers as well as church registers. They were in Polish and one copy stayed in the town or village and the other went to the nearest civil court, which subsequently passed them on to the Vital Statistics Office. If you find the church registers are missing, these civil records may fill the gap.

Catholic Registers

These start in about 1670 and are scattered in several locations: provincial archives, church archives, parish churches, and in the Vital Statistics Office (since 1850). Generally speaking, Catholic records were kept in Latin until the middle of the last century.

Some of the registers from the eastern territories are in the Main Archive of Ancient Documents (Archiwum Główne Akt Dawnych, ul. Długa 7, 00263 Warsaw) and others (since 1850) in Archiwum Zabuzańskie, Nowy Świat 18/20, Warsaw.

Information about the location of a particular register can be obtained from the church archives listed below—if you know the geographical location of the church in which you are interested. Write to Archiwum Diecezjalne in the appropriate one in the following cities:

15087 Białystok	10020 Olsztyn
42200 Częstochowa	83130 Pelplin
80330 Gdańsk	09900 Płock
62200 Gnieźno	61108 Poznań
40053 Katowice	37700 Przemyśl
25013 Kielce	27600 Sandomierz
31004 Kraków	08110 Siedlce
90458 Łódź	33100 Tarnów
18400 Łomża	00288 Warsaw
37600 Lubaczów	87800 Włocławek
20105 Lublin	50328 Wrocław

Two other sources of information are:

Catholic Church Headquarters (Prymasa Polski)
ul. Miodowa 17, 00246 Warsaw

Catholic University Library (Biblioteka Uniwersytecka)
ul. Chopina 27, 20950 Lublin

Many of the registers of all denominations have been microfilmed by the LDS Church.

Birth Registers (Liber Natorum or Księga Urodzin)
These give names of child, parents, and grandparents, as well as addresses and occupations.

Marriage Registers (Liber Matrimonium or Księga Małżeństw)
These give names, ages, and addresses of bride and groom, names and addresses of parents on both sides, names and addresses of witnesses, and ages and occupations.

Death Registers (Liber Mortuorum or Księga Zmarłych)
These give name, address, and parents; surviving spouse or next of kin; date, place, and cause of death; and all surviving children by name.

Evangelical and Evangelical Reformed Registers (Parafie Ewangelicke)
These started in 1595 and contain the same general information you will find in the Catholic registers. These records are in German.

Eastern Orthodox Registers (Parafie Prawosławne)
These started at the same time and have the same information. These records are usually in Russian.

Tombstone Inscriptions (Nagrobki i Tablice)
These lists or extracts are in churches, public cemeteries, and cemetery administration offices in the larger cities. They started in 1380, and because of the widespread destruction of church registers they may be the most valuable source of information you will have available.

Printed Funeral Sermons (Druki)
For some two and a half centuries from 1650 it was the custom for very effusive funeral orations to be made at the graveside or in the church. Sometimes these were given by the priest or pastor, and often by a close relative or family friend or business associate. Afterwards they were printed and distributed among all the relatives, friends, and associates of the dead.

Allowing the fulsomeness of the language and the archaic principle of never speaking ill of the dead, they were surprisingly accurate. After all, everyone knew the dead man or woman, and there was no way the family could get away with gross exaggerations or downright lies. If the man was known to beat his wife, it could be said he was active in the affairs of his family. If he had fathered several bastard children in the village, this might be over-looked, and emphasis placed on his close and happy relationship with his legitimate children, and the interest he always took in the youth of the area.

Many of these have been collected and indexed and are in local libraries.

Marriage Records (Allegata do Akt Ślubu)

These are now mainly in provincial archives and give details of the family background of the bride and groom, and their financial status. The records started in about 1790 and had been discontinued by 1900.

Notarial Records (Akta Notarialne)

These date from about 1800 and include such items as wills, estate inven-tories, marriage contracts and settlements, wills being contested by rela-tives (often with details of out-of-court settlements), and land transfers and disposals of property. They are in the various provincial archives.

Wills (Testamenty)

There are also details of wills and probate records outside of notarial records. They go back to the fifteenth century and are in provincial or municipal archives.

County Court Documents (Akta Wiejskie)

These cover the period from the late 1400s to the early days of the present century, and are in the provincial archives. Not many have survived, but those that have cover reports of county court decisions in local litigation, often over land boundaries, and may include useful genealogical informa-tion, provided that you know, or can discover, the actual village from which your ancestor came. In that case, by all means try a letter to the appropriate provincial archives.

City Documents (Akta Miejskie)

These will be of value if your ancestor came from a city, although there are documents that have survived in a few other municipal areas. They date from the fourteenth century and contain names and addresses of citizens, property transactions, taxes paid, assessments, wills, estate inventories, and details of family relationships. They are in the provincial archives and some of the earlier ones have been published and indexed.

Guild Records (Akta Cechowe)

These cover the period from the early 1600s to the late 1800s; some are earlier and some are later. If your ancestor was a skilled craftsman working in jewelry, leather, clocks and watches, decorative iron, or a dozen other skilled crafts, he would have belonged to a guild. After his long apprenticeship he would not be able to practice his craft without joining the guild. Their records are reasonably complete and include very full personal details, information about his apprenticeship, and reports about his competence, plus his address, place of origin, and marital status. If he was accepted, he was established for life, because he could be assured of controlled competition, stable prices, generous support in times of illness, and a great deal of social status in his community.

Passports (Akta Paszportowe)

These records started in 1851 and continue to the present. The early records are in the Main Archive of Ancient Documents and those after 1945 are in the Department of Internal Affairs. They give the usual personal information you would expect to find.

Concentration Camp Records (Akta Obozów Koncentracyjnych)

These cover the period 1940–45 and refer particularly to the camps at Auschwitz and Majdanek. The lists include names of prisoners, date and place of birth, name and address of parents, physical appearance, date of entry into the camp, and date of death. The records are in the museums in the two locations (see European Jewish Records, page 23), as well as in the Jewish Historical Institute in Warsaw (Żydowski Instytut Historyczny, ul. Gen. Świerczewskiego 79, Warsaw) and in the custody of the Department of Justice.

Emigration Records

These do not exist in Poland itself, but until 1918 your emigrant ancestor would have been either Austrian, German (Prussian), or Russian so far as jurisdiction was concerned. You should, therefore, read the Austrian and German chapters of this book for information about the emigration records of those countries. It is regretted that specific information is not at present available from Russia, Ukraine, and Belarus.

However, the majority of emigrants from what is now Poland left Europe through the port of Hamburg and good records exist there. Here again, please read the German chapter for detailed information.

University and School Records (Akta Instytucji Oświatowych)

These are located in various places and should certainly be consulted. So far as university lists are concerned these are in the archives of Jagiellonski University at Kraków and date from the early 1400s to the present. They include details of students attending foreign universities as well, and give very complete personal details. Similar information is available about students at secondary schools dating back to the nineteenth century; these records are in the various provincial archives up to 1950, and in the schools since then.

Military Records (Akta Wojskowe)

These date from the fifteenth century and include muster-rolls of regular regiments, local militia, and conscription lists. They are in the Main Archive of Ancient Documents; military records after 1918 are in the Central Military Archives. So far as Austrian-occupied Poland is concerned the Kriegsarchiv in Vienna handed over all its records under the terms of the Peace Treaty of 1919.

Court Records (Akta Instytucji Wymiaru Sprawiedliwości)

Many events were within the jurisdiction of a court of justice besides the usual criminal cases. The courts dealt with wills, estates, marriage contracts and settlements, inheritance, and transfer of property. The early records are fragmented and of doubtful value; the period covered is 1480–1795 and they are in the Main Archive of Ancient Documents.

If your family is descended from the Polish nobility, there are many records of value to you. It is estimated that a century ago ten percent of the Polish population claimed to be of noble birth and that the other ninety percent lived in abject poverty, semi-serfdom, and downright slavery. Since the great majority of people of Polish descent are not connected with the favored few, I will not list every available noble record but only the main ones.

Royal Court Records (Księgi Kancelarii Królewskiej)

If your noble ancestors held some kind of office in the Royal Court, you may find out something about them from these records; they are in the Main Archive of Ancient Documents and cover the period from the mid-1400s up to 1794. They list names, estates, social status, and family relationships.

Estate Employees (Akta Personalne Pracowników)

If your ancestors worked on one of the great estates of the Polish nobility, you will probably find quite a bit of information in these records. They are in the provincial archives, but before writing you must know the correct name of the owner of the estate, its location, the period of employment, and the full name of the ancestor. If you cannot supply this information, don't bother to write.

Genealogical Collection (Kolekcje Genealogiczne)

There has always been an interest in genealogy among people of political and social importance. In the Main Archive of Ancient Documents there is a very large genealogical collection of family trees and family histories, but it is almost entirely concentrated within the narrow ten percent limit mentioned above.

Genealogical Organizations

The Towarzystwo Genealogiczno-Heraldyczne was founded in 1987. It is involved in several research projects, including indexing vital records and compiling bibliographies and inventories of archival sources. Although they do not do research for the public, ancestor-hunters from outside Poland may join the society and receive copies of their quarterly magazine as well as the Genealogical Data Bank, which lists surnames being researched by society members. For more information write to Towaryzstwo Genealogiczno-Heraldyczne, Wodna 27 Pałac Górków, 61781 Poznań.

Land Records (Dokumenty Gruntowe)

These records, many of which are missing or fragmented, are mostly from the areas occupied by Austria and Prussia. Those from the Russian area are not available. They are in the provincial archives and date from 1795 to 1920.

Mortgage Registers (Akta Hipoteczne)

Unusually for European countries, these listings are separate from land records and property transfers. They started in 1808 and ended in 1945 and are located in the provincial archives or district courts. Details are given of all land and property transactions involving a mortgage or a promissory note, and include names, parentage, amount of mortgage and length of term, location of property and addresses of the parties concerned, and actual survey details.

Heraldry

The Poles do have an heraldic organization even if they lack genealogical research into ordinary families. It is the Heraldic Section of the Historical Society of Poland, Rynek Starego Miasta 29/31, Warsaw.

As I mentioned earlier, and as you will now have realized yourself, there are many problems in doing your own research in Poland: the need to understand one, two, or even three languages; the immense destruction of records; the great lack of centralization; the problems with names, name changes, and name duplication; and the general attitude of the authorities. So far as the latter is concerned, you will find that there is no common pattern. Some archivists are as kindly and helpful as you could find anywhere in the world, while others are most reluctant to provide anything beyond one-word answers.

Finally, remember to do your best to have any letters of inquiry translated into Polish (this will increase your chances of success), and be sure to be polite and express your gratitude in advance. The Poles have very good manners and react favorably to the same good manners on your part.

PORTUGAL

The area that is now Portugal was first occupied by a tribe called the Lusitanians in about 1000 B.C. They were followed by other tribes, and eventually by the Romans, who conquered the region in about 200 B.C. Then came the Visigoths and the Moors. In 1140 Portugal declared its independence after a series of successful battles with the Moors. Spain recognized the new country in 1143 and the Pope did the same in 1179. The southern part of the country, the Algarve, remained under the control of the Moors until 1249, when it was retaken by the Portuguese. Portugal has retained its independence from 1140 until the present except for a brief period under Spanish rule from 1580 to 1640. It has the oldest fixed frontiers of any European country.

Portugal, in alliance with Great Britain, fought against Napoleon from 1807 to 1814 and the country was fought over by both sides (so much better than fighting in your own country)! In 1910 the monarchy was abolished and a republic established. In the First World War the country was neutral at first but joined the Allies in 1916. Portugal was again neutral in the Second World War but did provide air and naval bases for the United States and Great Britain.

At one time Portugal had vast colonial possessions in South America (Brazil), Africa (Angola, Mozambique, Guinea, St. Thomas), India (Goa, Daman, and Diu), and Asia (Timor and Macao). Of these, only Macao remains under Portuguese administration. The Atlantic islands of the Azores (Açores) and Madeira have always been regarded as an integral part of Portugal. The great majority of Portuguese emigrants to North America came from these islands.

The country is divided into eighteen administrative districts on the mainland, three in the Azores, and one in Madeira. The districts, which are listed below, are named after the chief town in each district. Each district has its own archives (Arquivos Distritais), which are located in the administrative center. Most of them have their own separate headquarters but some are part of other organizations, and details are given in the following list:

District Archives

District Archives are located in the following administrative districts: Aveiro, Beja, Braga, Bragança, Castelo Branco, Coimbra, Évora, Faro, Guarda, Leiria, Lisboa, Portalegre, Porto, Santarém, Setúbal, Viana do Castelo, Vila Real, and Viseu.

Note: The district archives in Lisboa are part of the National Archives, those at Coimbra are part of the University Museum and Library, and those of Braga and Évora are in the local public libraries.

In addition to the district archives on the mainland there are others in the Azores and Madeira:

AZORES: Angra do Heroismo, Horta, and Ponta Delgada.
MADEIRA: Funchal.

Other Archives

The National Archives are located in Lisbon (Lisboa) at the following address:

The National Archives
(Arquivo Nacional da Torre do Tombo)
Largo de S. Bento, 1200 Lisbon

There are also other archives of interest in Lisbon: the Civil Registration Archives (Conservatórias do Registo Civil); the Property Registration Archives (Conservatórias do Registo Predial); and the National Identification Archives (Centro de Identificação Civil e Criminal).

If you are of noble descent and your family has been granted the right to use a coat of arms, you can obtain much information about your forebears from the Portuguese Institute of Heraldry (Instituto Português de Heráldica, Avenida da República 20, 1000 Lisbon).

Civil Registration (Registo Civil)

This is not centralized, although copies of the registration are on file in the Civil Registration Archives mentioned above. The records are in the various district archives so far as genealogical research is concerned.

Civil registration began officially in 1878 but had been in existence in many areas on an optional basis since 1832. In reality it was used only by non-Catholics, since all Catholics continued to have their vital events recorded in their church registers (Registos Paroquiais). It was only in 1911 that civil registration was made compulsory.

The records are in the local registry offices (Conservatórias do Registo Civil) in each municipality. When they are 100 years old they are transferred to the district archives (Arquivos Distritais) with a copy to the National Archives in Lisbon. Before compulsory civil registration in 1911 the

registration was done by the local priest. After 1911 the records were transferred to the local registry office.

Church Registers (Registos Paroquiais)

These are still in the original churches, but when churches have been closed
or destroyed by fire the registers are sent either to the district archives or to
the National Archives (if they are among the very earliest known records).

In the church registers you will not find, as you will in many countries,
marriage contracts, engagements, communion lists, and confirmations, but
you will find frequent notes about local events, and personal comments by
the local priest about members of his flock. Who knows what you may
discover about your ancestors? Judging by the entries in one of the Coimbra
parishes you may find "a worthy man and a good Catholic, but I cannot say
the same about his wife" or "Baptized his fourth child today—the first one
born in wedlock."

The oldest parish register in existence is that of Nabainhos, near Gouveia,
which started with a baptism in 1529. Other early ones are Sameice (Seia),
Cheleiros (Mafra), Santiago (Torres Novas), Várzea (Alenquer), and Santa
Eulália (Seia). The name in parentheses is that of the commune or municipality. There is reference to the registration of marriages as early as 1390 in
a letter sent to King Alfonso IV. All these very early records are in the
National Archives.

The entries for baptism include the names of parents, grandparents, and
witnesses or godparents (and their relationship to the child). The marriage
entries also contain full details of parents, grandparents, and witnesses.
Burials include the next of kin and all surviving family members.

If you are writing to the parish priest you should also ask if he has a list
of the names appearing on the tombstones (Pedras Tumulares). You may
well find a great deal of new information from this source.

Although the majority of the church registers have survived the centuries,
there were three events that caused great destruction of registers in particular areas:

1. The 1755 earthquake in the area of Lisbon.
2. The French invasions that devastated the provinces of Beira Baixa
   and Ribatejo.
3. The invasion of Alentejo by the Spanish.

In most cases, after these disasters the parish priest persuaded his church
members to give him dates of family events so that to a degree he could
reconstruct the most recent entries. This helped, but it did not, of course,
replace the irreplaceable.

It should be mentioned that because of the close ties between Great

Britain and Portugal and the number of British businessmen resident in the country, there were Church of England churches in Lisbon and Madeira. Registers for the period 1721–1890 are in the custody of the Bishop of London, in England.

Wills (Testamentos)

These date back to the early fifteenth century but of course are only of value to you if your Portuguese ancestors owned land or property of some kind. Wills are kept in the local notarial registry (Cartórios Notarais) and are transferred every thirty years to the district archives.

Passports (Passaportes)

These were first issued in 1757 and continue up to the present. They are in the district archives and list name, date, place of birth, date of the voyage, and destination.

University Records

If your ancestor attended a university, his personal records will be on file. The information dates right back to the fourteenth century and gives names and places of birth up to the early eighteenth century; since then it also includes the names of the parents and grandparents.

Inquisition Records

During the days of the notorious Catholic Inquisition (fifteenth to eighteenth centuries) there were many trials in Lisbon, Coimbra, and Évora. The reports often include very detailed personal biographies of the accused people and they are all in the National Archives.

MADEIRA

The Regional Archives of Madeira (Arquivo Regional da Madeira) are located in the Palácio de S. Pedro, 9000 Funchal, Madeira. However, this archive does not do any genealogical research and only issues certificates of vital events to inquirers providing an exact parish and date. If research is required, you should write to the Bureau of Genealogical Research, Rua da Ponte Nova 42, 9000 Funchal, Madeira.

The archive has no census records, and any inquiries about them should be sent to the Instituto Nacional de Estatistica in Lisbon. Madeira wills date back to the fourteenth century and are all in the archive. All vital records prior to 1860 are located there too, and the registers from 1860 are in the different county Conservatórias do Registo Civil, which are listed later.

Church Registers

The registers of the undermentioned parishes are in the custody of the archives and date from as early as 1539:

Achadas da Cruz, Agua de Pena, Arco da Calheta, Arco de São Jorge, Boaventura, Calheta, Camacha, Câmara de Lobos, Campanário, Canhas, Caniçal, Caniço, Estreito da Calheta, Estreito de Câmara de Lobos, Faial, Fajã da Ovelha, Gaula, Jardim do Mar, Machico, Maria Madalena do Mar, Monte, Paul do Mar, Ponta Delgada, Ponta do Pargo, Ponta do Sol, Porto da Cruz, Porto Santo, Ribeira da Janela, Santa Cruz, Santa Luzia, Santa Maria Maior, Santana, Santo António, Santo António da Serra, São Gonçalo, São Jorge, São Martinho, São Pedro, São Roque, São Vicente, Sé, Seixal, Serra d'Agua, Tábua.

Civil Registers

As mentioned above, registers up to 1860 are in the Conservatórias do Registo Civil and are located in eleven counties; the parishes concerned are listed after the names of the counties:

CALHETA: Arco da Calheta, Calheta, Estreito da Calheta, Fajã da Ovelha, Jardim do Mar, Paul do Mar, Ponta do Pargo, Prazeres.

CAMARA DE LOBOS: Câmara de Lobos, Curral das Freiras, Estreito de Câmara de Lobos.

FUNCHAL: Monte, Santa Luzia, Santa Maria Maior, Santo Antonio, São Gonçalo, São Martinho, São Pedro, São Roque, Sé.

MACHICO: Agua de Pena (part), Caniçal, Machico, Porto da Cruz, Santo António da Serra (part).

PONTA DO SOL: Canhas, Madalena do Mar, Ponta do Sol.

PORTO DO MONIZ: Achadas da Cruz, Porto do Moniz, Ribeira da Janela, Seixal.

PORTO SANTO: Porto Santo.

RIBEIRA BRAVA: Companário, Ribeira Brava, Serra d'Agua, Tábua.

SANTA CRUZ: Agua de Pena (part), Camacha, Caniço, Gaula, Santa Cruz, Santo Antonio da Serra (part).

SANTANA: Arco de São Jorge, Faial, Santana, São Jorge, São Roque.

SÃO VINCENTE: Boaventura, Ponta Delgada, São Vicente.

AZORES (AÇORES)

The Regional Archives of the Azores (Arquivo Regional da Açores) are located in the Palácio Betancourt, Rua Conseilheiro, Angra do Heroismo, Azores.

In view of the large numbers of Portuguese emigrants to North America from the Azores, the records there are of major importance, and it is unfortunate that it is so difficult to obtain information from the archives. You will need patience and a willingness to write several times in order to get an answer to your queries. The LDS Church and the American-Portuguese Genealogical Society have some information, and if you know the name of the particular place in the Azores from which your ancestor came, it will be worthwhile getting in touch with these two organizations.

I set out below the limited information I have been able to obtain. The islands include the districts of Angra do Heroismo, which contains the smaller islands of Terceira, São Jorge, and Graciosa; Horta, which includes Faial, Pico, Flores, and Corvo; and Ponta Delgada, which includes the islands of São Miguel and Santa Maria.

There are district archives in the main town of each of the three districts mentioned above. The main records these archives hold are the following:

Passport Records

Angra do Heroismo: 1775–1818, 1844–45, 1857–1924.
Horta: 1836–39, 1856 to date.
Ponta Delgada: 1836–39, 1856 to date.

Passenger Lists

These are available from 1841 to 1929 and are in the regional archives in Angra do Heroismo.

Parish Registers

These date back to the seventeenth century and in some cases to the sixteenth. They are located in the three district archives and certified copies can be obtained for a small fee. You must supply an approximate date and place, as the archival staff will not undertake protracted searches. In such cases you will be referred to a local researcher.

It has not been possible to obtain detailed information about the parish registers of Angra do Heroismo and Ponta Delgada, but the starting dates of the Horta registers are listed below:

FAIAL: Angústias, 1666; Capelo, 1680; Castelo Branco, 1706; Cedros, 1629; Conceição, 1705; Feteira, 1752; Flamengos, 1661; Matriz, 1655; Pedro Miguel, 1657; Praia do Almoxarife, 1703; Praia do Norte, 1840; Ribeirinha, 1643; Salão, 1728.

PICO: Bandeiras, 1850; Calheta do Nesquim, 1746; Candelária, 1636; Criacao Velha, 1801; Lajes do Pico, 1733; Madalena, 1664; Piedade, 1699; Praínha, 1664; Ribeiras, 1697; Santa Luzia, 1666; Santo Amaro, 1673; Santo António, 1815; São Caetano (missing); São João, 1711; São Mateus, 1673; São Roque, 1582.

FLORES: Caveira, 1860; Cedros, 1860; Fajã Grande, 1861*; Fajãzinha, 1860*; Fazenda (missing); Lajedo, 1860*; Lajes das Flores, 1860*; Lomba, 1862; Mosteiro, 1861*: Ponta Delgada, 1860; Santa Cruz, 1860.
CORVO: Corvo, 1860.

Please note that the starting dates given are those for baptisms. The dates for marriages and deaths may be earlier or later. Those parishes in Flores marked with an asterisk have their baptismal records missing and the dates given refer to marriages and deaths.

One final word if you are going to do your own research in Portugal. The archives are very fussy about identification. Be sure you bring with you a letter of introduction from your parish priest (if you are a Catholic) or from an official of some kind, or from a doctor or lawyer, written on letterhead paper. Then, when you get to Lisbon, visit the United States Embassy there and ask them if they will be kind enough to make a translation of the letter of introduction so that you can present it at the same time. Also, take with you half a dozen passport-sized photographs so that you can make one available to any archive that issues an identity card to you for that particular archive.

Unless your ancestors came from a district hit by one of the three calamities I mentioned, you should have great success in your ancestor-hunting in Portugal. The records are good, they go back a long way, and most of the archivists you meet will be very helpful.

One organization that you should join because you will find it most useful is the American-Portuguese Genealogical and Historical Society (Cecilia M. Rose, Executive Secretary; P.O. Box 644, Taunton, MA 02780). The society has a growing Portuguese section in the Taunton Public Library, which includes much information about sources in Portugal as well as in other countries in the world to which the Portuguese emigrated.

ROMANIA

Romania covers the approximate area of the Roman province of Dacia which existed in the second and third centuries, after the conquest of the ancient tribe of the Daci by the Roman emperor Trajan. After the Romans left, successive invasions brought in the Goths, Huns, Avars, Bulgars, and Magyars. The two principalities of Moldavia and Wallachia were the base on which the state of Romania was built; they were vassals of the Ottoman Empire but were semi-autonomous. By 1601 Michael the Brave, of Wallachia, controlled the two states. In 1711 the Turks asserted their control once more, but Russian influence increased in the area and in 1828 Russian forces occupied the two principalities.

They became, in reality, Russian protectorates while remaining technically within the Ottoman Empire. Several risings against the Russians led to their withdrawal in 1856. In that year the Congress of Paris recognized Moldavia and Wallachia as being under Turkish control and also awarded Bessarabia to Moldavia. The two countries united in 1861 under the name of Romania. Prince Alexander Cuza was elected ruler. He was deposed five years later and replaced by a German prince, who reigned as Carol I. In 1878 Romania became completely independent of the Ottoman Empire but ceded South Bessarabia to Russia, and was awarded the north of the Dobrudja in its place. The country became a kingdom in 1881.

Romania remained neutral in the First Balkan War (1912) but declared war on Bulgaria in 1913 and gained the southern part of the Dobrudja. In 1916 Romania declared war on Germany and the Austro-Hungarian empire and most of the country was occupied immediately by the armies of the two powers. In February 1918 Romania's resistance collapsed, but after the Allies invaded Romania in November it re-entered the war on the Allied side.

After the Armistice Romania took Bessarabia from Russia, Bukovina from Austria, and Transylvania and the Banat from Hungary. In 1919 part of the Banat was ceded to Yugoslavia.

In 1940 Romania became a "neutral partner" of Germany and Italy. As a result, Bessarabia was officially Russian again, and North Bukovina was also ceded to the USSR; the south of the Dobrudja went to Bulgaria, and part of Transylvania returned to Hungary. In 1941 Romania joined Germany in the attack on the USSR.

In 1944 the Red Army invaded Romania and in 1947 Romania recovered all the territories except Bessarabia, North Bukovina, and South Dobrudja, which were returned to the USSR and Bulgaria. Romania became a republic in 1947. The country is divided into forty-one administrative districts, but the seven historic and geographic regions are still widely recognized: Wallachia, Moldavia, Transylvania, part of Bukovina, Crisana-Maramures, the Dobrudja, and the Banat.

The Romanian authorities under Communism were totally non-informative so far as genealogical records were concerned. During a visit to the country, I picked up a few odds and ends of information, and have been informed of one or two other sources since then. The government is more cooperative now but is not equipped to find records.

Civil Registration

This began in 1831 in Wallachia and in 1832 in Moldavia, but in actual fact the priests of the Romanian Orthodox Church, who were responsible for the records of registration, had started earlier in many areas. Registration began in Transylvania in 1895, when it was part of Hungary. In 1865 the recording of vital events was taken over by the state.

Copies of certificates can be obtained from the Office of Vital Statistics (Oficiul Starii Civile) of the city or town in which you are interested. In the case of small villages, the office will be in the nearest large town. The records are kept locally for seventy-five years and then transferred to the National Archives.

Archives

The National Archives (Archivelor Statului) are located at Bulevardul M. Kogălniceanu 29, 70602 Bucharest (Bucureşti). There are also archives in each administrative district (Judet) and details are given below.

Church Registers

Church registers up to one hundred years ago are still in the original churches, those before that date are in the local archives listed.

Administrative Districts (Judets)

The forty-one districts are listed below, with the name of the district capital given in parentheses. If you are trying to find family records in these areas you should write to the Director, Archivelor Statului, followed by the name of the city. Please enclose a self-addressed airmail envelope and two International Reply Coupons. Write a nice, friendly letter and keep away from politics!

Alba (Alba Julia)
Arad (Arad)
Argeş (Piteşti)
Bacău (Bacău)
Bihor (Oradea)
Bistriţa-Năsăud (Bistritţa)
Botoşani (Botoşani)
Brăila (Brăila)
Braşov (Braşov)
Buzău (Buzău)
Călăraşi (Călăraşi)
Caraş-Severin (Caransebeş)
Cluj (Cluj-Napoca)
Constanţa (Constanţa)
Covasna (Sfîntu Gheorghe)
Dîmboviţa (Tîrgovişte)
Dolj (Craiova)
Galaţi (Galaţi)
Giurgiu (Giurgiu)
Gorj (Tîrgŏ Jiu)
Harghita (Miercurea Ciuc)

Hunedoara (Deva)
Ialomiţa (Slobozia)
Iaşi (Iaşi)
Maramureş (Baia Mare)
Mehedinţi (Drobeta-Turnu Severin)
Mureş (Tirgu Mureş)
Neamţ (Piatra Neamţ)
Olt (Slatina)
Prahova (Ploieşti)
Sălaj (Zalău)
Satu Mare (Satu Mare)
Sibiu (Sibiu)
Suceava (Suceava)
Teleorman (Alexandria)
Timiş (Timişoara)
Tulcea (Tulcea)
Vaslui (Vaslui)
Vîlcea (Rîmnicu-Vîlcea)
Vrancea (Focşani)
Bucureşti (Bucharest)

These district archives contain church registers (of all religions) up to one hundred years ago. Since that day they are in the local churches. The archives also hold wills, land records, and other legal documents up to thirty years ago.

The State makes no charge for a short search and visitors are welcome to do their own research in the various archives, provided that prior arrangements are made with the local archivist.

Religions

The majority belong to the Romanian Orthodox Church, with 11,000 parishes. The Catholic Church has two archbishoprics, at Bucharest and Iaşi; the Reformed Church two dioceses, at Cluj-Napoca and Oradea; the Evangelical Church of the Augustan Confession a bishopric at Sibiu; the Evangelical Church of Synodo-Presbyterian Confession a bishopric in Cluj-Napoca; and the Unitarians a bishopric in the same place. If you do not get an answer from a local priest, you should write to the church headquarters in one of these cities. (Do try to get your letters written in Romanian.)

RUSSIA AND THE FORMER SOVIET UNION

Russia, Belarus, and Ukraine were part of the Soviet Union until its break-up in the early 1990s. They are, at the time of publication, part of the Commonwealth of Independent States (CIS), which includes the major part of the old Soviet Union. Both the name CIS and the states within it may be changed again. The chaos that has followed the break-up of the USSR has brought poverty and suffering to many millions of people, and the dust has not yet settled. Ironically, it has brought slight benefits to those people whose ancestors fled the Russian Empire or the Soviet Union. The door is now unlocked, and very slightly ajar, for genealogical research.

In addition to the European countries of Belarus, Russia, and Ukraine, the CIS includes the central Asian republics of Kazakhstan, Kyrgyzstan, Tajikistan, Turkmenistan, and Uzbekistan, and several small autonomous regions. However, the five "stan" states are talking about breaking away and forming their own federation. The treaty forming the CIS was also signed by Armenia, Azerbaijan, Georgia, and Moldova, but these four states have since decided not to join. The first three countries—all in the Trans-Caucasian region—have bitter and bloody ethnic disputes within their own boundaries and with each other, and their future as independent states is uncertain. Moldova has a Romanian majority and a large and belligerent Russian minority. It is not yet clear whether it will survive in its present form or whether it will be split between Romania and Russia.

The three major partners in CIS—Belarus, Russia, and Ukraine—are fairly free of border disputes, apart from dissension over the Crimean Peninsula between Russia and Ukraine. Stalin transferred the area in 1954 from the former to the latter, even though the population was mainly Russian.

The remaining republics of the former Soviet Union—Estonia, Latvia, and Lithuania—are now completely independent. The national archivists are anxious to be of help to genealogists and, of course, to earn hard currency! They are being helpful in all possible ways, and also welcome overseas visitors to do their own research in the local and national archives. You will find separate chapters in this book for Estonia, Latvia, and Lithuania, giving the genealogical resources for those countries.

So much for the political legacies from the USSR. Let us now talk about genealogical research in Belarus, Russia, and Ukraine.

I suppose the most important development in the post-Soviet period is a complete change of attitude on the part of many persons of authority in the CIS area—both diplomats overseas and archival authorities at home. It is now possible—believe it or not—to fax a query to a Russian Embassy and receive a reply within the hour! It is also possible to get immediate answers to letters sent to archives at lower levels in some of the countries. Embassies and consulates in North America are now answering letters and providing limited information. The main barriers still confronting ancestor-hunters are in the archives themselves. I was in both Moscow and St. Petersburg in late 1990 and my conversations in both places left me with a clearer understanding of the problems of research in Russia.

Generally speaking, many archivists are anxious to be helpful, but there are many obstacles to be overcome before any wide-open and unrestricted research can come about:

1. Few archivists can speak English.
2. It is hard for any Russian citizen to understand why anyone should want to trace their ancestors.
3. There is built-in resistance to the idea that a person should be able to walk in off the street and look at archival material.
4. There are few catalogues or finding aids.
5. The archives exist to serve the State and not the individual citizen.

The situation is changing very, very slowly. Western archivists have visited Moscow, St. Petersburg, Minsk, and Kiev and there have been return visits. Some individuals such as the leading Jewish genealogist, Miriam Weiner, with her determination and dedication to a cause, and Dr. Lawrence Klippenstein, the noted Mennonite Church researcher, have worked miracles in overcoming bureaucratic resistance.

The archives in the three countries mentioned are in a Catch-22 situation. They are in desperate need of money so they can buy typewriters, computers, microfilm and microfiche viewers, and other mechanical aids. However, they can only obtain this money by providing information for genealogists for a fee, and they cannot provide the information until they have the mechanical aids. In addition, the financial regulations are so absurd that in many cases bank drafts or cash cannot be converted into rubles!

I doubt if this century will witness an "open sesame" situation for the individual researcher. It is true that I have received reports of successful visits to various archives by individual visitors doing their own research, but these are few and far between, and do not yet establish a pattern. I think it is wiser at the present time to seek the help of an accredited individual or organization with established contacts in the CIS.

Organizations Providing Research

There are now at least three organizations that are providing research for individual ancestor-hunters. The most important is the Russian-American Genealogical Archival Service, known by the acronym of RAGAS, which was created in April 1992 when the United States National Archives Volunteer Association (NAVA) signed an agreement with the AROS Society Limited (Archives of Russia). This was the result of several years of exchange visits between archivists of both countries, and consequent discussions on future cooperation. Genealogical searches were specifically included in the agreement.

RAGAS will accept inquiries from genealogists, distribute the necessary inquiry forms, and then forward the completed forms to AROS. The latter will create a computer database of genealogical information from orders received from the American side, translate the requests into Russian, and ensure the inquiry is sent to the right archives. RAGAS now operates in Russia, Belarus, and Ukraine. Negotiations are taking place with Moldova.

The rates for inquiries and research through AROS were as follows at the time of this writing:

1. To obtain a copy of a specific document, a *non-refundable fee* of $22 must be paid.

2. For answering more detailed genealogical inquiries linking generations or family members within a single generation, or for confirmation of several events in the life of a single individual, AROS will charge $6 per hour. There will be a consent form to be signed for each order. This will authorize up to fifty hours of research at the $6 per hour rate.

The address of RAGAS is P.O. Box 236, Glen Echo, Maryland 20812. Be prepared to wait at least six months for results. The costs are on the high side but are more likely to produce results than independent correspondence with the countries' archives. There is also the benefit of dealing through the National Archives of the United States rather than with some other organizations.

Two other organizations that provide research for individual ancestor-hunters are BLITZ and URBANA, which are commercial organizations. BLITZ (907 Mission Avenue, San Rafael, CA 94901) has been "blessed" by the Historical Archives in St. Petersburg. At the time of this writing there is a charge of $100 for a preliminary search of family history records in this one archive. The main thrust of this organization is research into Russian nobility, as well as German nobility and Baltic settlement. URBANA Technologies, Inc. (2011 Silver Court East, Urbana, IL 61801), at the time of this writing, charges $12 per hour for research and $1 upwards for document copies, and a possible further fee charged by a particular archive. It must be pointed out that this organization does not claim any close association with, or sponsorship by, any government or archive.

There have been recent instances of individuals obtaining helpful advice by writing directly to the Russian Archives Service (P.O. Box 27, Moscow 109180, Russia). The letters were written in Russian and a couple of dollar bills were attached to cover postage, and an offer made to pay a fee for information received.

There are also several Russian entrepreneurs operating out of Moscow and St. Petersburg and offering genealogical assistance on a fancy fee basis. One optimistic individual offers his services for an initial non-refundable fee of $500! He obviously has a very inflated idea of the wealth of the West! My advice is to have nothing to do with these con-artists.

If your ancestors are Jewish I suggest you make contact with Miriam Weiner, the genealogist I mentioned above. You can contact her at 136 Sandpiper Key, Secaucus, NJ 07094 (Phone: 201-866-4075 or Fax: 201-864-9222).

Now, let us deal with the historical background of Belarus, Russia, Ukraine, and Moldova, and the addresses of the major archives.

Belarus

Belarus has previously been known as White Russia or Bielorussia. It was originally part of Kievan Russia but was conquered by Lithuania in the early thirteenth century and passed under the control of Poland in 1569. As a result of the three Polish partitions of 1772, 1793, and 1795 it became a part of Russia. In 1919 the Bielorussian Soviet Socialist Republic was declared, and in 1990 Belarus became an independent republic within the CIS. The capital is Minsk, and the Central State Archives (Tsentral'ny Dziarzhaŭny Histarychny Arkhiŭ) are located at ul. Kozlova 26 in that city.

Russia

This country is, by far, the largest of the states within CIS. It stretches from Severnaya Zemlya in the north to the Black Sea in the south, and from St. Petersburg in the west to Vladivostok in the east. For over a thousand years the Russian Empire expanded constantly, absorbing many ancient kingdoms and principalities. There is no specific date for the establishment of the once-mighty Empire, but 882 is an acceptable starting date as Kievan Russia came into existence in that year. By 1547 Ivan the Terrible was crowned as Czar.

In 1917 the Romanov dynasty was overthrown and Russia officially became the Russian Soviet Federated Socialist Republic. In 1922 it joined with the Bielorussian, Ukrainian, and Transcaucasian republics to form the USSR. It became a separate independent state again in 1990 when the Soviet Union disintegrated and the CIS was established. The capital is Moscow, and the Central State Archives are located in Bolshaia Pirogovskaia ul. 17, in that city. These archives hold censuses for 1720–1930, and records of Jewish rabbis for 1839–1875.

Ukraine

This country has existed since the twelfth century. It became part of Lithuania in 1386 and part of Poland in 1569. The name Ukraine came into general use in the sixteenth century. In 1654 it came under the control of Moscow. As the result of a war in 1667 the country was partitioned between Russia and Poland. Russia took the left bank of the Dnieper River and Poland the right. The various partitions of Poland in the late eighteenth century resulted in Russia gaining control of the whole country. There were a number of unsuccessful revolts against the Russians in the next century. It finally gained independence in 1918 but the Red Army occupied Kiev and a Soviet Republic was declared in 1922. With Stalin's approval Ukraine annexed the Crimean Peninsula in 1954. This transfer is now under dispute between the two countries. Ukraine declared its independence in 1990.

The Central State Historical Archives of Ukraine, which are located at vul. Solomianska 24, Kiev 110 and also at pl. Vozziednannia 3a, Lviv 4, contain genealogical material.

Each county (oblasty) has its own archives, and in several places you appear to be more likely to receive a reply from them than from the Central State Archives in Kiev. Genealogist Miriam Weiner, mentioned above, has had some luck establishing a contact with the Kiev archives. I, however, have written many letters to the Chief Archivist there (Boris Ivanenko) without ever getting any reply.

The Ukrainians who emigrated directly to the United States came from a number of different areas in Ukraine but those who went to Canada trace their origins from four oblasts, and here are the addresses of the archives in these four locations. Since many of the people of Ukrainian descent living in the United States are, in fact, descended from people who went to Canada first, these addresses may be useful to them:

State Archives of Lviv Oblast
vul. Pidvalna 13, Lviv 6

State Archives of Ternopil Oblast
vul. Pershoho travnia 14, Ternopil

State Archives of Chernivtsi Oblast
vul. Shevchenka 2, Chernivtsi

State Archives of Ivano-Frankivsk Oblast
vul. Hriumvandska 3, Ivano-Frankivsk

Sources of information in the United States about Ukrainian
immigrants are:

Ukrainian Museum and Archives
1202 Kenilworth Street, Cleveland, OH 44113

Balch Institute for Ethnic Studies
18 South 7th Street, Philadelphia, PA 19106

Moldova

This country has had a very checkered history and its future is still being
resolved. It was originally an independent principality back in the Middle
Ages but came under Ottoman Empire rule in the sixteenth century. Part of
it passed to Russia in piecemeal fashion between 1791 and 1812, while the
remainder stayed under Turkish control until 1918. It then passed to Romania—with which country it has strong ethnic ties—and finally to the Soviet
Union in 1940. It was retaken by Romania in 1941 but became a Soviet
republic in 1944. When it announced its independence in 1990 it began to
consider re-union with Romania. The large Russian minority declared an
independent republic in the eastern part of the country, and appealed to
Russia for protection. The dispute is not yet resolved, and the state may yet
be divided between the two neighboring countries. The capital of Moldova
is Kishinev (Chisinau) and the Central State Archives are located in that city
(Serviciul de Stat de Arhiva, str. Gh. Asachi 67, Kishinev).

To sum up this chapter, the situation politically in the former Soviet
Union is in a state of flux, and no one can foresee the future. Genealogically,
there is great improvement and some hope for an eventual wide-open door
for research. Every ancestor-hunter can help by ignoring silence or discour-
agement, and continuing to write, write, write to national and local archives.
The more genealogical inquiries are received, the more likely the archive is
to appreciate the worldwide demand for information, and the potential in-
come in hard currency.

If you can write in the language of the country it will certainly help. Of
course, you will probably receive your reply in the same language, and that
will have to be translated. A local ethnic organization can probably help, or
even a nearby consulate. If you are willing to gamble you might try sending
a five dollar bill with your letter as a donation to archival funds. Maybe you
will say "Goodbye!" to your money, or maybe it will be the key that opens
the door.

THE LI-RA-MA COLLECTION

This is a collection of Russian consular records in the Public Archives of Canada. Do not be misled by the word "Russian." This fabulous collection may very well solve genealogical problems for many Canadians and Americans whose ancestors were Armenian, Estonian, Finnish, Georgian, Jewish, Latvian, Lithuanian, Mennonite, Polish, Russian, and Ukrainian who came to Canada from Czarist Russia before 1922. Many of them eventually joined relatives who were already in the United States.

At the time of the Russian Revolution in 1917 there were three Russian consuls in Canada: Serge Likacheff in Montreal, Constantine Ragosine in Vancouver, and Harry Mathers in Halifax. All three lost their jobs when the new government in Russia ordered the closing of the consulates. However, the Canadian government, which did not recognize the new regime, offered them positions in the Immigration Service so that they could continue to meet the needs of Russian citizens in Canada. This arrangement continued until 1922, when the Canadian government officially recognized the government of the Soviet Union.

The files of the consulates contained records of immigration, settlement, military service in both Canada and Russia, education, Russian police permits, details of place of origin, and family histories. There were hundreds of thousands of photographs, letters, certificates, and a variety of other documents. The three consuls appear to have had a passion for collecting everything they possibly could about anyone with whom they had occasion to deal. For example, during the First World War the Russian government tried to get Russians overseas to return home to fight in the army. If a man had already done his military service under the conscription laws of the Czar, he was under no legal obligation to return. When he received his orders to do so, via one of the consulates, he would, of course, get in touch with the consul and produce his release papers and his police permit to leave Russia. The consul would apparently inform the Russian government and then retain the documents in his files.

In 1922 the consuls decided the Canadian government might send their files back to Moscow and, knowing that the U.S. government had not recognized the government of the USSR, they had them shipped to the Russian consulates in New York and Boston (the U.S. government did not recognize the USSR until 1933). From the consulates the records were sent to the Russian Embassy in Washington. When the first Soviet ambassador arrived, he insisted that the embassy building be cleared of all traces of "imperialism." His request was granted and everything was removed.

As time went by, all trace of the files was lost, but rumors circulated that this genealogical treasure was somewhere in an underground vault belonging to the National Archives of the United States. After some years of searching, and some very astute detective work by Canadian officials, files consisting of over a hundred large cartons were found in a subterranean repository and returned to Canadian custody in 1980.

The records have been catalogued, copied, and sorted (a mammoth task), and the collection is open to anyone who can prove a relationship with any family mentioned. This rule is to protect the privacy of individuals. Some of the people concerned left Russia because they were wanted by the Okhrana (the Czar's secret police). They were not wanted for any criminal act but simply because they had taken part in demonstrations against the government, or circulated anti-Czarist literature. The Okhrana would discover they were in Canada and order the consuls to arrange their return to Russia because they were "dangerous terrorists" or "murderers." Although these charges were totally untrue, they are listed in the files, and if free access were granted it would lead to embarrassment to people still living.

It should be noted that, though the records stop in 1922, the information they contain goes back in many cases well into the nineteenth century. For further information you should write to the National Ethnic Archives of Canada, Manuscript Division, Public Archives of Canada, 395 Wellington Street, Ottawa, Ontario K1A 0N3.

So far as direct emigration from Russia to the United States is concerned, similar consular records are available in the Washington National Records Center, Suitland, Maryland. These files come from the consulates in Boston, Chicago, Honolulu, New York, Portland, Philadelphia, San Francisco, and Seattle.

When considering the Canadian or U.S. records in relation to your own family you must remember that Russian immigrants who had acquired citizenship will not be mentioned from then on, as they would be under no legal obligation to have anything further to do with a Russian consulate.

SAN MARINO

This tiny independent country of about 32 square miles is located in the Apennine area of Italy. It is believed to have become an independent country in about 380, but there have been a number of occasions since then when it was occupied temporarily by its more powerful neighbors. It is governed by two elected regents and a general council.

All genealogical records are either in the local churches or in the State Archives (Archivio di Stato), Palazzo Valloni, Via Carducci 141, San Marino.

SLOVAKIA

Slovakia was joined with the Czech Republic to form Czechoslovakia until Slovakia became an independent country in 1993. See the chapter on the Czech Republic earlier in this book for a history of the area.

The rules and regulations governing genealogical research in Slovakia are, as of this writing, very similar to those of the Czech Republic; however, you should check ahead because laws in this new country might change over the next few years. Much of the information about the availability of records in the Czech Republic also applies to Slovakia, so be sure to read through the Czech Republic chapter as well. However, from a genealogical point of view, Slovakia had a very different history than the Czech Republic because it was ruled by Hungary for nearly a thousand years. For this reason, you should also check the chapter on Hungary for information about records.

In 1949 administrative districts were set up in Czechoslovakia. The three that are now in Slovakia are listed below, together with the name of the chief administrative city in each district:

Západoslovenský (Bratislava)
Středoslovenský (Bánská Bystrica)
Východoslovenský (Košice)

The three districts listed above each contain the following counties:

ZÁPADOSLOVENSKÝ: Bratislava-Mesto, Bratislava-Venkov, Duhajská Streda, Galanta, Komárno, Levice, Nitra, Nové Zámky, Senica, Topol'čany, Trenčin, Trnava.

STŘEDOSLOVENSKÝ: Bánská Bystrica, Čadca, Dolní Kubín, Liptovský Mikulaš, Lučenec, Martin, Považská Bystrica, Prievidza, Rimavská Sobota, Stara, Ždiar nad Hronom, Žilina, Zvolen.

VÝCHODOSLOVENSKÝ: Bardéjov, Humenné, Košice, Michalovce, Poprad, Prešov, Rožňava, Spišská Nová Ves, Trebišov.

A very useful book to consult is *Die Deutschen in der Tschechoslowakei, 1933–1947* by Vacloc Kral, which lists place-name changes from German to Slovak and Czech.

Language

Try to buy a good Slovak dictionary and study it. A good book about ancestor-hunting in the area is *Genealogical Research for Czech and Slovak Americans* by Olga Miller, which provides some first-rate information about the Slovak language.

Civil Registration

This started in 1894. The records are not available for search by an individual but the National Archives will supply copies of certificates for a fee. Application should be made in writing either to your nearest Slovakian embassy or consulate, or directly to the National Archives in Bratislava, the capital city of Slovakia (Archívní Správa, Kriškova 7, 811 04 Bratislava). You must supply the date and place of the vital event, but the archives will usually check over a period of five years to allow for error.

Church Registers

The churches of all denominations retain the registers in the original churches. Their responsibility to record vital events ended in 1894 with the introduction of civil registration, but they still continue to keep their own records.

Although some Catholic registers in Slovakia date back to 1650, not many church registers exist before 1800 because of destruction during the Turkish invasions, or Slovak revolts against the Hungarians. Slovakia was a stronghold of the Lutheran faith and this is reflected in the church records. There are more surviving Protestant registers than Catholic for this very reason. Up to 1720, entries in the registers were in Hungarian, and after that year in Slovak or Latin. In 1840 the use of Hungarian was again ordered and this lasted until 1868, when a choice of either Slovak or Hungarian was allowed, depending on local choice and the population balance.

The LDS Church has begun microfilming church registers of all religions in the former Czechoslovakia from 1599 to 1896. Check with your nearest family history center for up-to-date information.

Census Returns

In Slovakia censuses were held in 1809, 1880, 1890, and 1910, and then in 1920 and every ten years since. They are in the National Archives (Archívní Správa, Kriškova 7, 811 04 Bratislava). Copies of the pre-1920 ones are in the National Archives of Hungary (Magyar Országos Léveltár, Bécsikapu tér 4, Budapest).

Wills

These date from the fifteenth century and are in the Archívní Správa in Bratislava. They are open to public search.

Land Records

These are not open for public search, but the archives will supply information from them for a fee.

Military Records

Earlier records are in the National Archives in Bratislava and are available for search. More recent records are not available.

State Archives

The Slovakian archives, which are listed below, can be visited by a foreigner who wishes to do his or her own research, but only after written application has been made through the nearest Slovakian embassy or consulate, or by writing directly to the Archívní Správa in Bratislava. You will have to give full personal information about yourself, explain the object of your search, and give proof of your Slovak descent. You should apply, giving the date of your visit, at least four months in advance.

The various state archives in Slovakia are listed below:

Štátný Oblastný archiv v Banskej Bystrici
Sládkovičova 77, 976 04 Bánská Bystrica

Štátný Oblastný archiv v Bratislava
Kriškova 7, 811 04 Bratislava

Štátný Oblastný archiv v Bytči
014 35 Bytča-kaštiel

Štátný Oblastný archiv v Levoča
Mierové nám. 7, 054 80 Levoča

Štátný Oblastný archiv v Nitre
Novozámocká ul. 388, 949 08 Nitre

Štátný Oblastný archiv v Prešove
ul. Slovenskej Republiky rád 137, 080 01 Prešov

Archiv hlavného mesta Bratislavy
Primaciálne nám. 2, 814 71 Bratislava

Note: All the above archives are district archives except for the last one, which is confined to the city of Bratislava.

The Calendar

Before searching records, do not forget the changes in the calendar. In 1582 Pope Gregory XIII ordained that ten days be dropped from the calendar, and that the beginning of the year be changed from March 25 to January 1. Catholic churches observed the change almost immediately; Protestant ones were slower to follow. In Slovakia the year started on 1 November 1587.

Emigration

No lists have survived, except in a few unrelated places, but most Slovaks emigrated overseas through the German ports of Hamburg and Bremen. Although the latter records were destroyed during the Second World War, the Hamburg records exist for the period from 1850 to 1934 (except for Jan.–June 1853 and Aug. 1914–1919). You will find many more details about these records in the chapter on Germany.

SLOVENIA

Slovenia was originally part of the empire of Charlemagne. In 843 it came under the control of the Duke of Bavaria, but from 1335 until 1918 it was part of Austria. In 1918 the country, together with Serbia and Croatia, formed the new kingdom of Yugoslavia—the kingdom of the Serbs, Croats, and Slovenes as it was called. In World War II it was divided among Germany, Italy, and Hungary. In 1945 it rejoined the new republic of Yugoslavia, and was awarded part of the Italian area of Venezia Giulia. It was never happy under the increasing domination of Serbia and declared its independence in 1991.

There are various archives in Slovenia. The National Archives are in Ljubljana, the capital (Zvezdarska 1, 61001 Ljubljana). There are other archives in the various main centers of the country. The addresses are:

HISTORICAL ARCHIVES:	Mestni trg 27
	61000 Ljubljana
	Muzejski trg 1
	62250 Ptuj
	Trg Svobode 10
	63000 Celje
PROVINCIAL ARCHIVES:	Glavni trg 7
	62000 Maribor
	Cevljarska 66
	66000 Koper
	Trg Edvarda Kardelja 1
	65001 Nova Gorica

Civil Registration

This started in 1926. Before that, dates of vital events were recorded in the churches of the various denominations—mainly Catholic with some Orthodox in some small areas.

Church Registers

The patronymic system was in operation until the late 1800s in certain areas, but the registers usually bracketed together both types of names. Early entries are in Latin. Many registers were destroyed during rebellions and invasions.

Censuses

Several of these were taken during the period from 1857 to 1910 but their present location is doubtful. They are thought to be in either provincial or historical archives.

Other records common to the whole area of the former Yugoslavia are described in the chapter on that country.

SPAIN

Over the years Spain has suffered a succession of invaders and civil uprisings. These, plus its isolation on the Iberian Peninsula between the Pyrenees and the sea, have produced a unique race—proud, brave, deeply suspicious of strangers, and yet with a passion for exploration and the conquest of lands beyond the sea.

The Romans were the first conquerors of Spain, then the Vandals, the Visigoths, and most important, the Moors in 711. For four hundred years and more these warriors from North Africa occupied nearly all of the area of present-day Spain. At the time of the invasion and for many years after, Spain was a collection of small kingdoms: León, Navarre, Aragón, Castile, and so on. It was not until 1492 that the Moors were finally expelled and a united Spain was created, ruled by a single king. During the next three centuries the central government extended its control over the old kingdoms and semi-autonomous provinces, and then turned its eyes westward to the Americas.

In 1808 Spain was invaded by the French armies of Napoleon, who placed his brother Joseph on the throne for a few years. The Spaniards proved to be superb guerrilla fighters and by 1814, aided by the British Army under Wellington, they drove the French from the country. During the occupation and fighting, a number of local genealogical records were destroyed or damaged.

In the next one hundred years there were a number of rebellions, caused partly by poverty and oppression in some areas, and partly by a deep-rooted provincial patriotism in others. The great tragedy of the present century was the Civil War, 1936–39, with its great loss of life. More records were destroyed, too, but a surprisingly small number in proportion to the whole, even in areas of the fiercest fighting. There are, or were, 13,000 parishes in Spain and only a handful lost their registers.

Spain is divided into fifty provinces, but you will find many more references to the fifteen historical divisions based in the main on the original small kingdoms. You will find below a list of the fifteen regions, and under each one the names of the present-day provinces within that region. In this way, if you only know that your ancestor came from Catalonia, you will at least now know the names of the four provinces within Catalonia:

ANDALUSIA: Almeria, Cádiz, Córdoba, Granada, Huelva, Jaén, Málaga, Sevilla.

ARAGÓN: Heusca, Teruel, Zaragoza.

ASTURIAS: Oviedo.

BALEARES: Baleares.

BASQUE PROVINCES: Álava, Guipúzcoa, Vizcaya.

CANARY ISLANDS: Las Palmas, Tenerife.

CASTILE (OLD): Ávila, Burgos, Logroño, Santander, Segovia, Soria.

CASTILE (NEW): Ciudad Real, Cuenca, Guadalajara, Madrid, Toledo.

CATALONIA: Barcelona, Gerona, Lérida, Tarragona.

EXTREMADURA: Badajoz, Cáceres.

GALICIA: La Coruña, Lugo, Orense, Pontevedra.

LEÓN: León, Palencia, Salamanca, Valladolid, Zamora.

MURCIA: Albacete, Murcia.

NAVARRA: Navarra.

VALENCIA: Alicante, Castellón, Valencia.

Archives

In Spain there is an embarrassing richness of archives: national, regional, provincial, municipal, parish, military, governmental, and finally, those of private and noble families.

The major archives in these various categories are listed below, but I make no claim that the list is complete. I am sure it is not, because I doubt if anyone knows where all the Spanish archives are. My information was collected from a variety of sources in Spain and elsewhere over a period of several years. I have only listed the name of the archive in some cases, and in others have given the name of the city or town as well, but not the street address. There is a great deal of changing of location going on in Spain and any detailed list would soon be out of date. Every archive is, of course, well known in its own area and letter-writing or a personal visit will still be quite easy without an exact address.

Whatever you do, do not neglect the local city, town, or village archives. They are of much greater importance than in most other countries, where the tendency has been to centralize records in counties or provinces, or in central archives in the capital city. For over five centuries the Spaniards have been storing material in local archives and little attempt has been made to either centralize these records or even put them on microfilm or microfiche, and to lodge original material in major archives or in secure storage.

With the mass of archival material available at the local level, you have a good chance of being able to trace your Spanish ancestors back for 500 years. The key to it all is the knowledge of the place from which your ancestor emigrated—not the port from which he or she sailed, but his or her place of birth or origin.

So far as church registers are concerned, the vast majority are in the original churches, except in a few dioceses where an attempt is being made to collect all the registers into a diocesan archive. There is great local resistance to these projects even on such a limited and local scale. There are no registers in the main archives of the state.

There are eleven different National Archives, based in the main on the ancient divisions of what is now a united country:

Archivo Histórico Nacional
Serrano 115, Madrid

Archiva General de Indias
Avenida de la Constitución,
Seville

Archivo General de Simancas
Villadolid

Archivo de la Corona de
 Aragón
Zaragoza

Archivo del Reino de Valencia
Alameda 22, Valencia

Archiva General de Navarra
Pamplona, Navarra

Archivo Regional de Galicia
San Carlos, La Coruña,
Galicia

Archivo del Reino de Mallorca
Ramón Llull 3, Palma de
 Mallorca

Archivo de la Real
 Chancilleria
Valladolid

Archivo de la Real
 Chancilleria
Plaza Suárez 17, Granada

Archivo General del
 Ministerio de Asuntos
 Exteriores
Madrid

There are also important archives (Archivo Municipal) in all major centers as well as in smaller towns and villages. It is not possible to list all of these but the following major centers have excellent archives:

Alicante, Barcelona, Cáceres, Córdoba, La Coruña, Gerona, Guadalajara, Guipúzcoa, León, Madrid, Orense, Palencia, Pamplona, Salamanca, Santander, Segovia, Seville, Teruel, Vizcaya, and Zamora.

There are also archives in Mahón, in the Balearic Islands.

There are three types of very important records that will be found at the local level: civil registration, church registers, and notarial records. Let us talk about these in turn.

Civil Registration (Los Registros Civiles)

This started officially in 1870 and it is easy to discount its importance because it commenced so recently. However, to do that is wrong, because civil registration certificates will take you back another two generations so far as the births are concerned, and at least one more generation in the case of marriages and deaths.

Although the official starting date was 1870, it had already been in operation in a few municipalities for a number of years. The responsibility for organizing the new system was given to the local court, the Court of the First Instance (Juzgado de Primera Instancia), as it was called. All vital events—births, marriages, and deaths—had to be registered within eight days of the event.

The civil registers are still kept in the same courts. In large cities there may be several Juzgado and in underpopulated areas one office will serve a score of municipalities. The volumes in which the registers are kept are indexed by surname, but in the very early days of registration of births the indexes were by given, or Christian, name, and this can make searching a little hard at times.

When you write for a copy of an entry, be very sure you ask for a *full* copy, because if you don't you will receive an extract, and you will miss the fund of information contained in the original entry. The Spaniards are even more thorough than the Finns in the amount of detailed family information recorded.

The *birth* entries contain the usual day and date of birth, names, town and street address, and names, ages, and birthplaces of both parents, but in Spain this is only the beginning! You will also find the dates and places of birth of the grandparents, and the occupations or professions of the two generations, plus the names of the witnesses, and the signatures of all those present. Finally, there is full personal information about the person who registered the birth.

The *marriage* entries are less detailed. They give names of the bride and groom, addresses, ages, places of birth (in some cases the date of birth), names and addresses of the parents on both sides, and their places of birth.

The *death* entries give the names of both the deceased and the surviving spouse, with their addresses and places of birth; the full names of the parents of the deceased, and whether they are living or dead; the cause and place of death; the names of all surviving children; and the particular cemetery where the burial took place.

As I mentioned above, civil registration started in 1870, but be sure you always check whether it started earlier in the parish in which you are interested. There are a number of churches with records dating back to 1840.

There is no central index for civil registration, so you must know a place to start. The government department responsible for the administration of the system is the Ministry of Justice (Ministerio de Justicia), and the official directly concerned is the Director-General (Dirección General de los Registros y del Natariado), Madrid.

Church Registers (Registros de Parroquia)

The parish churches of Spain contain records that go back at least to 1650, and in many cases much earlier. The oldest baptismal entries found so far are those of Alcala de Henares, which date back to 1437. The earliest known parish papers are those of Solsona and are dated 1394. A guide to the various parishes was published in 1954 (*Guia de la Iglesia en España,* Vol. 4). Ninety percent of the parishes are listed. A few of the registers have been copied by the LDS Church.

Apart from the registers of baptism, marriage, and burial, the parish records also include confirmations, parish censuses, the church account books, inventories of parish property, and the minutes of meetings of the Cofradias (a society of laymen, which organizes social and religious events within the parish). The three most important records named above are usually each in a separate book, and confirmations are generally recorded in a separate section of the birth registers.

A **baptismal** entry contains a great deal of information from about 1760 to the present, but earlier registers will not contain as much information; for example, the names of grandparents did not appear much before 1780.

In recent times the baptismal entry will give the name of the child being baptized; paternal and maternal surnames; the date of the baptism; the names, addresses, and birthplaces of the parents and grandparents; the birth date and birthplace of the child; whether the child is legitimate or illegitimate; the names of the godparents, and their addresses and birthplaces.

A **marriage** entry contains the full names of the bride and groom; their marital status; their occupations; their addresses and birthplaces; their ages; and the names, addresses, and birthplaces of the parents on both sides. Earlier marriage entries omit mention of the grandparents.

The **death** entry is by no means as detailed and there is tremendous variation from parish to parish as to the information given. Some mention the date of death, but not of burial—or vice versa. Usually, the entry will give details of name of the deceased, address at the time of death, age, birthplace, name of surviving spouse or of the spouse who had died earlier, names of the parents, names of the children, and a notation stating that the will was made before a lawyer (notario) or written down by the priest.

Confirmation, although a sacrament of the church, is treated quite differently in that it is not performed by the parish priest but by the bishop. Consequently a person might have to wait many years to be confirmed. In the present day, with ease of travel, such delays no longer exist. The confirmation entry will give the date it was performed, the name and address of the person, and the names of the parents.

The **Cofradias** records will not help you with your family tree, but if your ancestors were active in the church you will find out quite a lot about them; what their views were on different subjects, when they joined, how active they were, and when they died.

The **Padrones** or censuses were taken in parishes at various times and on various occasions. There was no particular pattern, or any regularity, but you may find in some parish archive a census entry for your family that tells you the place they came from and, suddenly and almost miraculously, a major problem has been solved.

You will also find the church account books, which contain details of payments received for masses for the dead, and this may give you the date of death of an ancestor, or you may find in the land records (capellanías) details of a gift of land from your ancestor to the church. You may also find copies of wills (testamentos) and petitions (expedientes). These latter were applications to the priest for a marriage, signed by bride and groom, usually including copies of their baptismal records—another valuable document in an unlikely location, judged by our present-day experiences.

You must always be prepared to find that church records have been destroyed, either in the French invasions at the end of the eighteenth century, or during the Civil War, or by vandalism or fire. In that case, you should try the archives of the diocese in which the parish is located; sometimes there are duplicate records or registers in the custody of the bishop, or diocesan censuses that may help you go further back. If you don't know the exact diocese, you should write to the headquarters of the Catholic Church (Conference Episcopal Española, Oficina de Estadistica y Sociologia, Alfonso XI 4, Madrid 14), give them the name and province of the village, and ask for the name of the diocese and the address of the diocesan office.

Civil Censuses (Padrones Civiles)

These records are kept in local municipal offices (Ayuntamiento) and are very complete. The name of each family member is listed, with date and place of birth and relationship to the head of the household, and length of time in present town or village. In addition, details are given of education and military service. The records are not indexed but in smaller places this is no great drawback, as one page in the register is devoted to one family, and it is just a question of turning the pages for a short time. The family name at the top of the page is usually quite legible. A search in a large city can be a monstrous chore, but it may be worth all the effort. Only you can decide.

Civil censuses have been held in various places at very frequent intervals since the 1500s. There is no official list of these censuses and I doubt if anyone knows how many there are. As dusty old documents are sorted in dusty old archives, dusty old census lists are always being discovered. All you can do is to check with the municipal offices (Ayuntamiento) or the provincial archives for information about early civil censuses in the area of your own interest. National censuses have been held since 1857 but the ones open to public search do not contain very much personal information. The most comprehensive census of them all was the one called Catastro del Marques de la Ensenada, in 1752. Copies are preserved in the appropriate archives throughout Spain and are readily available, and in some cases indexed.

Notarial Records (Protocolos)

Notaries are, of course, lawyers and they can be involved in almost every aspect of life (particularly Spanish life). If you know the exact place of origin of your emigrant ancestor, you may be able to make good use of the great mass of information contained in these records, assuming your ancestor had some reason to make use of the services of a notary. Notarial records include such items as wills, real estate sales, property transfers, marriage settlements and contracts, dowries, apprenticeship records and indentures, adoptions, guardianships, boundary disputes, inheritance disputes, building contracts, etc.—ad infinitum.

However, there are problems in searching for the records. They can be found in any one of a variety of archives—provincial, district, local, municipal, historical, ecclesiastical, governmental—and, of course, in notaries' offices. The law states that records over twenty-five years old must be given to the district notary, and that the district notary, in turn, must give all records over one hundred years old into the custody of the provincial archives. These regulations are not strictly enforced in all places, due to local resistance, and so these time periods should not be accepted without question. There is also a law that restricts access to the records younger than one hundred years except by a direct descendant. In this case you must produce sworn evidence of descent, fully documented.

Notarial papers are filed under the name of the notary. This means you must first discover the name of the notary in your place of ancestral origin. My advice is to forget the whole idea if your ancestor came from a city or a large town. If he or she came from a small place, the provincial archives will be able to give you the names of notaries who practiced in that place at that particular time, and for a small fee will search the lists for you for mention of any documents connected with your ancestors.

There is one very important aspect of notarial records, apart from those listed above. Until about the middle of the last century, anyone wishing to emigrate from Spain had to complete three documents before a notary. One was a certificate of permission to emigrate (if under twenty-five) from his or her father or elder brother; the second was a contract with the captain of the vessel on which he or she was to sail; and the third was a bond by which a relative or friend agreed to be liable for any unpaid debts of the emigrant. These documents may be found among the notarial records mentioned.

Passport Applications

Many of these are on file in the Archiva de Gobernación, in Madrid.

Military Records (Hojas de Servicio)

These records are in the Military Archives in Segovia (Archivo General Militar) and contain the complete personal records of every Spanish soldier and sailor from the early 1600s up to the present day. The lists have been published and indexed in the earlier years. Other records for the navy are in the Archives of the Ministry of the Navy (Archivo Central del Ministerio de Marina), and in the Naval Museum (Archivo del Museo Naval).

Passenger Lists (Listas de Pasajeros)

In Spain, as in many other European countries, genealogists have been searching in vain for records of emigrants sailing on passenger ships from their country. It is true there are lists of people sailing out of the port of Seville to the Americas in 1509–1701, but these are limited in value. They exist because Seville was the port from which emigrants and others always left. The people listed were, in very many cases, going overseas on government or private business and would eventually be returning to Spain.

The lists end in 1710, though records of licenses issued for travel continue to about 1790. Both types of records give details of the head of the family and his place of birth or residence. If your ancestors emigrated before the latter date, these records may be invaluable to you. They are located in Archivo General de Indias, in Seville. It must be remembered that the lists are not infallible; many emigrants went unrecorded, by accident or design. Some attempts are being made to index the very early lists. No emigration or passenger lists after 1790 are known to be in existence.

Genealogical Societies

There are believed to be two genealogical organizations in existence in Spain, but since no replies have been received from either of them to several letters, I do not know if they are still in existence:

Instituto Salazar y Castro
La Calle de Medinaceli 4, Madrid

Instituto Internacional de Genealogia
Apartado 12079, Madrid

As you will realize by now, the amount of genealogical material available for you in Spain is immense, but it is not centralized and is poorly organized. If you speak fluent Spanish and have plenty of time, you will accomplish a great deal with a very leisurely visit. If you have to depend on correspondence, be prepared for very long waits for answers. " Mañana" may even mean "Nunca."

SWEDEN

The Swedes, like the Danes and the Norwegians, are descended from the Vikings, but, unlike their neighbors who went west to conquer the British Isles, France, and the Low Countries, the Swedes turned east. For centuries the wars between Sweden and Russia left their marks on the populations of both countries. From time to time the Swedes also fought with the Danes and the Norwegians, with an occasional foray into Finland.

Sweden and Norway joined forces in 1319 and in 1397 Queen Margaret of Denmark united the three countries in the Kalmar Union and ruled from Copenhagen. Sweden became independent again in 1523. During the next century the Swedes conquered Livonia, Karelia, Pomerania, and parts of the area that is now Germany. In 1720 after the Peace of Westphalia they returned the conquered territory. In 1814 they lost Finland to Russia at the Congress of Vienna, but were given Norway as compensation. Norway then remained a separate kingdom in personal union with Sweden until 1905.

Ancestor-hunting in Sweden is probably easier than in any other country in Europe, with the exception of Switzerland. However, it is particularly important that you start off by researching within your family. First, try to find out the name of the parish from which your ancestor came; there are over 2,000 parishes in Sweden. Check your surname very carefully. Your emigrant ancestor may have anglicized it upon his or her arrival in the new country; many thousands did so. Olsson became Oliver, Persson became Perkins, Stalhammar became Steel. Check your family papers; you may find the official exit permit from Sweden issued by the pastor of your ancestor's church. It will give a full name, date and place of birth, and a character reference. This is called a flyttningsbetyg.

Superb as the records are, you will need to know the name of the place where your ancestor was born, or lived prior to emigration. Unless you know this you will have problems.

The country is divided into twenty-four districts or counties (län). Sometimes these län are identical with the province (landskap), although there may be more than one län in a landskap. In seven counties there are archives, known as Landsarkivet.

Each län is divided into smaller units known as fögderi. These, as well as the cities and towns, have their own separate administrations. From a judicial point of view, each län is divided into other units known as härad. Each län is further divided into smaller ecclesiastical units similar to parishes. These were originally known in Swedish as socknar, but are now called församlingar. There are over 2,000 of these, too many to list in this chapter.

The following archives are in existence in Sweden:

Landsarkivet in Uppsala
(län of Stockholm, Uppsala, Södermanland, Örebro, Västmanland, and Kopparberg)
P.O. Box 135, 751 04 Uppsala

Landsarkivet in Vadstena
(län of Östergötland, Jönköping, Kronoberg, and Kalmar)
P.O. Box 126, 592 00 Vadstena

Landsarkivet in Visby
(län of Gotland)
P.O. Box 142, 621 01 Visby

Landsarkivet in Lund
(län of Blekinge, Kristianstad, Malmöhus, and Halland)
P.O. Box 2016, 220 02 Lund

Landsarkivet in Göteborg
(län of Göteborg and Bohus, Älvsborg, Skaraborg, and Värmland)
P.O. Box 3009, Geijersgatan 1, 400 10 Göteborg

Landsarkivet in Härnösand
(län of Gävleborg, Västernorrland, Västerbotten, and Norrbotten)
P.O. Box 161, 871 01 Härnösand

Landsarkivet in Östersund
(län of Jämtland)
P.O. Box 664, 831 27 Östersund

Stadsarkivet in Malmö
St. Petrigången 7a, 211 20 Malmö

Stadsarkivet in Stockholm
P.O. Box 22063
Kungsklippan 6
104 22 Stockholm

Stadsarkivet in Borås
P.O. Box 851, 501 15 Borås
(*Note:* All church records in Borås have been transferred to Landsarkivet in Uppsala.)

Stadsarkivet in Västerås
721 87 Västerås
(*Note:* All church records in Västerås have been transferred to Landsarkivet in Uppsala.)

Stadsarkivet in Örebro
701 01 Örebro

Stadsarkivet in Uppsala
P.O. Box 216
751 04 Uppsala

Stadsarkivet in Gävle
P.O. Box 552
Kyrkogatan 22, 801 07 Gävle

Stadsarkivet in Karlstad
Stadshuset, Drottninggatan 32
652 25 Karlstad

Stadsarkivet in Eskilstuna
Careliigatan 8
632 20 Eskilstuna

Stadsarkivet in Norrköping
Norrköpings Kommun
601 81 Norrköping

There are also other archives that will be referred to in this chapter:

Riksarkivet (The National Swedish Record Office)
Fyrverkarbacken 13-17, 100 26 Stockholm

Kammararkivet (The Cameral Archives)
(same address as Riksarkivet, above)

Kungliga Utrikesdepartementets Arkiv (Foreign Affairs Archives)
P.O. Box 16121, Gustaf Adolfs Torg 1
103 23 Stockholm

Riddarhuset (House of Nobility)
P.O. Box 2022, 103 11 Stockholm

Krigsarkivet (Military Record Office)
Banérgatan 64, 104 50 Stockholm

Emigrantregistret (Emigrant Register)
P.O. Box 331, S:a Kyrkogatan 4
651 05 Karlstad

Statistiska Centralbyrån (Central Bureau of Statistics)
Karlavägen 100, 102 50 Stockholm

Civil Registration

This does not exist in Sweden. The responsibility for recording births, marriages, and deaths rests with the ministers of the Lutheran Church, which became the official church in 1527. Since then it has also become the official recorder of the vital events of Sweden.

Church Registers

In 1571 a royal proclamation ordered that books should be kept in each church in which statistics could be recorded. In 1608 the church urged its ministers to obey the law and maintain the records. The clergy does not seem to have paid much attention to these royal and ecclesiastical urgings, because few registers exist before 1686, when a new law specified that a record be kept of all married couples, together with the names and addresses of parents; the births of all children, with the names of parents and witnesses at the baptism, the dates of birth and baptism, and the place of birth; the name of each dead person, with a short account of his or her life, and age at death; the name of those moving in or out of the parish, with details of where they came from, or where they were going; and, finally, a book containing the names of all parishioners being instructed in the catechism before being confirmed (this was called the katekismilängder).

There was still resistance to the law and many did not comply until the early 1700s. On the other hand, some started much earlier, for example, Skultuna, in the län of Västmanland (1607), and Holy Trinity Parish (Trefaldighets) in Uppsala city (1608).

Each parish maintained its own books. Some were kept in the church, some in the minister's house, and some in outbuildings. As a result many were lost, burnt, or damaged. In 1888 all the registers were transferred to the Landsarkivet. However, there was some opposition to this transfer, particularly in the län of Kopparberg. It was finally agreed that individual churches could retain their registers if certain standards of storage could be observed. Over the years many of these retained registers have been transferred and very few now remain in the churches. In the latter cases there are copies in the Landsarkivet. No exemptions have been granted since 1916. Churches, of course, retain the current registers.

The kinds of records that were, and are, maintained in the churches are births and baptisms, banns and marriages, deaths and burials; church accounts; catechism, confirmation, and communion records; records of arrivals and departures; and since 1750, house examination rolls (husförhörslängder).

The house examination rolls are invaluable—if only every country maintained such records! They are a record kept by the minister of his visits to his church members (in the days when clergymen, like doctors, made house calls). The rolls give details of the social status of the individuals, their education, their character, their occupation, their state of health, their journeys away from the parish, and the names of any visitors in the house when the minister called. In 1895 some changes were made in these records and they became known as församlingsböcker. These records are still kept up to the present day and do not differ in any substantial way from the husförhörslängder.

It should be noted that in 1860 the ministers started sending a copy of the entries in the parish registers to the Central Bureau of Statistics. These records are filed by year, county, and parish and are still in operation. In cases where the original registers have been lost, the copies in the Bureau of Statistics will fill the gap.

Personal Records (Personakt)

In 1946 all Swedes were given personal records (personakt) that contain a précis of the information in their parish records. When they move, they take the records with them. If they die or leave the country permanently, the personakt is sent to the Central Bureau of Statistics. Here the records are divided into two sections, one for deaths and the other for emigration.

Censuses (Mantalslängder)

These started in 1620 in various places and at irregular intervals. The information contained in the early censuses varies a great deal. A good rule of thumb is, the later the census the more detailed the information. Copies are in the Cameral Archives in Stockholm, and in the Landsarkivet.

Property Lists (Jordeböcker)

These date back as early as 1540 and record all transactions in property, together with tax information relating to the property. The names of all owners of property are given in great detail and the genealogical value can be very great. These records are also in the Landsarkivet.

Probate Records (Bouppteckningar)

These are inventories of the real and personal property of deceased persons. They date back to about 1660 and give details of birth and death, heirs and their relationship to the deceased, together with their ages and locations. They are to be found either in Landsarkivet, Stadsarkivet, or district courts (Rådhusrätt).

Tax Lists (Boskapsräkningar)

These only existed for a short period (1620–42) before they were incorporated in other records, and they are located in the Cameral Archives in Stockholm.

Court Records (Dombÿcker)

These very comprehensive records start in 1620 and continue to the present day. They include details not only of court cases and prosecutions, but also of real estate transfers, mortgages, guardianships, and marriage settlements. Recent records are in local courts, and earlier ones are in the Landsarkivet.

Trade Guilds (Skråhandlingar)

These cover the period from 1604 to about 1890 and are usually found in city archives (Stadsarkivet). In almost every European country the trade guilds were immensely powerful. They were the equivalent of today's trade unions and in each trade they regulated that particular craft or industry. Membership was a jealously guarded privilege, because only members could practice their trade in the city or community. To qualify for membership you had to be an upright and honest citizen of impeccable character; to have served your apprenticeship in the craft; to have passed an examination of your skills by a board of examiners; and, most important, to have an opening in the craft in your community available for you. Once in, you were a success in life. You were protected against competition and were a respected figure in your community. You were also told where you should live, and if you were single a marriage could be arranged for you with the daughter of another guild member. You had duties and responsibilities to your guild, but you obtained rights and privileges in return.

The guild records list full personal details about each applicant, including date and place of birth, and parents and their place of residence.

Emigration Records (Emigrationshandlingar)

I have left these most important records to the end. Nearly all emigrants from Sweden passed through the ports of Malmö and Göteborg, though a few emigrated overseas via Hamburg, Germany. (For information about the records there, see the chapter on Germany.)

All emigrants passing through the two Swedish ports had to register with the police, who recorded the names and addresses of the emigrants, age and sex, occupation, place of birth, and intended destination. These police records did not start until 1867, but most emigration from Sweden started after that date. In any case, do not forget that the parish records I mentioned earlier give details of people leaving a particular parish and their destination. The police records are almost completely indexed and are in the Landsarkivet and the Stadsarkivet.

In addition, the national government also kept emigration records from 1851. These are in the Central Bureau of Statistics, Stockholm, and also in the Landsarkivet in Göteborg.

Finally, there are all the records and correspondence of the Larsson Brothers, emigration agents in Göteborg. These date from 1876 to 1913 and are in the Landsarkivet there. They give not only details of emigrants and their families, but in many cases names and addresses of relatives who had emigrated previously.

From all these sources you should be able to find out all there is to know about your emigrant ancestor. Certainly no other country has such detailed records in this particular area of genealogical research. If, after searching all of them, you are still in need of information, there are still the records of passports issued. These are in the War Archives in Stockholm and in the Landsarkivet and the Stadsarkivet.

One final word about Swedish records. Be prepared for poor writing in many areas, and also for the fact that however good your spoken Swedish may be, you will be dealing with Swedish in a German script up to about 1790. Because of this you may need to employ an expert in Sweden on occasion; a list of researchers can be obtained from the archives in your area of interest.

There are also two active genealogical organizations in Sweden:

Personhistoriska Samfundet
Riksarkivet, 100 26 Stockholm

Genealogiska Föreningen
Arkivgatan 3, 111 28 Stockholm

In addition, there is an active organization in the United States:

Swedish Genealogy Group
P.O. Box 16069
St. Paul, MN 55116-0069

Counties (Län)

The borders of the twenty-four counties have been almost unchanged since 1634. Nowadays, the counties are usually named by a letter instead of the full name, and this can be very confusing for genealogists. I list each county below with its letter equivalent. For example, Gotland is I-Län.

Älvsborg (Elfsborg)	P	Malmöhus	M
Blekinge	K	Norrbotten	BD
Gotland	I	Örebro	T
Gävleborg	X	Östergötland	E
Göteberg and Bohus	O	Skaraborg	R
Halland	N	Södermanland	D
Jämtland	Z	Stockholm	B
Jönköping	F	Uppsala	C
Kalmar	H	Värmland	S
Kopparberg	W	Västerbotten	AC
Kristianstad	L	Västernorrland	Y
Kronoberg	G	Västmanland	U

The Use of Patronymics

These were used by the working class until about 1860. The nobility, clergy, and guild members adopted surnames in the seventeenth century—in some places much earlier. Women often retained their surnames.

SWITZERLAND

The federal capital of Switzerland is Bern. In the early centuries the Swiss were conquered by the Romans and, later, the Franks. Finally, in 1291, three cantons—Schwyz, Unterwalden, and Uri—formed a confederacy to protect themselves against attempts by the Hapsburg dynasty to control them. (This was the period of the famous William Tell and his equally famous apple.) Other cantons joined the confederacy over the centuries and in 1648 the independence of the Swiss Confederation was recognized in the Treaty of Westphalia. In 1815 the perpetual neutrality of the country was endorsed by the Treaty of Paris and the Congress of Vienna.

The country is divided into twenty-six federated cantons or states, of which twenty are full cantons and six are half cantons. The latter are joined in pairs to form three full cantons. The list of the cantons is given below, together with the chief city of each. The German-speaking cantons are listed under their German names, with the French variation, if any, in parentheses; the reverse applies for the French-speaking cantons; and the only Italian-speaking one is listed in Italian, with the French and German variation in parentheses. In the "Remarks" column is noted an additional appropriate language to use when writing.

German-speaking Cantons	Chief City	Remarks
Aargau (Argovie)	Aarau	
Appenzell—Ausser-Rhoden, Inner-Rhoden (Rhodes-Extérieures, Rhodes-Intérieures)	Herisau and Appenzell	
Basel—Basel-Stadt, Basel-Land (Bâle-Ville, Bâle-Campagne)	Basel and Liestal	
Bern (Berne)	Bern	also French
Glarus (Glaris)	Glarus	
Graubünden (Grisons)	Chur	also Italian and Romansch

German-speaking Cantons	Chief City	Remarks
Luzern (Lucerne)	Luzern	also French
St. Gallen (St. Gall)	St. Gallen	
Schaffhausen (Schaffhouse)	Schaffhausen	
Schwyz	Schwyz	
Solothurn (Soleure)	Solothurn	
Thurgau (Thurgovie)	Frauenfeld	
Unterwalden (Unterwald)— Nidwalden, Obwalden	Stans and Sarnen	
Uri	Altdorf	
Zug (Zoug)	Zug	
Zürich (Zurich)	Zürich	

French-speaking Cantons	Chief City	Remarks
Fribourg (Freiburg)	Fribourg	also German
Genève (Genf)	Genève	
Jura	Delémont	
Neuchâtel (Neuenburg)	Neuchâtel	
Valais (Wallis)	Sion	also German
Vaud (Waadt)	Lausanne	

Italian-speaking Canton	Chief City	Remarks
Ticino (Tessin)	Bellinzona	also German

The Swiss Confederation deals with foreign affairs, transport and communications, and tariffs. All other matters are the responsibility of the individual cantons.

Generally speaking, unless you are writing in English, you will find the above guide to cantonal languages reliable. If, however, you are a fluent German speaker and are going to visit the German-speaking areas of Switzerland on an ancestor-hunt, a word of caution. Be prepared to find great difficulty in understanding and being understood. The Swiss-German dialect is an amalgam of Middle High German (1200–1500) and numerous regional dialects.

Civil Registration

Government registration of births, marriages, and deaths started in Switzerland on January 1, 1876. Before that date, such records had been the responsibility of the churches. When civil registration began, there were two types of registers kept. The first contained records of the *local* vital events; the second was a list of vital events affecting local people that occurred elsewhere. This system continued until 1928, when the second register was discontinued.

However, a second register was again started but in a very different form. The second register became a family register, recording and collating the vital events that occurred in each family. This information comes to the registrar from the first, or local, list and also from information from authorities in other areas. This information can be very complete. For example, a Swiss couple living in Canada will report the births of their children to the local Swiss consul. He, in turn, will pass on the information to the hometown of the couple and the entry will be made in the family register. Such records are invaluable, and they are signed, witnessed, and officially endorsed. Photocopies are obtainable for a small fee by writing to the Civil Registrar (Zivilstandsamt or Greffier Civil) of the particular district. All records for the pre-civil-registration period (1834–75) are also in the District Registry Office. The general principle governing civil registration in Switzerland is that all vital records—including birth, marriage, death, divorce, and nullity—are kept in the place where the citizen was born. There is no central index, so it is essential that you know the place to begin your research.

Church Registers

These are known by a number of names: Kirchenbücher, Pfarrbücher, Matriken, Kirchenrodel, or Rodeli. They include the usual entries of baptism (Taufen), marriage (Trauungen, Heiraten, Verehelichungen), and burial (Begräbnisse, Beerdigungen), but also confirmations (Konfirmationen) and, until 1875, the information now found in the civil registries. Generally speaking, the Protestant church records started in about 1550, but some early baptismal entries have been found that date back to 1481. The Catholic records start about 1580, but in fact the record-keeping in that church did not really come into full effect until about 1610.

As you may imagine, the efficiency of the records depends very much on the efficiency and energy of the priest or pastor of the time. There are gaps; there is indecipherable writing; there are mysterious abbreviations (Xopher for Christopher, for example); and, of course, the entries are in German, French, Italian, or Latin.

Family registers (Familienregister) were started in many parishes in the late 1700s, but here again there are exceptions. Some have been found that date back to 1620 and others did not start until 1812. Be sure you check thoroughly to see if a family register is available for the parish in which you are interested. The great advantage of this register is that it was created from the church registers and includes all the entries in chronological order. You may find three or more generations on the one page, with the earliest member at the top and the most recent at the bottom. In other words, you will find a complete family tree spanning at least three generations, and you will also find references to other entries elsewhere in the register linking up with your family. Bear in mind, though, that you are exposed to human error and always try to cross-check with the church registers.

In church records you may also find citizen books (Bürgerbucher or Bürgerregister). To a large degree these duplicate the information in the family registers but they often contain details of emigration from the town or village to another place (either in Switzerland or overseas). A number of these have been published and you should always check for them with the local Standsamt (municipal office) or Archiv.

Population Registers (Bevölkerungsverzeichnisse)

These are also known as Burger Rolls or Status Animarum, and are found in the cantons of most of Switzerland, but particularly in the German-speaking areas. These records, like others, often duplicate information to be found in other places, like church registers and Family Books, but some-times they include information left out of the other sources.

Censuses (Volkszählungen)

The first city census was taken in Bern in 1764, and the first federal census in the period April 1836 to February 1838. The latter is very incomplete. In 1841 the quality improved. In 1850 the census only included people with rights of residence and not the actual people present at a place during the census. In 1860 the census as we know it was instituted and has continued every ten years ever since. Copies can be obtained from both state and city archives.

Wills (Testamente)

The location of wills is a good illustration of the problems in a federated state. Because of the autonomous situation of the cantons, each has devel-oped its own systems and ideas over the years. The earliest wills date back to the twelfth century and they can be found in state or city archives, or in local or district courthouses. Until 1912 the probating, or proving, of wills was entirely the responsibility of the cantons, but in that year the law was changed and the responsibility devolved on the federal government. In the case of death, the will has to be submitted to a judge, or other authority, who is dealing with matters of succession for proof of probate, regardless of whether the will has been retained in private hands or lodged in the office of a notary. Searching for wills, therefore, involves making contact with both courts and notaries. However, persistence pays off, and I know of several instances where wills have been eventually found as far back as 1600.

There are a variety of other records that you will need to search, some of them peculiar to Switzerland.

Notarial Records (Notariatsregister)

These date from the fourteenth century and include land records (Katasterbücher), which list the inheritors of land for several generations, together with details of their addresses, ages, and occupations; marriage contracts (Eheverträge), which were always drawn up when property was involved and give the full names of the couple, ages, names of parents, places of birth, and current residence; inventories (Bestandsaufnahmen), which list all property and possessions left by the deceased, together with name and age, address, occupation, and surviving family members; mortgages (Hypotheken), which list not only mortgages, but loans against property, contracts for real estate sales, and the full names and addresses of the parties involved.

The more recent of the above records are in the local courthouse (Kantonal- und Amtsgericht). Older records are in the canton and state archives and some of them have been indexed.

Genealogical City Registers
(Genealogische Stadtregister)

Four localities have such registers: Bern, Glarus, Zürich, and Schaffhausen. The first three are in the state archives and the fourth in the city courthouse. The registers include pedigrees of local families, some of which date back for six centuries. These records, of course, are over and above the many printed genealogies you will find in local libraries. Always check with a local library for any information they have about your family. You may be astonished at what you will discover. My wife and I had quite an experience once in Scotland. We were working on her paternal grandmother's family, the Coplands. We knew that recent generations had come from the area of the city of Dumfries. While we were there we called in at the local library and found that they had, in manuscript form, a complete history of the family for 500 years, fully documented, and completed some fifty years ago by a member of the family. Our own research joined in with the manuscript material and saved us many, many hours of work. You see what can happen!

Military Records (Militärakten)

Each male citizen of Switzerland must spend time in the army and then go on the reserve. These records date from 1800 and are in the Military Department of the federal government (Eidgenössisches Militärdepartement, 3000 Bern).

University Registers (Universitätsmatrikeln)

If your ancestor graduated from a university (Basel, Geneva, Lausanne, Zürich) you will find him or her listed. The registers go back to the fifteenth century in Basel, to the sixteenth century in Geneva and Lausanne, and to 1832 in Zürich. Old records are in the state archives and more recent ones in the various university archives.

Guild Records (Zunftbücher)

In Switzerland, as in most other European countries, the trade guilds were powerful organizations, controlling who could enter a trade, where he could practice it, whom he married, and in which area he could live. These records cover the 300 years from the early sixteenth century and are in either state or city archives.

Passports (Passkontrollen)

A list of passports issued in the eighteenth and early nineteenth centuries up to 1848 is in the state archives; a list of passports after 1848 is in the Offices of the Federal Government (Schweizer Bundesregierung, Bundeshaus, 3000 Bern). This gives very full personal information, including place of birth as well as current address and, usually, a list of family members traveling with the passport-holder. If you know your ancestor left the country in, say, 1842 but you don't know his or her place of origin, the passport records may solve your problem very easily.

Other Records

There are many other more specialized or localized records in the various state archives. These are listed below, together with major city archives and church archives. In addition, the LDS Church has microfilmed many parish registers in the cantons of Appenzell, Basel, Luzern, St. Gallen, Thurgau, Zürich, Genève, and Vaud. It also has the research papers of a Swiss genealogist named Julius Billeter who traced the descent of over 1,200 families. These are also on microfilm and can be inspected in your nearest LDS family history center. The federal archives of Switzerland are located in Bern (Schweizerisches Bundesarchiv, Archivstrasse 4, 3003 Bern), but because of the local nature of Swiss government the individual cantonal archives (see below) are much more useful.

State or Cantonal Archives
German-speaking Cantons

AARGAU:	Staatsarchiv
	5000 Aarau
APPENZELL (AUSSER-RHODEN):	Staatsarchiv
	9100 Herisau
APPENZELL (INNER-RHODEN):	Landesarchiv
	9050 Appenzell

BASEL (LAND):	Staatsarchiv
	4410 Liestal
BASEL (STADT):	Staatsarchiv
	4001 Basel
BERN:	Staatsarchiv
	3012 Bern
GLARUS:	Landesarchiv
	8750 Glarus
GRAUBÜNDEN:	Staatsarchiv
	7000 Chur
LUZERN:	Staatsarchiv
	6003 Luzern
ST. GALLEN:	Staatsarchiv
	9000 St. Gallen
SCHAFFHAUSEN:	Staatsarchiv
	8200 Schaffhausen
SCHWYZ:	Staatsarchiv
	6430 Schwyz
SOLOTHURN:	Staatsarchiv
	4500 Solothurn
THURGAU:	Staatsarchiv
	8500 Frauenfeld
UNTERWALDEN (NIDWALDEN):	Staatsarchiv
	6730 Stans
UNTERWALDEN (OBWALDEN):	Staatsarchiv
	6060 Sarnen
URI:	Staatsarchiv
	6460 Altdorf
ZUG:	Staatsarchiv
	6300 Zug
ZÜRICH:	Staatsarchiv
	8001 Zürich

French-speaking Cantons

FRIBOURG:	Archives de l'État
	1700 Fribourg
GENÈVE:	Archives de l'État
	1211 Genève 3
JURA:	Chancellerie de l'État
	2800 Delémont
NEUCHÂTEL:	Archives de l'État
	2001 Neuchâtel
VALAIS:	Archives de l'État du Canton
	1951 Sion

VAUD: Archives Cantonales
1022 Chavannes-Renens VD

Italian-speaking Canton
TICINO: Archivio Cantonale
6500 Bellinzona

City Archives (Stadtarchiv)

Aarburg (Kanton Aargau)
Arbon (Kanton Thurgau)
Baden (Kanton Aargau)
Biel (Kanton Bern)
Bischofszell (Kanton Thurgau)
Bremgarten (Kanton Aargau)
Brugg (Kanton Aargau)
Diessenhofen (Kanton Thurgau)
Kaiserstuhl (Kanton Aargau)
Klingnau (Kanton Aargau)
Laufenburg (Kanton Aargau)
Lausanne (Canton Vaudoise)
Lenzburg (Kanton Aargau)

Luzern (Kanton Luzern)
Mellingen (Kanton Aargau)
Murten (Canton de Fribourg)
Olten (Kanton Solothurn)
Rheinfelden (Kanton Aargau)
Schaffhausen (Kanton
  Schaffhausen)
Steckborn (Kanton Thurgau)
Stein am Rhein (Kanton
  Schaffhausen)
Winterthur (Kanton Zürich)
Zofingen (Kanton Aargau)

Church Archives (Kirchliche Archiv)

Archiv des Kapuzinerklosters Appenzell
9050 Appenzell

Archives de l'Ancien Évêché de Bâle
2900 Porrentruy

Bischöfliches Archiv des Bistums Basel
4500 Solothurn

Stiftsarchiv Beromünster
6215 Beromünster

Bischöfliches Archiv Chur
7000 Chur

Stiftsarchiv Disentis
7180 Disentis

Stiftsarchiv Einsiedeln
8840 Einsiedeln

Stiftsarchiv Engelberg
6390 Engelberg

Provinzarchiv der Schweizerischen Kapuzinerprovinz
6006 Luzern

Klosterarchiv Mariastein
4115 Mariastein

Archiv Institut Menzingen
6313 Menzingen

Stiftsarchiv der Benediktinerabtei Muri-Gries
3910 Gries-Bozen

Stiftsarchiv St. Gallen
9001 St. Gallen

Archives de l'Abbaye de Saint Maurice
1890 Saint-Maurice

Genealogical Organizations

The following organizations will answer simple inquiries if you enclose
two International Reply Coupons and a self-addressed airmail envelope.
For more detailed searches or problems they will refer you to a list of
available researchers among their membership:

Schweizerische Gesellschaft für Familienforschung
Eggstrasse 46, 8102 Oberengstringen

Verband Schweizerischer Berufsfamilienforscher
Rietstrasse 25, 8703 Erlenbach-Zürich

Genealogisch-Heraldische Gesellschaft Zürich
Eggwiesenstrasse, 8332 Russikon

(This organization is only concerned with the area of Zürich and district.)

The Zentralstelle für genealogische Auskuenfte was founded in 1987 as a
central genealogical inquiry center for the whole country. For more information write to the center at Steinbühlallee 189, 4054 Basel, Switzerland.

YUGOSLAVIA

Let me say at once that ancestor-hunting in Yugoslavia will not be easy, for many reasons. (1) It was only created as an independent country in 1918 by uniting various parts of the Austro-Hungarian Empire and Serbia and Montenegro. (2) The boundaries of the country changed in 1992 and much of what was Yugoslavia now makes up the independent countries of Bosnia-Herzegovina, Croatia, Macedonia, and Slovenia. (3) The records (many of which were destroyed during World War II and the civil wars of the early 1990s) are scattered in many different locations, both inside and outside the country, and have never been properly catalogued, and (4) there is practically no interest in genealogy among the population.

The present situation in Yugoslavia is very complicated. Four republics that were part of Yugoslavia—Bosnia-Herzegovina, Croatia, Macedonia, and Slovenia—declared their independence in the early 1990s. For details of the genealogical records and their location in these four former republics, check the individual chapters on Bosnia-Herzegovina, Croatia, Macedonia, and Slovenia. Other records, which cannot be separated easily, are listed in the following pages.

Present-day Yugoslavia consists of two republics—Serbia and Montenegro. In addition, Yugoslavia also includes two provinces—Kosovo and Vojvodina—which are governed by Serbia. Everything in the area is so chaotic that a great deal of the information given about Yugoslavia may be out-of-date by the time this book is published.

SERBIA

The capital city is Belgrade (Beograd), which is also the capital of the Federal Republic. It was an independent kingdom by 1217, but in 1389 it fell under the control of the Ottoman Empire and became a Turkish province in 1521. There were frequent insurrections over the next centuries, and in 1878 its independence was assured by the Congress of Berlin. In the Balkan Wars of 1912 and 1913 the Serbs fought against both the Austro-Hungarian and the Ottoman empires in an effort to liberate the whole Balkan area from foreign domination. It also fought and won a short war against Bulgaria in order to secure a major part of the Macedonian area of that country. When a Serbian nationalist assassinated an Austrian archduke in 1914, the Austro-Hungarian Empire declared war on Serbia and precipitated the First World War. In 1915 the country was overrun by Austria-Hungary, Germany, and Bulgaria. The government and part of the army were evacuated to the island of Corfu (Kérkira), and in 1917 on that island representatives of Serbia, Croatia, Slovenia, and Montenegro proclaimed a Union of the South Slavs. In 1918, with the end of the First World War, the Kingdom of the Serbs, Croats, and Slovenes was officially recognized. Its name was changed to Yugoslavia in 1929.

MONTENEGRO

The capital city is Titograd (originally Podgorica). The area was originally the principality of Zeta, within the Serbian kingdom. By the late fifteenth century part of the area was ruled by Turkey, part by Venice, and a small part was still independent. From 1515 until 1851 this latter area was under the rule of the prince-bishops of Cetinje. During this whole period Montenegro never accepted foreign domination, particularly that of the Turks, and fighting against the invaders went on almost continuously. In 1799 the Sultan of Turkey recognized its independence. In 1878, at the Congress of Berlin, Montenegro was awarded its lost territories and its new boundaries were officially recognized.

In the First World War Montenegro invaded Albania to obtain further territory, and also declared war on the Austro-Hungarian Empire. It, in turn, was occupied by Austria and Germany. In 1918 it joined with Serbia, Croatia, and Slovenia in the formation of Yugoslavia. In 1946 it became one of the founding republics of the new federal state.

KOSOVO

This area is in southeast Yugoslavia and the capital city is Priština. From the fourteenth century until 1913 it was part of the Ottoman Empire. It was then partitioned between Serbia and Montenegro, and incorporated into what is now Yugoslavia in 1918. The population is mainly Albanian, with some Serbian and Montenegrin minorities. There is considerable unrest in this area at the time of this writing.

VOJVODINA

This is in northeast Yugoslavia and the capital is Novi Sad. It was part of Hungary and Croatia before its conquest by the Turks in the sixteenth century. It was restored to Hungary in 1699 and the whole area was resettled by Croats and Serbs from the Ottoman Empire, and a little later by German colonists. As a result, the population is a very mixed one, including Serbs, Croats, Magyars, Romanians, and Slovaks. The region was ceded to Yugoslavia under the terms of the Treaty of Trianon in 1920, and became autonomous in 1946. There are three sections to the region: the Srem, in the southwest, which was part of Croatia-Slavonia until 1918; the Backa, in the northwest, which was part of Hungary; and the western part of the Banat of Temesvar, which had also been Hungarian. (The eastern part of the Banat went to Romania.)

It has been necessary to explain at some length the political divisions of what is now Yugoslavia, and the history of the various regions over the centuries. Without this knowledge you will have difficulty in knowing just where to look for the records of your ancestors.

There is more to follow before we discuss specific records and their locations, because you must also know about the various religions and languages within Yugoslavia, two more factors that will have a great influence on your success or failure.

Religions
The major religion is Orthodox but there are large Muslim minorities in the south, especially in Montenegro and Kosovo, and Catholics in the north, especially in Vojvodina. It is a genealogical misfortune that these religions are not tidily assembled in particular parts of the country. If you do not know the religion of your Yugoslav ancestors you must tread with care and check all the religious sources available to you. It should also be noted that the religions are not confined to a particular area within a particular republic.

Language
The principal language of present-day Yugoslavia is Serbo-Croatian. Although *Serbs* and *Croats* speak variations of the same language and have no difficulty understanding each other, the Serbs use the old Cyrillic alphabet

and lettering, and the Croats the Latin. The *Montenegrins* share the same language and alphabet as the Serbs and are regarded, historically, as of similar ethnic stock.

It should also be mentioned that there are over half a million Hungarians in the Vojvodina, some 70,000 Romanians in the same area, and about two million Albanians in Kosovo.

So much for the background; now for the details.

Church Registers

Many of these have been destroyed or lost during rebellions and invasions. There are some exceptions. In Dubrovnik, for example, there are baptismal records dating back to the early seventeenth century. Generally speaking, the Catholic registers go back further than the Orthodox or Muslim ones. The early church registers are in the various archives (national, regional, and municipal). Unfortunately, no central list of the parishes and the dates is available.

One further complication with the church registers is that in many areas of Yugoslavia surnames did not stabilize until about 1870. As a result, registers can show someone being born, married, and buried under three different names. However, a close search will usually show two names bracketed together, the patronymic and the earlier family name. This is particularly true of Catholic registers but also applies to most Orthodox ones.

There are also a number of surviving Church Books that record the life of the local church and its members, church meetings, and clergymen's visits within the parish. These are also in the various archives.

Civil Registration

Registration of births, marriages, and deaths did not commence in Yugoslavia until 1946; before that only the various churches recorded these events, and, as I mentioned, many of these church records are missing. Certificates of birth, marriage, and death are issued by the local registrar in small towns and villages. In the larger cities, registration is done on a ward or small-district basis. When applying for a copy of a certificate, you should write to the registrar (Maticar) in the small town or village, and also in the large city—there are over twenty maticars in Belgrade, for example, but your letter will reach the right one provided you give the address where the person was living at the time of birth, marriage, or death.

There are early civil-registration records available in the Dalmatian area (back as far as the sixteenth century, but with many gaps). Records for 1550 exist in Zadar, for example. Civil registration started in Vojvodina in 1895, when it was part of Hungary.

Census Returns

Modern census returns are located in the National Statistical Bureau (Savezni Zavod Za Statistiku, Kneza Milosa 20, 11000 Belgrade). Earlier ones are in the various provincial archives.

Records of earlier censuses (and some go back to 1453 in Turkish-held areas) have suffered in the same manner as the church records. Many have been destroyed, and those that still exist are by no means complete; you will just have to hope you will be lucky in your particular area of interest. When you do find an entry, bear in mind that it was the custom to round off the ages of the people listed, so that 67 became 70, 43 became 40, and so on.

Once again we have to face the fact that there is no centralization of records, or even of information about those records. I can tell you a little about early censuses in the various areas but cannot guarantee that the records mentioned are in any way complete.

Serbia

There were censuses in this area as early as 1528 but only males were listed. The only complete census of earlier years is that for 1863 and this is in the Serbian Provincial Archives. Austria took a census of Belgrade in 1733–34. It was done by the various priests and gives full names, ages, and relationship. It also is in the archives. Serbian censuses were taken in 1890, 1895, 1900, 1905, and 1910, but most are missing or incomplete. The census of 1884 is complete but so far unpublished and not normally available for research.

Vojvodina

A census was held in this area in 1715 and there were later ones between 1855 and 1910 but only portions are in the archives.

Occupied Areas

The Turks held regular censuses from 1453, and they give personal names, relationship, unmarried mature males, and sometimes, widows who were heads of households. There are also Turkish Population Lists dating from the early nineteenth century, and many of these included physical descriptions; for example, in the Sarajevo (which is in present-day Bosnia) list of 1841 you will find "Selim, short and bearded, Pyotr, tall and no beard."

Some of the Turkish records are in the various archives and others are believed to be in the National Archives of Turkey in the Topkapi Palace in Istanbul.

Other census information is in the National Archives of Hungary, Austria, and Italy. However, some of this has recently been handed over to the appropriate Yugoslavian archive and has not yet been sorted and catalogued.

Wills

Early wills and probate records are in the various regional archives but the collections are small. Not many people had any money or possessions in the area we now call Yugoslavia. More recent ones are in the local municipal court.

Tax Rolls

There are some sixteenth-century Turkish Tax Rolls (Defter) and these have been published and indexed by the Belgrade Museum of History (1107 Novi Beograd, Palmira Toljatija 1).

Records of Serfs

Some records exist of serfs bound to nobles or religious institutions. For example, the archives in the Kosovo region have Serf Lists (or Chrysobulls) dating back to 1357.

Other Records

These include feudal taxes and tributes, voter registration, conscription lists, and genealogical collections mostly referring to noble families. Such records are in many of the various regional archives. Some of them, particularly in Belgrade and Serbia, have been printed and indexed. Here again you must check with the archives.

In addition, since the Second World War there have been a number of sociological studies of village life made by professors and students from overseas, particularly the United States. Many of these studies were of no value genealogically but in some cases the research was centered on recording oral histories and this may be of value to you. The various archives will tell you which villages in their area have been studied.

Oral history has been prevalent in the area that we are discussing. There was very little movement of population until the Second World War, and the majority of people lived in remote and mountainous areas far from civilization. The winter nights were long and each family had its storyteller who could recount the members of the family and their activities and accomplishments back for many generations.

Below you will find a complete list of archives in Yugoslavia at all levels: provincial and regional, district, and municipal. You will have to write to the ones in your area to find out just what they have. If you can write in Serbo-Croatian so much the better, but if not, then English is the next best thing. When you write, always send return postage (two International Reply Coupons) and a self-addressed airmail envelope. Be sure you say "Please" and "Thank you" (Molim and Hvala).

I have been told that foreigners making inquiries at archives have encountered difficulties in obtaining cooperation. I doubt this. Personally I have found archivists in Yugoslavia very helpful both in my personal visits and by correspondence. The story may possibly apply to some remote mountain villages, but I think they would be the exception.

YUGOSLAV ARCHIVES

The National Archives are located in Belgrade at the following address: National Archives (Arhiv Jugoslavije), Vase Pelagica 33, 11001 Belgrade.

Serbia

Archives of Serbia
Karnedžijeva 2
11001 Belgrade

Archives of Belgrade
Palmira Toljatija 1
11007 Novi Beograd

Historical Archives
Pop Lukina 25
14000 Valjevo

Partizanska
18500 Vranje

Maršala Tita 160
19000 Zaječar

Trg Avnoj - a-3
34000 Kragujevac

Karadjordjeva 1
36000 Kraljevo

Zgrada Doma Sindikata
Trg Maršala Tito
37000 Kruševac

Dr. Rade Svilara 25
16000 Leskovac

Branka Perića 13
19300 Negotin

Tvrdjava
18001 Niš

Oslobodjenja 23
36300 Novi Pazar

Dr. Voje Dulića 10
12001 Požarevac

Trg Narodnih Heroja 5
11420 Smederevska Palanka

Milana Mijalkovića 14
35000 Svetozarevo

Maršala Tita 52
31000 Titovo Ižice

Vojvode Mišića 52
15000 Šabac

Svetozara Markovića 2
32000 Čačak

Vojvodina Region

Archives of Vojvodina
Trg Branka Radičevića 8
21205 Sremski Karlovci

Historical Archives
Trg Slobode 10
23000 Zrenjanin

1 Oktobra 40
26340 Bela Crkva

Maršala Tita 3/1
23300 Kikinda

Tvrdjava
21131 Novi Sad

Nemenjina 7
26001 Pančevo

Trg Maršala Tita 1/II
24400 Senta

Trg 7 Jula 5
25000 Sombor

Pinkijeva 4
22000 Sremska Mitrovica

Trg Slobode 1/III
24000 Subotica

Kosovo Region
Archives of Kosovo
Naselje Kodbolnice 3
38000 Priština

Historical Archives
Nikole Tesle 43
38000 Priština

Bratstvo—Jedinstvo 7
38400 Prizren

Bore Vukmanovića 13a
38300 Peć

29 Novembra 21
38220 Titova Mitrovica

Maršala Tita
38250 Gnjilane

Borisa Kidriča 46/I
38320 Djakovica

Communal Archives
38313 Glogovac

Communal Archives
Trg Slobode 27
38214 Vučitrn

Maršala Tita 336
38240 Podujevo

Communal Archives
38322 Dečane
38232 Lipljan

Montenegro
Archives of Montenegro
Njegoševa 208
81330 Kotor

Communal Archives
Marka Vojnovića 9
81340 Herceg Novi

Osnova Škola 52
81380 Budva

Note: Many of the above archives located in small towns also have archival records from nearby places.

BIBLIOGRAPHY

This is a very short bibliography because of limitations of space. I could have included an additional several hundred books but (a) very many of them would have been in one of the European languages and (b) most of them would have referred to certain specific areas within a particular country. There is also the problem that although your ancestors came from Europe you may not speak the language that they spoke. In that case, a list of genealogical books in Bulgarian, or Hungarian, or Swedish would be of little use to you.

After much soul-searching I have decided to include only a representative collection. You can find out what other books are available (either in English or in your ancestral language) by writing to one or all of the following:

1. The National Archives of your ancestral country.
2. The National Library of the same country.
3. The Genealogical Society of the Church of Jesus Christ of Latter-day Saints, Salt Lake City, Utah.
4. A genealogical organization (if one exists) in the country in which you are interested.
5. A genealogical organization in North America that concentrates exclusively on the one country (some of these are listed at the end of this section, but I cannot guarantee the addresses, since the secretaries may have changed since I compiled the list).

Be sure you enclose a self-addressed airmail envelope and return postage (two International Reply Coupons with any overseas mail).

AUSTRIA
Finsterwalder, K. *Tiroler Namenkunde*. Innsbruck, 1978.
Senekovic, D. *Handy Guide to Austrian Genealogical Records*. Logan, Utah, 1979.

BELGIUM
Belgian Government. *Het Rijksarchief (De Vlaamse Provinciën)*. Brussels, 1975.

_____. *Les Archives de l'État (Provinces Wallonnes)*. Brussels, 1975.

_____. *Registres Paroissiaux (Brabant)*. Brussels, 1976.

Sabbe, P.D., and L. Buyse. *Belgians in America*. Tielt, 1960.

BULGARIA

Tosheva, Snezhina. *Spravochnik na Bibliotekitev Bolgariya*. Sofia, 1963.

CROATIA

Prpic, G. *Croatian Immigrants in America*. New York, 1971.

CZECH REPUBLIC AND SLOVAKIA

Kral, Vacloc. *Die Deutschen in der Tschechoslowakei*. Prague, 1964.

Miller, Olga K. *Genealogical Research for Czech and Slovak Americans*. Detroit, 1978.

Procházka, R. *Genealogisches Handbuch Erschlosener Böhmischer*. Neustadt, 1973.

Society for the History of Czechoslovak Jews. *The Jews of Czechoslovakia*. Philadelphia, 1968.

DENMARK

Baisler, B. *History of the Danish Jews*. Copenhagen, 1932.

ESTONIA

Penmar, Parming, and Rebanc. *The Estonians in America, 1627–1975*. Dobbs Ferry, N.Y., 1975.

FINLAND

Brenner, A. *Staktforskning: Practisk Handbok*. Helsinki, 1947.

Kolehmainen, J. *The Finns in America*. New York, 1947.

FRANCE

Audin, Margaret. *Barking Up That French Tree*. Utica, N.Y., 1980.

Beattie, W. *The Waldenses or Protestant Valleys of Piedmont*. London, 1938.

Beaucarnot, J.-L. de. *Chasseurs d'Ancêtres*. Paris, 1980.

Durye, Pierre. *Genealogy*. New Orleans, 1977.

Fleury, M., and L. Henry. *Des Registres Paroissiaux*. Paris, 1956.

Hézelles, N., and Nadine Vigier. *La Généalogie*. Paris, 1979.

Levy, P. *Les Noms des Israélites en France*. Paris, 1960.

Reaman, G. E. *The Trail of the Huguenots*. Toronto, 1963 (repr. Baltimore, 1972).

Tupigny, J. de. *Guide des Recherches Généalogiques aux Archives*. Paris, 1956.

GERMANY

Bahlow, H. *Deutsches Namenlexicon*. Munich, 1967.

Baxter, Angus. *In Search of Your German Roots*. Baltimore, 1991 (repr. 1992).

Henning and Ribbe, *Handbuch des Genealogie*. Neustadt, 1972.

Jensen, L.D. *Genealogical Handbook of German Research*. Pleasant Grove, Utah, 1980.

Kessler, G. *Die Familiennamen der Juden in Deutschland*. Jerusalem, 1935.

Minerva Handbücher. *Archiv in Deutschsprachigen Raum*. Berlin, 1974.

Smith, C. and A. *Encyclopedia of German-American Genealogical Research*. New York, 1976.

Thode, Ernest. *Address Book for Germanic Genealogy*. Baltimore, 1991.

GREECE

Saloutos, T. *Greeks in the United States*. Cambridge, Mass., 1964.

HUNGARY

Brandt, Edward Reimer. *Contents and Addresses of Hungarian Archives*. Baltimore, 1993.

Judák, Margit. *Egyházi Anyakönyvek Mikrofilmmásolatai*. Budapest, 1977.

Kempelen, D. *Magyar Forangu Csaladok*. Budapest, 1931.

Pamlenyi, E. *A History of Hungary*. Budapest, 1973.

Suess, Jared. *Handy Guide to Hungarian Genealogical Records*. Logan, Utah, 1980.

Szeplaki, J. *The Hungarians in America*. Dobbs Ferry, N.Y., 1975.

ICELAND

Jonasson, E. *Tracing Your Icelandic Ancestors*. Winnipeg, 1974.

Lindal, W. *The Icelanders in Canada*. Winnipeg, 1967.

Ólason, P.E. *Íslenzkar Aeviskrár*. 5 vols. Reykjavik, 1940.

Thorgeissen, O. *Almanach Fyrir*. Reykjavik, 1895.

ITALY

Colletta, John Philip. *Finding Italian Roots*. Baltimore, 1993.

Fucilla, J.G.S. *Our Italian Surnames*. Evanston, Ill., 1949.

Musmanno, M. *The Italians in America*. Garden City, N.Y., 1965.

Preece, P.P., and F.S. Preece. *Handy Guide to Italian Genealogical Records*. Logan, Utah, 1978.

Roth, C. *Stemmi di Famiglia Ebraice Italiane*. Jerusalem, 1967.

LATVIA

Akmentińs, O. *Latvijas Ideja Amerika*. Boston, 1969.

LITHUANIA

Michelsonas, S. *Lietuviu Iśeivija Amerikoje*. Boston, 1961.

LUXEMBOURG

Bruck, A. *Fondations des Bourses d'Études Instituées en Faveur des Luxembourgeois*. Luxembourg, 1928.

Krieps, R. *Luxemburger in America (1609–1974)*. Boston, 1975.

MALTA

Xuereb, P. Catalogue of Books and Articles in the University of Malta Library. Malta, 1974.

NETHERLANDS

De Jong, G.F. *The Dutch in America*. Boston, 1975.

Van Resandt, W. Wijaendts. *Repertorium DTB* (Dutch Parish Registers). The Hague, 1969.

NORWAY

Andersen, A.W. *The Norwegian-Americans*. Boston, 1974.

Norlie, O. *History of the Norwegian People in America*. New York, 1973.

POLAND

Chorzempa, Rosemary A. *Polish Roots*. Baltimore, 1993.

Lewanski, R.C. *Guide to Polish Libraries and Archives*. Boulder, Col., 1974.

Weinryb, B. *The Jews in Poland, 1100–1800*. Jerusalem, 1975.

PORTUGAL

Cardozo, M.S.S. *The Portuguese in America*. Dobbs Ferry, N.Y., 1976.

De Sousa, A.C. *Indice General da História Genealógica*. Coimbra, 1955.

Mattos, A. *Manuel de Genealogica Portuguesa*. Pôrto, 1943.

Tavares, B.E. *Portuguese Pioneers in the U.S.A.* Fall River, Mass., 1973.

ROMANIA

Bodea, C., and V. Cândea. *Heritage and Continuity in Eastern Europe: The Transylvanian Legacy in the History of the Romanians*. Boulder, Col., 1982.

Wertsman, V. *The Romanians in America*. Dobbs Ferry, N.Y., 1975.

RUSSIA

Stumpp, Karl. *The Emigration from Germany to Russia, 1763–1862*. Lincoln, Neb., 1978.

Wertsman, V. *The Russians in America, 1727–1970*. Dobbs Ferry, N.Y., 1977.

SPAIN

Baer, Y. *A History of the Jews in Christian Spain*. Philadelphia, 1961.

Catholic Church. *Guia de la Iglesia en España*. 4 vols. Madrid, 1954–57.

SWEDEN

Furtenbach, B. *Slaktforskning for alla*. Stockholm, 1971.

Hildebrand, B. *Hand Bok i slakt-och personforskning*. Stockholm, 1961.

Johanssen, Carl-Erik. *Cradled in Sweden*. Salt Lake City, 1972.

Ottervik, Gösta. *Libraries and Archives in Sweden.* Stockholm, 1964.
Royal Ministry of Foreign Affairs. *Tracing Your Swedish Ancestry.*
Uppsala, 1977.

SWITZERLAND
Editions Polygraphiques. *Familiennamen Buch der Schweiz.* Zürich,
1968–71.
Faust, A., and G. Brumbaugh. *Lists of Swiss Emigrants in the Eighteenth
Century to the American Colonies.* 2 vols. Washington, D.C., 1920,
1925 (repr. Baltimore, 1968).
Suess, Jared H. *Handy Guide to Swiss Genealogical Records.* Logan,
Utah, 1978.
Von Grüninga, J.P. *The Swiss in the United States.* Madison, Wis., 1940.

UKRAINE
Wertsman, V. *The Ukrainians in America, 1627–1975.* Dobbs Ferry,
N.Y., 1976.

YUGOSLAVIA
Govorchin, G. *Americans from Jugoslavia.* Gainesville, Fla., 1961.
Jovanovic, S., and M. Rojnic. *A Guide to Jugoslav Libraries and
Archives.* Columbus, Ohio, 1975.
Rojnic, M. *Jugoslav Libraries.* Zagreb, 1954.
Vujnovich, M. *The Yugoslavs in America.* Minneapolis, 1977.

JEWISH (GENERAL)
Beider, A. *A Dictionary of Jewish Surnames from the Russian Empire.*
Teaneck, N.J., 1993.
Fraenkel, J. *Guide to Jewish Libraries in the World.* London, 1959.
Gorr, S. *Jewish Personal Names.* Teaneck, N.J., 1990.
Gruber, R. *Jewish Heritage Travel.* New York, 1992.
Kagan, B. *Sefer Hapremumerantin.* New York, 1975.
Kurzweil, A. *From Generation to Generation.* New York, 1982.
Kurzweil, A., and Miriam Weiner. *The Encyclopedia of Jewish Geneal-
ogy.* Northvale, N.J., 1991.
Mokotoff G., and S. Sack. *Where Once We Walked.* Teaneck, N.J., 1991.
Stern, M. *First American Jewish Families.* 3rd ed. Baltimore, 1991.

GENERAL
National Archives of the United States. *Guide to Genealogical Research
in the National Archives.* Washington, D.C., 1983 (revised 1985).

GENEALOGICAL ORGANIZATIONS

The following "ethnic" genealogical organizations exist in North America, i.e., organizations devoted to genealogical research in a country, or a group of countries, in Europe. I make no claim to completeness, since information of this kind has to be obtained from many different sources, and I am sure there are others about which I know nothing. You should always check with your local library for further information:

Balkan and East European American Genealogical Society, c/o Adam Eterovich, 4843 Mission St., San Francisco, CA 94112.

Belgian Researchers, Fruitdale Lane 62073, La Grande, OR 97850.

Czechoslovak Genealogical Society, P.O. Box 16225, St. Paul, MN 55116.

Croatian-Slovenian-Serbian Genealogical Society, 936 Industrial Avenue, Palo Alto, CA 94302.

Croatian-Serbian-Slovene Genealogical Society, 2527 San Carlos Avenue, San Carlos, CA 94070.

Danish American Heritage Society, 29681 Dane Lane, Junction City, OR 97448.

Federation of East European Family History Societies, c/o Charles M. Hall, P.O. Box 21346, Salt Lake City, UT 84121.

Finnish-American Historical Society of Michigan, 19885 Melrose Street, Southfield, MI 48075.

(Finnish) Immigration History Research Center, University of Minnesota, 826 Barry Street, St. Paul, MN 55114.

(Finnish) Minnesota Historical Society, 690 Cedar Street, St. Paul, MN 55101.

Franco-American Historical Society, P.O. Box 668, Manchester, NH 03105.

American-*French* Genealogical Society, P.O. Box 2113, Pawtucket, RI 02861.

German-American Genealogical Club, P.O. Box 24 APO, New York, NY 09012.

German Genealogical Society of America, 2125 Wright Avenue, Suite C9, La Verne, CA 91750.

German Research Association, P.O. Box 711600, San Diego, CA 92171-1600.

Mid-Atlantic *Germanic* Society, P.O. Box 2642, Kensington, MD 20892.

(German) Palatines to America, P.O. Box 101, Capital University, Columbus, OH 43209.

(German) Pommerscher Verein Freistadt, P.O. Box 204, Germantown, WI 53022.

American-*German* Historical Association, 4246 South 3100 Street East, Salt Lake City, UT 84117.

American Historical Society of *Germans* from Russia, 631 D Street, Lincoln, NE 68502.

Germans from Russia Heritage Society, 1008 E. Central Avenue, Bismarck, ND 58501.

Italian Genealogy and Heraldry Society of Canada, 2951 S. Clair Avenue, Windsor, ON N9E 4A1 Canada.

Jewish Genealogical Society, P.O. Box 6398, New York, NY 10028.

Jewish Genealogical Society, P.O. Box 446, Station A, Willowdale, ON M2N 5T1, Canada.

Norwegian-American Museum, 502 West Water Street, Decorah, IA 52101.

Norwegian-American Historical Association, Northfield, MN 55057.

Supreme Lodge of the Sons of *Norway*, 1312 West Lake Street, Minneapolis, MN 55408.

Polish Genealogical Society, 984 North Milwaukee Avenue, Chicago, IL 60622. (There are affiliated branches in California, Connecticut, Massachusetts, Michigan, New York, Ohio, Texas, and Wisconsin.)

Polish Genealogical Society of Connecticut, 8 Lyle Road, New Britain, CT 06053.

Polish Genealogical Society of Greater Cleveland, 906 College Avenue, Cleveland, Ohio 44113.

Polish Genealogical Society of Michigan, 5201 Woodward Avenue, Detroit, MI 48202.

Polish Genealogical Society of Minnesota, P.O. Box 16069, St. Paul, Minnesota 55116.

Polish Genealogical Society of Wisconsin, P.O. Box 37476, Milwaukee, WI 53237.

Polish Museum of America, 984 North Milwaukee Avenue, Chicago, IL 60622. (This has a large collection of Polish-American newspapers on microfilm.)

Polish Nobility Association, 529 Dunkirk Road, Baltimore, MD 21212.

Polish Archives, St. Mary's College, Orchard Lake, MI 48033.

American-*Portuguese* Genealogical Society, P.O. Box 644, Taunton, MA 02780.

Russian Historical and Genealogical Society, 971 1st Avenue, New York, NY 10022.

Scandinavian-American Genealogical Society, P.O. Box 16069, St. Paul, MN 55116.

Schleswig-Holstein Heritage Society, P.O. Box 21, Le Claire, IA 52753.

Swedish Pioneer Historical Society, 5125 North Spaulding Avenue, Chicago, IL 60625.

American-*Swedish* Institute, 2600 Park Avenue, Minneapolis, MN 55407.

Swiss-American Historical Society, 216 East 39th Street, Norfolk, VA 23504.

Swiss-American Genealogical Committee, 2526 Jackson Avenue, Evanston, IL 60201.

Ukrainian Genealogical and Heraldic Society, 573 N.E. 102nd Street, Miami Shores, FL 33138.

Ukrainian Genealogical and Historical Society of Canada, 1530 23rd Avenue, Calgary, Alberta T2M 1V1.

INDEX